Advance Praise for
Saturday's Child

"In her searingly honest memoir, Deborah Burns unpacks what it means to be the daughter of a mistaken-for-a-movie-star mother who refuses to be defeated by life, no matter its disappointments. At once painful and uplifting, and rich with period detail; you will fall in love with both generations."

—Sally Koslow, international best-selling author of *Another Side of Paradise*

"Riveting and affecting; timeless and timely—a stunning debut."

—Bethany Ball, author of *What to Do About the Solomons*

"A beautifully written love letter to a fascinating mother. I was immediately drawn in by both the prose and the mysteries at the heart of this unique mother-daughter relationship."

—Andrea Jarrell, author of National Book Critics Circle Award nominee *I'm the One Who Got Away*

"Mesmerizing. A must-read for any daughter who's ever tried to figure out where her mother ends and she begins."

—Lynnda Pollio, author of *Trusting the Currents*

"A poignant, candid exploration of the bond between mother and daughter. In allowing herself to see her mother as a real person, flaws and all, Burns not only sets herself free—she shows the rest of us how to do the same."

—Gayle Brandeis, author of *The Art of Misdiagnosis: Surviving My Mother's Suicide*

"A heartfelt tale of love, honor, and becoming . . . wise and wonderful."

—Agapi Stassinopoulos, author of *Wake Up to the Joy of You*

"In this captivating memoir, the relationship between an unconventional and fiercely independent mother and the daughter who idolized her is revealed in all its complexity. A story of identity, self-discovery, and forgiveness."

—Jennifer Kitses, author of *Small Hours*

"Deborah Burns fearlessly reveals the hidden truths of a compelling and challenging mother-daughter relationship. Vividly written and thoroughly rewarding!"

—Barbara Novack, Writer-in-Residence, Molloy College, author of Pulitzer Prize–nominated *J.W. Valentine*

"With a journalist's eye and a poet's hand, the author unveils the unique texture of her glamorous mother's elusive love. Heartbreaking and hopeful, searing and soulful, *Saturday's Child* is unputdownable—this generation's *Terms of Endearment*."

—Meghann Foye, author of *Meternity*

"A cinematic memoir that reads like fiction, with lush, elegant prose that belies a raw, honest narrative of a daughter coming to terms with the narcissistic mother whom she idealized. An unforgettable journey of discovery, understanding, and self-love."

—Lisa Anselmo, author of *My (Part-Time) Paris Life: How Running Away Brought Me Home*

SATURDAY'S CHILD

SATURDAY'S CHILD

A Daughter's Memoir

DEBORAH BURNS

SHE WRITES PRESS

Published 2019
Printed in the United States of America
ISBN: 978-1-63152-547-6
ISBN: 978-1-63152-548-3

Library of Congress Control Number: 2018958411

For information, address:
She Writes Press
1569 Solano Ave #546
Berkeley, CA 94707

Interior design by Tabitha Lahr

She Writes Press is a division of SparkPoint Studio, LLC.

Dedicated to Elizabeth, who sparked the journey
and to Dorothy, who was the flame.

Every Mother contains her daughter in herself and every daughter her mother and every mother extends backwards into her mother and forwards into her daughter.

—Carl Jung

London Dawn

The dream. Again. I shot up at 3:30 a.m. in a London hotel room, my heart full of remorse and racing with panic. The nightmare hadn't surfaced for years but was now breaking through the veil once or twice a week. Nearly two decades after my mother's death, the recurring illusion unfolded anew—that she was really alive and somehow, I hadn't called her in months. A notion that could not have been more absurd.

How could I be such a terrible daughter? So ungrateful? She was sick and alone. I'd been absent when she needed me most. Sharp metal prongs were pulling me under, drowning me in murky water, my mouth open, arms flailing. *How could I possibly have forgotten to call for so long?* But I couldn't call. Because in the dream I had forgotten something else—her phone number. The frantic search began again. *What was it?* Back in my childhood apartment, it was missing from the center of the rotary dial. In a frenzy, I dug into address books, through paper fragments, pocketbooks, and closets. Through strange new rooms, unfurnished and dim, their low doorways making me crouch and crawl. *Aaahh!* A guttural sound, equal parts frustration and fury. *Where was that number?* If only I could find it, I would get to her, make everything all right once more. But despite my mad scrabbling for clues, I could never once make the call.

When she was alive, I had always been in chasing mode, in longing pursuit of something fleeting. In death, my mother continued to elude and haunt me, holding fiercely on to answers that only she could offer.

Now fully awake, I slid slowly out of bed and glanced at my sleeping daughter. Elizabeth had conceived of and planned the entire trip, a carefully timed one-week respite from her job.

"Let's go to London, just you and me," she suggested.

It was an easy yes, and off we went to steep ourselves in the British history she loved. What she couldn't have fully realized was just how perfectly timed this escape was for me.

The dreams weren't my only upset. Lately, the waking world had me white-knuckled as well, reaching for something just beyond my grasp while I felt a familiar slipping away. The women's magazines I worked for were collapsing—they had looked their digital future in the eye and didn't know what to say next. I could read the cards, and it was just a matter of time before my role as Chief Innovation Officer imploded, taking my livelihood and professional realm with it. Secretly, part of me welcomed a change. I'd had enough of corporate life to know how it hardened you, constantly forcing you to cut back on what *was* to make way for a newer, smaller what *is*.

All I was really sure of was that I would soon need to reinvent my bewildered self in an uncertain future. The returning dream seemed like one more emotional hijacking, reminding me of how I still yearned for my mother; of how I needed to fully understand all that had been withheld between us. Had she somehow broken my little girl's heart all those years before, knotting me up in ways that still cried out to be unraveled?

"Are you OK?" Elizabeth asked. That's the gift of a daughter— she senses, she knows.

"Totally." A whispered mom lie. "Sorry. Just my morning routine." My eyes filled at the sound of her voice in the dark.

I reached for the tiny coffeepot that sat under an eighteenth-century gilt-framed landscape, flicked on a low-light at the far side of the room, and unzipped the closeted suitcase. There, the blank journal. I decided that I would finally reflect on this trip about the emotions trapped inside me, about searing loss and something not quite found.

I inhaled, eyes closed, and waited, unsure of how much time had passed before I picked up the pen and wrote:

> *I just turned the age my mother was when the illness began to take hold of her; when errant cells, undercover and uninvited, began to grow wildly beyond her control.*

I stared at the words. *Of course,* I thought, suddenly hit with the realization. This was the reason for the dreams, the longing, the panic. *I am now as she was then.*

Country

My hand started waving as soon as I sensed my mother's car about to round the last curve before the hotel. I never failed to anticipate her arrival every summer Saturday, not even once, not even by a second. When she stepped out, I threw my arms around her waist, careful to angle my body back a bit so my bathing suit would not dampen her. A half embrace, but we were together again. Even if her hug wasn't quite as tight as mine, I could tell that she had missed me too.

A quick change into one of her Emilio Pucci–inspired sarongs, and then we would trek to the enormous pool with all the other guests. My towel was already on the hill's coarse grass from the morning, and she would join me on it for a few moments so I could cover her back with oil. Then I'd watch as she first glossed her face, then her chest and arms and finally her legs, slightly raised to reach her arched feet. Even now, the scent of Bain de Soleil transports me to another time and place.

Back in the water, I kept one eye on my mother as I swam with all of the other children. Always holding a cigarette aloft, she'd laugh with the friends who orbited her, admirers who vied for proximity, seeking some sort of rub-off effect—or so it seemed to me. She seduced the world, and I was no exception.

Once an hour she'd pin up her tumbling red mane, tie a sheer kerchief around it, and come in for a dip. Everyone knew to stop splashing. She slowly submerged up to her shoulders and began to do her sidestroke once around the circumference of the pool. That signature stroke was completely her, effortlessly gliding sideways through life without ever going too deep. After all, leaving the surface would wet her hair.

When I was very young, our pool ritual was both a public and private gift. Before or after the side-stroking—sometimes before *and* after on a really great day—my mother would press her body down on the rope that separated the children's side of the pool and slide across. Scooping me up, she'd ease back over to the grown-up side (where it was almost as shallow but still felt as though you were entering a forbidden zone). She would bend her slippery knees so the water just reached her neck and I'd climb on to face her, weightless, my little hands, arms, and feet sliding on her shoulders and legs. A smiling pause to build the anticipation, and then she'd begin her bouncing game. "Bah-dum, bah-dum," she would singsong, "bah-dum, bah-dum," as we bobbed and turned round and round together. Her breath, her closeness, her blue eyes on me as the cool water beaded on our skin was like nothing else. If I close my eyes, I can still feel that joy.

The ramshackle little hotel that my father's family had built was upstate New York's Italian safe haven. And my mother—Dorothy, a.k.a. Dotty—reigned supreme as its brightest non-Italian star. The grounds of the resort and its cast of characters anchored us both in the country for three months every year. As soon as school was over, I was ready to leave the city, impatient—for once—as if I were some unruly child. I'd roll down the window as we drove and tick off the markers to the *almost there* stop in throwback Marlboro. The town's two storefronts were ready to greet us—a bakery and Jack's Variety Store, which seemed to hold all the plastic and paper mysteries of the universe behind its screen door. We'd emerge with a bag of toy horses, coloring books, crayons, and enough paint-by-numbers sets to last the summer, and a second bag filled solely with connect-the-dot books. My fascination with drawing lines between randomly placed dots to reveal something surprising knew no bounds.

Then fifteen minutes more on the narrow looping roads, up and down hills, past dense trees, and over a little stone bridge. *Almost there, almost.* A straight patch and then there it was, the grand field with the pool in the distance on my right, the house my grandfather had once lived in on the left, and straight in front of me the three-story hotel he had named the Canzoneri Country Club. Arriving, I felt like I was finally home.

Bought by my father's brother, Tony Canzoneri—also known as the lightweight boxing champion of the world—it had been, in its 1940s heyday long before me, *the* Italian destination for anyone who was anyone with a vowel ending their last name. Some of the colorful guests were on the sketchier side; some even signed the check-in register with aliases, parking their families at the hotel for the summer season while they traded sunshine for shady city business during the week. What those men actually did was anybody's guess. No one dared ask too many questions.

My grandfather, however, must have heard many of their secrets. He was, I learned many years later, also known as "the Sicilian mediator." Apparently, he resolved underworld disputes from his high-backed chair flanked by one temperamental Great Dane and two Boxers, their long tongues hanging from the sides of their mouths. He ran the hotel for my uncle when it first opened, with help from his other children, including my father, Jay. All summer long, movie-worthy personas dove into the pool, played pickup handball, baseball, and badminton, and later in the day, enjoyed boozing to live music in the smoke-filled cocktail lounge. The lounge's nicked chestnut bar spanned the room's length and was the resort's communal centerpiece. Bordered by maroon leather stools, it was backed by mirrors so the guests could keep a close eye on themselves—and each other. A giant framed sketch of Uncle Tony dominated the center mirror, his cocky grin and gloved fighter's fists pointing straight at the gold-chained, pinky-ringed crowd. Everyone had been drawn to the hotel by a shared universe of fame and vice and a certain circle-of-understanding that felt familial. And all of the guests were committed to having a blast.

Each day I could be found loitering around a flock of women sporting cropped skinny pants, ruffled midriffs, and beehive hairdos. Theirs was a slow communion, a passive mingling devoted to the endless discussing and dissecting of shared whispers. In contrast, the communion of the men at the resort was always active and loud enough to make you wary, with poker as their pastime of choice. I noticed early on that my mother was the only one who shared in both worlds.

The card room lived off the dining pavilion, which held thirty round and square tables set under massive oak beams. After dinner, some of the men would stretch, grab a scotch, and then retreat to the small side room for a few hours before the bar scene kicked into action. Lined with pine paneling that had been infused with the smoke of a thousand cigars, this high-testosterone province had well-defined borders as if the players had peed along the perimeter to mark their territory. The only estrogen ever permitted in that room and at that poker table was hers.

"Here she is. Have a seat." Hovering in the doorway, I'd notice how they all sat a chair apart from one another at the outset, hoping that perhaps she'd choose the seat next to them. She would slink into a chair alongside one or another, and whoever it was always looked down as if to conceal a grin that silently announced that he had already won.

"You deal, Dotty."

"Ante up." Somehow, she always managed the most professional shuffle despite her long nails. She'd do four or five in a row, each half deck elegantly bent back in her hands, the cards snapping and falling in line as she swiftly moved her fingers.

"Seven-card stud." It was dealer's choice, and she announced her game. After the cut, she'd toss the first two cards facedown to each player, then add another faceup for all to see.

"Don't kill me tonight," the most recent big loser said to get their easy laughter going.

"I'll try not to." My mother smiled.

"Whadya win last night?"

"I never count," she answered. But I knew she did. And I knew where she secreted away her hauls, stashing bills in velvet pouches deep within drawers, in folded stocking toes and tiny sequined evening bags stacked on closet shelves. I always begged her to tell me how much she'd won when she was done tallying and to teach me how to play. When to raise, call, or check—and when to bluff. Rules, which she adhered to rather loosely in life, were critical to her in poker. They were as strict as she was—meant to be understood, mastered, and followed to the letter. And one was never, ever to play with a joker or a wild card—those silly games were for girls. They would give you away. They would reveal you for who you were, not worthy of being taken seriously. Not a real player.

Sometimes she'd even let me come in and stand behind her chair. "You can watch, Debbie, but don't you dare let anything show on your face. Whether my hand is good or bad. You understand? Or else that's it, never again."

"I promise, Mommy." I quickly learned to never reveal anything. Missing the chance to see her compete in this world of men felt too important.

They'd play a round, and then another shuffle would open up the conversation. "You should be in Hollywood." One heavyset man always repeated that line as they watched her, a simple fallback when at a loss for words.

"She could probably run Hollywood," another growled. "How'd a smart girl like you end up in a place like this?"

"Sometimes I ask myself the same question." She said it lightly, in a way that didn't offend them given that they were there too—just a nonchalant acknowledgment of the obvious that made them all nod.

Their weekends, like mine, were lit by her presence. She always drove up to the hotel alone because by the time I was born, my father preferred to stay in the city on the weekends. Most summers I didn't see him at all. I was left in the country for three months with my father's sister, Aunt Lena, and my mother would always visit at the end of each week, staying in room 107—right next door to the one I shared with my aunt, room 105. There would only be an adjoining bathroom between us. That and a different brass key. The hotel rooms were rustic with no air conditioning, but each corner held some dusty magic for me. Twin beds with thin headboards and even thinner chenille quilts; drawers that never quite closed on the wood-knobbed dresser; worn curtains blowing prayer strings on cool nights. My young eyes saw past the run-downness of the place; only a child could see it so purely. For me, it was a faraway kingdom, a storybook land with a beautiful queen and her little princess of the meadow.

Idealizing it—and her—as a child helped me cope with certain uncomfortable truths. That's the insight of an adult looking back, one who now realizes that my penchant for exaltation served me well when I was young. Those magical wonder years between five and ten remain incredibly vivid, the memories flickering in my mind like scenes from an old film: splices of the swings at the base of the evergreen path that led to the pool, or the porch that spanned nearly the whole length of the hotel's façade. Its enormous screen walls were held together by flimsy wood trim and a loosely hinged door that groaned open and closed. Under a planked ceiling of forest green lived Ping-Pong and bumper pool, a pinball machine, and small card tables for no-rules games of Go Fish.

Nothing beat being on the porch when the sky darkened from an approaching storm. It was as close to nature as a city child could get—the safest place to experience the thrill of being unsafe, to forget oneself in the face of something larger and uncontrollable. Thunder stomped on the roof and lightning cracked with frightening closeness as the air's scent turned mossy and earthy. Wind and rain forced through the thousands of tiny holes in the screens, blowing hair and wetting feet as we played on. I spent years perfecting an almost unhittable Ping-Pong serve that still lives on in my muscle memory today. What I don't have any memory of is my mother watching. But even then, I knew the porch scene was not for her. I understood.

As much as summers in the country were a welcome antidote to my concrete, crowded city life, they did rouse a vague, diffused ache that back then I couldn't name. A.k.a. maternal longing, a yearning that was ever present in both locales. "A.k.a."—also known as—was a hallmark of my life with my mother, for almost nothing was as it seemed to be—or perhaps as it should have been. Illusions abounded.

Maybe it was wistful mommy-longing that made the resort's female guests seem perpetually fascinating with their circle of lounge chairs huddled around the pool. So preoccupied with women and their stories, I'd always swim close to the edge and eavesdrop, a waterlogged sponge for their conversational bits. I loved the warmth of their public privacies, especially when they were out of the earshot of men. Above the row of creaky cabanas, speakers played a never-ending loop of Frank Sinatra, Jerry Vale, Dean Martin, Perry Como, and Vic Damone—a background score that lent a certain gravitas to their observations and opinions.

"I thought it was a tumor. But I was pregnant again, dammit."

"I think he's seeing someone else."

"I'm in love."

"I told him: 'When I call, you better answer the phone.'"

"Really? I can't believe she did that! What was she thinking?"

"Do that again, and he's putty in your hands, I'm telling you."

"Listen to me—never, ever say that. He won't respect you."

"Oooooh! What a fuuuuuuuccccckkkk!"

"Tell his mother to shove it up her ass."

"I love a parade, but I'm not marching."

"Do you see how he's always ready to cop a feel?"

"I lost the baby."

"It was a helluva ride to go nowhere."

"I need this like a hole in my head."

"I looked him straight in the eye and said: 'You are trouble.' And then I walked away."

Pre-dinner every evening, my mother and the other women gathered on the patio, fresh in their outfits and ready for cocktails. "Debbie," one of them would always call out, tapping the spot beside them, "sit by me." Then she would maybe offer a story or a revealing insight that clued me into something new. I was always at the edge of my seat, my head swiveling between them to not miss a word. They all were so different and yet so much the same—whether extroverted or introverted, educated or not, funny or more serious, beautiful or not quite. At an early age, I learned to roll with all of them and never once had my fill as I took in everything from the flick of an ash to the twist of a phrase or a hip.

My favorite teacher—other than my mother—was always Annette. I would angle to be next to her on the patio, just as I dove under the water to swim closer whenever she shimmied down the steps in her white bikini. Annette was the knockout daughter of a guest who had become the owner of the resort when my family sold it. She was thirteen years younger than my mother, who was her idol, and thirteen years older than me, her worshipper. Annette sat between us literally and figuratively, a go-between in whom I could see my mother's influence. She held her cigarette just like her and tossed her head back the same way my mother did when she laughed. I saw myself in Annette, and not just because she also revered my mother. It was because she seemed within reach, someone I could actually grow up to be like.

When the dinner bell rang, we all poured into the dining room. Surrounded by oversized windows, our special Canzoneri table had a complete view of the expanse, a place of honor. I always sat beside my mother, soaking up her presence. Once in our seats, we'd put our pinky fingers together—a private gesture, as close to a secret handshake as we would ever get, and proof positive, I felt, that something about us was the same. She'd soon turn to play her starring role at dinners that were always lively and long, with guests hopping tables and mingling between courses like a wedding reception without the bride and groom. She was the only one who didn't move, though, since everyone came to her.

Every year in that dining room, my mother and I would celebrate our birthdays together. In this instance, what was mine was hers—I was born on July sixteenth and she on the seventeenth, which, in my mind, clearly anointed us as star-crossed, connected, and meant to be together. More pinky-like evidence collected in a slim folder. If only I had been able to quietly wait for another twelve hours, I used to reprimand myself, I could have actually appeared on her day—but it was still close enough to be considered the same by all. Our birthdays also came with an extra gift: my mother got into the routine of taking a whole week of vacation around our celebration, and I reveled in the bounty of additional togetherness.

On the night of the birthday bash, after the slightly tipsy guests had toasted us, our giant cake was everyone's dessert. My mother would bend down to help blow out our candles, her hair parted on the left so it flowed in waves over her right shoulder as she pursed her lips. How she shimmered above me, bronzed and radiant. I could only field a few candles, but she took over like some mythical wind goddess who could blow new promise into motionless sails. Everyone clapped once she had conquered all the tiny flames.

Next, I would read her a sentimental card that I had created on the screened-in porch during the week. Each year's version rephrased the same message reminding her that she was the best, most wonderful mommy in the world and of how lucky I was. The other women got misty hearing the sweet words of a young, devoted heart, and my mother would beam. Then I'd open her card to me, signed with love in flourished script, and reach for her gift, turning it over and over in my hands, trying to guess what it was. But the thrill was about more than just what was inside; it was about the fact that she had chosen something special for me. A bracelet or necklace or doll would be unwrapped, and while everyone watched, I'd reach up to kiss her.

Afterward, as with every other night, the lemminglike drift into the cocktail lounge would begin. The crowd would move past the lobby's corner reception desk, past the armless chairs grouped for idle talk, and past the rough-hewn white stone fireplace. Set with thick black mortar, the fireplace was startling, an uneven contrast between light and dark. Then we arrived at the low-lit lounge. Before you walked through the galvanized door, the live music hit you—a trio of guitar, drums, and accordion trying valiantly to sound like more than they were. The pack of us entered, our arms raised and laughing, and immediately hit the dance floor to start Lindy-ing and Mambo-ing the night away.

A jukebox was there to fill any moments when the musicians were on break, and we children were in charge of the music then. We pushed E45, A16, N60, B24—never a slow dance in a bingo of pop songs funded by the grown-ups. Children were welcome, and we all were good dancers, taught carefully by adults who believed that knowing the steps was sacrosanct, almost like the rules of card games. My mother never exercised, but she certainly did dance. Sometimes while she was getting dressed for the night ahead, she'd call me into her overheated room if the bathroom doors between us were open. She'd hike up her half-slip to just cover her cleavage (and barely everything else), and we'd squeeze in a minute of practice, both of us on our toes, hands lightly touching.

"Like this, Debbie. One, two. One, two, three."

"Cha-cha. Cha-cha-cha. I got it!"

"Now twirl around while you do the same three steps. There! See?"

I circled her, then floated back to be eye-to-eye, both of us smiling. She was free when she danced and so, I discovered, was I. Breaking down the steps and knowing the rules helped me to maneuver around them. Once I had the rhythm and routine down, I loved to improvise, to make it my own and shine. And to make my mother nod if I caught her eye.

When she wasn't dancing with one of her chosen partners, my mother held court at the first bar stool near the entrance. Since my father wasn't there, whenever she danced, it was with someone else's husband, but they all knew each other so well from summers past and present that none of the wives ever minded. There was no risk—she never flirted, and the men knew that chasing the unattainable would have been an embarrassing waste of time.

Black plastic ashtrays dotted the bar's length, and my mother's lipsticked stubs filled her own private one. With a scotch sour or a Manhattan in hand, she was the person to talk to, and when it was time for the most fun part of every night—the group sing-along—she was the siren who serenaded the audience.

Each evening, the ad hoc talent show began with guests singing upon request no matter how off-key. Most often they sang
as solos, sometimes in pairs or groups swaying with their arms
around each other. The first ones to take the microphone were
always the regulars, and the other guests shouted them out by
name. Each performer had a few minutes in the spotlight as one
after another belted out songs that ran the gamut, from ballads to
the blues, as the orchestra trio heroically kept pace. By the end of
the summer, we had often heard the same people sing the same
song fifty times, but it didn't seem to matter. This was the spirited,
spontaneous, slapstick core of each evening, an audience-partici-
pation tour de force that tightened everyone's kinship.

"Dotty, Dotty," the guests would yell. My mother would
make her way to the little step-up stage slowly, drawing out her
stride in the same way she stretched the opening lines to "Hey
Daddy," her best bring-down-the-house number. With each verse,
she'd raise her arms and gesture with parted fingers to receive all
the very best baubles the man in the song was providing.

My hit, on children's talent nights, was the more wistful
classic "Moon River," infused with dreams and total surrender
to the water's currents.

Aunt Lena would always sing "Till There Was You." Then
more women chimed in, hugging themselves as they sang, "You
Made Me Love You," or "I Put a Spell on You," or "You Don't
Have to Say You Love Me." And then came the heavyset Italian
matrons, their jellied bodies heaving as they belted out, "Arrive-
derci Roma," "Tarantella," "Volare," or "Non Dimenticar."

But one tenor always brought everyone to tears with his rendi-
tions of "Malafemmina" and "Mama." I didn't understand all the
words, but the two opposing songs—equal in majesty—made me
almost physically feel his voice, the notes echoing inside me as if I
were hollow. My young heart rose and fell as the emotional anthems
confirmed the power of both evil women—the literal translation of
"Malafemmina"—and motherhood night after night.

In between the singing and dancing, I had access to a continuous supply of orange and grape soda. "Put it on my tab," was

my favorite adult thing to say. Children weren't allowed to sit at the bar, so we claimed a few square tables against the back wall. Our sit-downs became more fun when some character joined us for a few minutes to tell jokes or do magic tricks. My favorite was the guest who was also an expert illusionist. Beyond his gambling and whatever else he did to earn a living, his métier was card tricks that no one could figure out. We all knew he was pulling a fast one, but the indiscernible *how* held us rapt.

"Debbie," he whispered to me one night after a twenty-minute exhibition that left us jumping up and down to know his secrets. "Here's a birthday present for you. Always remember that what looks normal is often not. Take this deck. It looks ordinary, but it isn't." He winked. "There's something you're not seeing. And you can't see it because you don't know it's there. You don't have a clue what you should be looking for. It keeps you guessing. That's what makes an illusion an illusion."

"Ohhh," was all I said, sensing that his words held some truth that I needed to know but didn't quite understand.

What I could never have guessed then was that the resort was to become a source of disillusionment for both my mother and me. What had once been her gateway to a new world eventually became a limiting yoke, chaining her to a past that no longer served. For me too, the years were unforgiving as the hotel faded along with the glory of those early enchantments. But for a long time, it was my summer solace, the lifeline to my roots and to the women who inspired me. I couldn't foresee when I was a child how completely it would lose its sheen, then decline and disappear, just as she would.

City

"**E**eeee! Please!" Each night's plea was to my Aunt Lena (also known as just Eeeee to me). Lena was my bunkmate at the hotel, and when we returned from our summer oasis to my family's apartment in Queens, New York, she also shared my tiny city bedroom.

"Stay with me," I begged.

"Debbie, be a big girl. Mommy will be back soon. I have to put the dishes away."

The door that separated my room from the kitchen was always slightly ajar, and a sliver of pale yellow light cut across the room to the end of my bed. I knew that I was safe. I could hear Aunt Lena puttering and see her shadow as she moved from sink to cabinet. But still. "Eeeee!" I knew not to call for her sister, my Aunt Lilly, who also lived with us. Bedtime was not her job. I needed Aunt Lilly for many other things, but not for this.

"Just a few more minutes," Aunt Lena answered. "Getting the coffeepot ready for the morning. Mommy will want a cup when she wakes up."

"Eeeee! Now!" I always tried to be good. I tried to fall asleep by myself. But I just couldn't unless she was there. Couldn't let my eyes flutter open to see the ceiling that looked like blood again.

Couldn't recite the prayer that my aunts had taught me one more time. The last two lines—*And if I die before I wake, I pray the Lord my soul to take*—weren't calming at all. I couldn't keep turning my head away from what was hanging above me, then turning back to check it again. That chandelier stared down as I lay there, enormous and menacing and forged from black wrought iron. Each prong's bulb had a shade like a top hat, and the whole effect was so jarring, I was too afraid to even think about why. But it didn't matter for long. Aunt Lena couldn't bear to hear my cries, so she always came to rescue me.

When the summer season ended, we all tripped over each other in a one-bedroom, one-bathroom apartment. Mine was the extra half room, the rental's dining room—a.k.a. my bedroom. The conversion was not a true one, however, as the space continued to maintain the adult air of its prior incarnation. My early years were spent in this fashion-forward room with a ripe tomato–red ceiling and full-length draperies hiding the one window that faced an alley. Meticulously selected by my mother, the curtains were like a work of art, an intricate pattern of black and red curvy lines dancing all over an ivory background, almost like floating musical notes waiting to be composed into song. The pattern complemented the abstract fabric on the chandelier's shades but was not the same; my mother viewed too much matchy-matchy-ness as a major decorating faux pas.

The walls still had a pair of Italianate diamond-shaped, gold-flecked mirrors hanging on them, which made my room feel like a Venetian wonderland without young Alice or any other reminder that a child lived within. I realize now—and only now—that some truth about the natural order of things took possession of me then and lingered deep inside. I had to fit into the room rather than the other way around.

A strange parallel universe to the hotel, that apartment was where my family and I coexisted for the other nine months of the year. It was confined, often chokingly so. There were no country freedoms; no fresh air wafting in from the first-floor city windows that remained forever closed; no escape from the tensions and hushed whispers. There was no room to wander; nowhere to breathe. It was a too-small box that one never left unless there was a purpose. Without some specific reason to go out, you remained inside, the walls closing in around you, like a bomb shelter or a safe house that might not live up to its name.

The apartment vibrated with secrets and its own assortment of adults to figure out—four very different grown-ups who were connected by impressionable, only-child me. I had to navigate between quick-tempered and quick-witted Dorothy; my always-striving-for-something father, Jay; *and* his two unmarried Canzoneri sisters—a.k.a. my substitute mothers. Nurturer Lena and cultured Lilly were as different from each other as they were from the woman who ruled over them. My mother had cleverly created a household that served her needs, one that flipped the 1950s homemaker stereotype upside down, eliminated anything she did not want to do, and allowed her to come and go freely.

After their parents had died and the resort no longer needed them, my aunts had to decamp to different shores. The only daughters among four Sicilian brothers, Lena and Lilly had been raised within traditional walls that strangled their own choices. No suitor was ever good enough for the Canzoneri sisters, and the result was a matched set of two fifty-something virgins with limited prospects. It was inconceivable that they would go out and work, so my mother stepped in with a way around her problem and theirs.

She never so much as washed a glass again once she had turned over every aspect of the home—and my daily care—to her sisters-in-law, from diapers to toilet training, socks to school. The apartment became a convenient, orderly hive that revolved around its queen. My mother breezed in and out like a VIP guest, full of pronouncements and air kisses and balanced by the pair of plump fairy godmothers who constantly fussed over me, the child they would never have.

My mother would rush in on her way back out, her cheeks flushed with some excitement. "My darling girl!" she'd exclaim. "How are you today? Come! Follow me and help me change."

I'd scamper alongside her, trying not to bump myself on the

dining table and chairs that had been placed in the foyer after I commandeered their former space. Like everything else in the apartment, it was a tight squeeze. You could get bruised if you weren't careful.

"Why are your bangs so short?" Suddenly fully noticed when we reached her room, I could tell my mother was displeased. "Lilly," she called, "did you cut her hair with a bowl around her head? Why do her bangs look like that?"

Aunt Lena would always scurry on command, but Aunt Lilly moved more slowly, attempting a certain bearing that was difficult to maintain when facing the person who provided the roof that shielded you, the food you ate, and the clothes you wore. I pressed down on my forehead to make my dark brown bangs longer.

"They really aren't that short, Dotty. It's humid today, so they just curled up a bit."

"Well, we all know her hair does that. You have to take that into account when you cut."

Hair fell into Aunt Lilly's bucket. My aunts had divided up the domestic labor, and each had specific areas of responsibility and oversight. Lovable, huggable Lena did all the shopping and washing and cooking—once the hotel's head chef, her culinary talents easily transferred to three meals a day for five people. Our apartment building had the most tempting lobby on the block, and every delicious aroma led right to apartment 1B. Any time of day, any day of the week, we were the source. Maybe that made my mother happy too.

Lilly was in charge of cleaning (except for the kitchen) and all aspects of me. As I grew, she was an adoring built-in tutor, overseeing school and homework and extracurricular activities. We got lost together on rainy afternoons with artsy crafts and arias soaring from the record player. She was a fine soprano, and I always begged her to sing along. I thought she could have been an opera star, but she didn't agree. Sometimes she wasn't in the mood to sing, but when Madame Butterfly's "Un Bel Di" played— full of the longing and sorrow of innocent love—her voice would always rise.

"Debbie, let's chisel these bars of soap like Renaissance sculptors." She'd hand me a plastic knife, and although I always tried to make a new shape, it somehow turned out to be the same white blob, its cast-off shavings spread all over the newspaper. But in my mind's eye, I was always whittling the woman I couldn't wait to grow up to be.

Even though everyone in our house spoke English, it was as if the three women came from different countries. I had to become trilingual, fluent in each of their distinct dialects to get by. My aunts spoke an ordinary language of food and simple pleasures and chaste propriety. My mother spoke another language entirely—one of parties and people; ideas and independence; adventure and fearlessness. It would have been impossible not to be reeled in by the romance of her language, so it became my mother tongue, uniting my dreams with hers.

The words they each strung together were often contradictory, and all their conversations demanded endless deciphering and interpreting. Like how one would define a woman's actions as either good or bad, while another would attach a different value entirely. "Oh, Lilly, please, she wasn't happy, so she left him," my mother dismissed her sister-in-law with quick certainty. "There's nothing wrong with that." I knew Aunt Lilly would never come back at her, but I felt like she might have a good reason to see it another way.

"Lena, Debbie doesn't need to learn how to cook or clean. It takes too much time away from school. She'll have to learn to do all that later on," my mother pronounced.

It was true, I noticed, that Aunt Lena had no time to do anything else. She never read or went out except for her daily walk to the supermarket three blocks away. And yet, she knew how to really do something that could be touched and tasted and felt. A creative skill that made something wonderful from nothing. Aunt Lena always tickled the back of my neck when she leaned down to put the plate in front of me and whispered, "For you." I knew she really wanted to teach me all the culinary secrets within her, but when I tried to watch, she'd gently shoo me away. "Now, Debbie,

Mommy wants you to read instead, not be in here with me. That's more important. Go find Aunt Lilly."

And there was one other woman in the mix—not a lead, but part of the supporting cast who also had a role in my upbringing. My grandmother, my mother's mother, was in charge of my religious education. In stark contrast to her own daughter, my grandmother was full of cautions and admonitions and prayers. Bespectacled and prim, she had short gray hair that stood like a skyscraper defying any style. Her only beauty tool was a black plastic comb. Every now and then, she'd pull it from a stiff, short-handled pocketbook to tend the wiry mass. It was impossible to believe she had birthed such gloriousness, and she was one more person that I struggled to interpret.

"Ma," my mother would reprimand her. "Don't tell Debbie that. She'll grow up afraid of men." But I still listened to my grandmother. When she walked me to church every Sunday morning, she told me things that sounded right. She seemed to know so much about crossing legs and never being alone with the wrong people. And how you always needed to be on guard. For what, I wasn't entirely sure.

There were distinct physical languages too. My aunts were affectionate big huggers and kissers—Lena's pillow chest was the best place for a worried mind; Lilly's arms went all the way around and never let go first. And my father was as mushy as his sisters. "Squeeze me with your eyes," he'd tease as he fake-tripped into a hug, always adding as he looked behind him, "Who pushed me?" His physicality was designed to amuse and spread warmth, while my mother's was cooler, more distant. From on high. It wasn't her nature to be demonstrative or overly affectionate. Easy to misinterpret, I imagine, even for someone as fluent as me.

My father's pretend stumbles had real meaning. He seemed a man on unsteady ground. A man who was absent as he tried to earn a living and make his mark, and absent sometimes when he was home as well because he didn't want to unsettle anyone or interfere with our routine. These dynamics were all unspoken, but they floated in the air strongly enough for me to sniff them out.

I'd try to make sense of what he was thinking when he sat some nights with his head in his hands, of the venomous sparring that happened when my parents' bedroom door was closed, of why they were so often apart. Somehow, I knew early on that he loved her more. It was as if he could only protest the situation up to a certain point, beyond which it could all rip apart. Then everything would dissolve, leaving him eviscerated and alone. How many silent messages and lessons had I absorbed from watching how my mother was with him? And how he was with her? He seemed beholden to a higher power, just like my aunts. And just like me.

My mother, on the other hand, was not beholden to anyone. She came and went as she pleased—not just for work, but most evenings each week—never questioned or restrained by her husband. Yet despite her stature in our household, there was never a meanness to her, no lording of anything over him. She just behaved like he wasn't there. Apart from the low anger that leaked from their bedroom—sometimes clear enough that I could decipher words like "money" or "crazy idea"—my mother never really fought with my father in front of me. But that just meant there were more mysteries to solve.

There was a kind of curious balance in our household, a gravity that held us all in our places and allowed us to coexist. Yet the impossibility of fitting our collective stuff into the limited closets surely had to mean that some important things were left out. How we even managed to coordinate a bathroom routine speaks to some hidden order; an invisible living system at work. My mother's needs were at the heart of it, and the rest of us just molded ourselves around that.

Aunt Lena had her cot stowed under my bed—she would pull it out at night and tuck it away each morning, her roommate status undercover. Aunt Lilly slept on a cot in the living room, stowed away daily in the hall closet. Not being the deeper thinker that her sister was, Lena was always jolly (not my favorite word, but it captures her life's attitude and contentment with the arrangement). Lilly, however, often seemed to quietly smolder about her fate. She was equally loving but had a firmness with me that was absent in Lena. "Because I have your best interests at heart, Debbie." It was clear that I had to put a little more effort into pleasing Aunt Lilly—and I did—but never so much that it took any energy away from my efforts to appease my mother.

Time with my mother was extra precious and alluring because I had to plug into her very busy schedule. I was, in essence, Saturday's child. City or country, we were mostly weekend pals. Every Saturday outing began with me dressed and ready to go extra early in the morning. I would sit on the long orange Chesterfield sofa in our living room, positioned so I had a sight line straight to her closed bedroom door. Knocking would have been unthinkable, so I'd wait—an hour, sometimes two, depending on how late she had been out the night before—my eyes on the brass knob, anticipating its turn. When the door finally opened, so did my world.

Off we'd go to the local clothes shop where I'd perch on the dressing room stool to watch my mother try on possibilities while the other women around her cooed. *Whoosh*, the curtain parted, and there she was—transformed. *Whoosh*, version after version appeared before me, each new vision receiving my delighted little clap when the drape pulled back.

After shopping, we'd carry any packages to lunch at the ice-cream parlor around the corner and sit across from each other, full of smiles. When summer was coming, we'd also stop at a children's clothing store and then it would be my turn to try on cute ruffled short sets and twirl in cotton dresses. The ones she approved would be purchased and quickly handed over to my aunts for our hotel packing.

Aunt Lilly stayed behind in the summer to take care of my father on the weekends and both of my parents during the week. Meanwhile, Aunt Lena and I lolled away the summer together—her only work was to keep a watchful eye on me. A plum assignment, except at night. Poor Aunt Lena could never escape my inability to sleep without her. Maybe it was because she was my assigned roommate wherever I was. Or maybe it was just me. She would tiptoe out of room 105 as soon as I drifted off and try to savor her one shot of sweet vermouth downstairs in the cocktail lounge. The guests, who all took turns listening at the foot of the stairs for sounds indicating that a sleeping child had awakened, would inevitably soon hear my screams. "Lena, Debbie's up again." Even when it was a weekend and my mother was there, they all knew to still tell Lena. What I was so afraid of every night no one ever quite figured out. I wonder now if maybe it was just what I wanted rather than what I feared.

I wasn't too certain of much then, save one thing. Whether city or country, the women around me seemed to fill voids I wasn't fully aware of; they got me closer to answers I hadn't yet even formed the questions for. But the one who always led me by the hand—whether she was holding it or not—was my mother.

Sometimes she occasionally held it on Sundays when our city outings would extend beyond shopping. Manhattan's Central Park was an end-of-May favorite, its blooming green acreage announcing that summer was mere weeks away. My aunts never came along when we went out, but usually, my grandmother would join to spend time with us. We were quite the trio, the gray-haired, hunched-over widow, the spectacular woman everyone thought was a movie star—the most frequent comparison was Rita Hayworth—and the cute little girl with big dark eyes who didn't look like she belonged to either of them.

We'd make our way to the entrance, always crowded with magical carriages attached to horses restrained by blinders. I'd find the ebony ones with white diamond patches and gaze as their heads dipped into the feedbags strapped to their necks. *If they had everything they needed right there,* I wondered, *why did they all seem so sad?* The coachmen in top hats and boutonnieres would all call to us to pick them, but I don't remember ever riding through the park. Those were the days when my mother dressed in full regalia for all her public travels, with fitted knee-length pencil skirts and high patent leather heels, and I think it would have been too hard for her to climb onboard.

She didn't much care for the smell of horses anyway, so we'd stroll past them into the park and walk the winding landscaped paths with trees and boulders, then circle the man-made lake, nodding at people who stared. One bright Sunday afternoon when I was almost seven, we found the park's zoo. Being so close to exotic, wild creatures made my heart beat faster and my mother, in a dazzling lime-green suit with a silver fox collar, led the three of us into the monkey house.

We had only been inside for a minute when an enormous gorilla with graying fur caught sight of her. He began to wildly pace and pant and issue the most guttural, rolling grunts. I had never heard anything like it; never imagined an animal instinct so frightening. I looked up to see my mother's expression, but she wasn't afraid at all. Her neck arched higher as she faced him, amused. He grabbed the bars of his cage and growled in a faster, higher pitch as he pulled at them in a frenzy. Pieces of dried grasses kicked up everywhere and a burning stench—overwhelming despite the open doors on either end of the cage corridor—intensified the more he moved and spread it all around. Some onlookers began to chant "*King Kong, King Kong!*" More chimed in, "Beauty and the beast. Look at that! Beauty and the beast," encouraging my mother to walk by his cage again and again and again so he would follow her. Agitated and pounding, the gorilla swung from one arm as he switched bars to keep pace and everyone who had cameras hanging from their necks snapped away, laughing.

By this time, I had already realized that restaurants would hush a bit when we walked in, all eyes turning and trying to figure out who she was. But this gorilla had figured it out instantly. He knew her. I stood back as the primal scene unfolded, a silent witness to the undeniable truth of my mother's power and an event that would become one more nugget of Dotty lore. When everyone had finally had enough, she and my grandmother walked on ahead as I lingered to put my hands on the barricade. I stared up into the gorilla's eyes, and he stared right through me as if I wasn't there. Aside from an exhausted glance as he turned away, there was no reaction. He didn't know who I was, apparently.

"Debbie, hurry up," my grandmother called back, a few steps

behind my mother. As I took her hand and then my mother's, she sang,

Miss Dotty Jane is the girl for me
Because even monkeys love her very much you see
She has red hair . . .

"I do think it was partly my hair," my mother interrupted.

"Yes, dear. The way it contrasts with the green. And those heels make you almost six feet tall! It was all too much for the poor creature." My grandmother chuckled in her tight, thin-lipped New England way. "Aren't you proud of your mother, sweetie heart?"

Was I? I wondered. *And for what exactly?* I remember feeling tears brimming as I stood between them, not knowing why I had such an urge to cry. I felt as if I would never be able to find the words to express what I was feeling without sounding resentful or ungrateful or unworthy. Best to just go along. "Yes!" I answered. "She's *my* Mommy!"

I sat balled up in Aunt Lena's lap when we got home, knees to chin, my ear right over her heartbeat. She just patted my back every few seconds for over an hour, humming softly. I didn't have to find any words for what was inexpressible then; how the gorilla had conjured up all that I felt was secretly true. That I was invisible, existing only as a part of her—and sometimes not even then. That she really did absorb all the energy in a room, never considering that others might need a share. Tucked into my aunt, it was all about me and her unquestioning, comforting presence. But it wasn't enough. I wasn't enough.

You never intended it, you couldn't help it, I thought many years later. *It all just happened because you were you.*

Halcyon Days

My father always carried a small black-and-white photo of my mother as a young girl, taken a year or so after they met. She was standing with him behind the hotel reception desk, under a framed portrait of my grandfather. Their picture had been cut down over the years to fit into my father's wallets, which were often as frayed as the edges of the photo. I loved to coax it out of its cellophane slot to get a glimpse of who she had been back then. In the image, my mother balances her seventeen-ish face on her hands and beams straight at the camera, radiating pure beauty and the kind of happiness that only springs from the heart. Alongside and holding papers in his hands, my father leans toward her behind the dark wood desk. Thirteen years older, his thirty-year-old self already appears more burdened with dashed dreams. As always, it looks and feels as if he is trying to smile through something.

A born storyteller—my father's winding, sometimes risqué jokes flowed freely whenever my parents were with friends—he often told me of their first meeting. He had been seated on the hotel's enormous tractor, wiping away dripping sweat with his hands. His champion boxer brother Tony had bought the land and then built the hotel across the road from a white-columned house that all the Canzoneris had moved into. Several hundred acres that included a working farm with a silo and stables, as well as an apple orchard on a small mountain, meant there was always work to do. Each of the six siblings had their role, and everyone was on board except my father. He went along with the arrangement but knew he didn't belong. He was the youngest, a creative, a city boy, a fan of the nights and the action. He had been sitting on the tractor, thinking, "What the hell am I doing in the country?" at the very moment their paths first crossed.

He saw my mother walking across the field with a group of nondescript girls making their way from the orchard toward the hotel. "The Farmerettes," they were called, part of a WWII summer program that enrolled young women to pick apples since the regular harvesters, the men, were off soldiering. Near the end of the war when my mother was still fifteen, the story went, she got on a bus alone to escape her parents after reading about a local farmerette chapter that sent girls from the city to upstate New York. Once she got the idea in her head, she made it happen, convincing her parents that she would be well-supervised. She might have lied about her age to qualify, but that wouldn't have been a problem for her—she was already so womanly that everyone always thought she was older anyway. No one at any of the part-time jobs that kept her in fashionable clothes ever doubted her when she claimed she was eighteen, and sometimes even when she said she was twenty-one. My mother was accepted into the program, and they had assigned her to this tiny hotel. That one decision would change the rest of her life.

"I can't imagine Mommy ever picking any apples," I'd always say, smiling.

"Maybe just one, like Eve," my father would always answer with the same smile.

That day in the field, he spotted her immediately. She didn't see him, didn't turn toward the throaty hum of the tractor engine in neutral. She just kept walking, giving my father full view from the front, then the side, then the back as she slowly moved beyond him. He could distinguish only the sound her feet made when they met the gravel path. All he knew at that moment was that she was the most beautiful creature he had ever seen and somehow, he had to win her.

Her eyes had been taking in the expensive black cars with dark windows in the parking lot, the men huddled together, their arms and hands gesticulating oddly in the heat, the women who walked quickly by the farmerettes, their piled-on bracelets chiming like golden bells. For as long as she could remember, my mother had been on a mission to escape a stifling, dreary life that was far beneath what she envisioned for herself, one that included an abusive, alcoholic father and a submissive mother whom she'd vowed never to be like. Now she turned to face the man who had walked across the field to stand in front of her.

"Hi De Ho," my father said. My mother was disheveled from her day in the apple orchard, but beautifully so. He could barely resist the urge to push back some of the strands of her hair that had fallen loose.

My mother looked up at him, smoothed her shift dress wet with sweat, and tried to smile. "You like Cab Calloway?"

"I *am* Cab Calloway," he grinned, launching into a little scat routine and doing a spin on his heels.

"Close." She tilted her head, her blue eyes piercing right through to the heart of him.

"You don't look too happy," he said. "Maybe when the summer's over I'll take you to the Cotton Club." He leaned in just a little. "We'll see Cab from a table right up front."

"Maybe. That's a long way from now. I'm Dotty." She motioned toward the orchard. "It all seemed like a good idea, but it's not for me."

"Man, do I know that feeling. We'll escape together one day. I'm Jay. My family owns the place."

He turned and started to walk away, instinctively knowing when to pull back. "I'll see what I can do to get you out of the fields."

She latched on to him and his promise, making her way to the bus that would return her to the farmerettes' camp-like barracks as she ignored the stares from the other girls. She didn't care. And she never picked another apple.

It was, as they say, the start of something big. My father enlisted his showgirl sister-in-law, the champion boxer's wife, Rita. An intensely beautiful brunette—and Jewish—her arrival and marriage to Tony had shaken the traditional Italian household and softened the way for whoever came next. Of all her in-laws, my father was the only one with whom Rita had a real kinship. And she came through for him.

Together, they convinced my grandfather that the hotel's first-floor cocktail lounge needed a hostess. And that they had found the perfect person who would do it just for tips. All she needed was a new place to stay, which they determined would be a small closet of a maid's room in the main house.

Rita and my father went to the farmerette compound a few towns over to remove her. Both of them reassured the program manager that my mother would be safely kept and tightly supervised by none other than the Canzoneri household. They lied and said that her parents had approved, producing a forged permission letter that Rita had written by hand. My mother quickly packed her bags, and the three of them escaped like bandits in a convertible with Rita's favorite Latin music blaring. The other farmerettes receded in the distance as my mother looked back. They stood like unwanted orphans, staring after her through the trail of dust.

"How old are you?" Rita shouted over the wind and the music.

"Twenty-one," my mother answered. She was almost sixteen.

"Another lie, I think." Rita smiled knowingly at my father.

"Doesn't matter. We're three of a kind."

My mother's hands shot up in the backseat, meeting the force of the wind as they drove. Finally free, her young aspirations were bursting with an almost giddy hopefulness that she could not restrain. She instantly fell in love with them both and would worship Rita until the day she died. My father was not quite as fortunate.

Rita taught her new protégé to feel and take command of her own power and talents for the first time. She lent my mother designer clothes, and together they practiced dancing and other charming arts. My father would stop by the house whenever he had a free moment. He'd lean against a doorframe as they balanced books on their heads, knowing that he was watching the birth of something extraordinary.

Night brought my parents together. After the cocktail lounge scene wound down around 2:00 a.m., they took walks across the open field, between the giant evergreens and around the pool, its water black in the moonlight. He was fascinated by her mouth. He named it "Lush." Also, "Lushtastic, Lushalicious, Lushpendous," and any other creative label that sprung to mind. He was never able to get enough of her, always struggling to rein himself in. She was the one, and he would not risk ruining anything. She would soon untangle herself from his arms, switching modes by laughing at the night's amusing antics in the bar.

Once in a while, their conversation revealed what they thought they knew about themselves. She believed in his creativity, that he would be a great songwriter one day and have his own clubs. How could he not be a success? He had talent, and his family was connected to everyone. She knew underneath that he loved her more than she loved him, but that was the way things were supposed to be. Her young self was sure that she loved him enough.

She felt like a star, and in the world of the Canzoneri hotel, she was one. When my father took the large silver microphone in the cocktail lounge to croon lines from one of his songs, all eyes in the bar smiled right at her.

Nothing could be better than to love you, to love you
To love you is such bliss
Nothing could be better than to kiss you, to kiss you
And kiss you just like this.

Once she'd left New York City and set foot on the grounds of the resort, my mother stepped into a world she had never imagined, one that was particularly alluring given the dreary janitor's apartment that was her home. A door had opened into a world of wealth, power, glamour, and sin. A world full of potential for someone so remarkable. She had known it was out there for her, and now here it was.

41

In a way, both of my parents fell in love with an illusion. When they married, she was eighteen and he had just turned thirty-two (in his defense, he thought she was twenty-four), and she felt that this secure, exciting life would go on forever, not seeing—or perhaps ignoring—the resort's frays around the edges. And he felt he had married his soulmate, not seeing—or perhaps ignoring—her real dreams: the hope for a financially secure life full of passion and refined living. Limitless options, with no restrictions and full control. A young girl's wish.

As the summer drew to a close, there was no doubt that she would find a way to come back to the hotel, and she did. The wallet photo shows her during the second summer she spent there, and by the following season, they were engaged. But that first end-of-summer goodbye after seeing each other every day was wrenching for both of them. He promised to take her out in the city since he took the bus down from Marlboro to Manhattan for a few days every week in the off-seasons. He didn't have a place of his own, but he always stayed with Tony and Rita at their sprawling apartment on the Upper West Side.

My mother's clever machinations were in full gear, but a blooming garden of lies requires more and more watering. Her parents never even knew that she'd left the farmerettes, so the next summer, she told them that the program had asked some of the "special" girls to come back—it was plausible, since WWII had ended and the operation needed to be shut down, that there was a lot of government paperwork to field. The following summer she told them that one of the upstate hotels she had picked apples for had offered her a job as a waitress for three months, picking a more generic-sounding name than the Canzoneri Country Club. Even then, my mother must have said everything with such authority that no one asked too many questions, if any at all.

The deception about her age also fueled a new pack of falsehoods. Especially because my father was so much older, she didn't feel it wise to tell him the truth, at least not in the early stages of their coupling. So, my mother hid the fact that she was really a high-schooler, using her after-school job on Wall Street as the cover. It was a lucrative side gig in the billing pool several days a week that underwrote her fashion and beauty necessities. My mother had lied to gain entry there as well—she told them that she was twenty-one and only wanted a job part-time because she modeled—and then she lied again to my father, telling him that she worked at the investment firm full-time.

My mother never had to put much effort into homework or studying to get good grades, so her nights were free for club-hopping, and she managed to see my father whenever she could. Leaving for and returning from their dates was easy—her own father fell into a drunken stupor relatively early each evening, and she could easily silence her mother, who was as cowed by her high-spirited daughter as she was by her husband.

She would meet my father for a drink at Tony and Rita's first. Their ten-year-old daughter, Denise, would come out of her room and say hello. A tentative little girl with long dark hair and almond eyes, Denise steered clear of Rita and seemed closer to her champion father. My mother found that even perfunctory, small doses of female attention made the little girl happy, and soon Denise opened the front door when she knew my mother would be on the other side.

My parents' courtship continued, and everything was progressing with only one remaining obstacle for my mother—her father. When and how to bring everyone together demanded careful consideration. Even though she knew she held the power in her relationship with my father because he was so in love, my mother feared giving him a firsthand look at such a depressingly humble life. And she knew there would be no warm welcome from her parents because my father was Italian—even though her father, Harry Adams, was a janitor, he seemed too Anglo-Saxon blue-blood for that. Embarrassed and worried, she had only shared stories of her father's drinking and unpredictable bad temper, and of her mother's hunched servitude.

"I will never be like her, Jay. Never."

"I'd never want you to be. You're meant for a different kind of life. With me."

He wrote a song for her on the spot—*If You Were Mine*—scribbling on the folded-up bar napkins he always had in his pocket, along with a little pencil, to capture his thoughts.

If you were mine just to love and hold
To feel your charm that my arms would unfold
If you were mine, you'd be just as you are
I wouldn't change a single thing by far
Through the years we would go hand-in-hand
Cherished by the slave at your command
You could expect a sweet life so divine
With love bold and true, if you were mine.

When they had been together two years, she graduated from high school with honors. One night, at the Copacabana, wearing a fitted black velvet off-the-shoulder dress, my mother announced that she was thinking of quitting her Wall Street job. She had bigger aspirations.

"You want that diamond ring?" my father proposed. "Say yes."

"Yes," she said, bewitched by her feelings for him and perhaps even more so by the world he was inviting her into.

Right after he proposed, my mother announced to her parents that she was getting married. It was a precisely timed reveal. She waited until her father was at the two-drink point, which gave him the best chance of being sedated enough not to object too much, but also aware enough to process the news. She never told my father how the discussion went, but she kept herself hidden for two weeks afterward. My father guessed what had happened, but she begged him not to intervene—that would only make the situation worse. She sounded so sad on the phone, he had a messenger deliver a song with a dozen red roses.

The moon when bright is dim to me
The touch of spring is far from me
And everything I see is strange to me
Darling, since you're away

Your sweetest lips are frost to me
The warmth of love feels lost to me
And everything in life is dull to me
Darling, since you're away.

My father never did see the inside of her family's basement apartment, but he took them all to dinner in the month following the announcement—my mother, her two slicked-back, handsome brothers, ages sixteen and nine, and his future in-laws—at one of the restaurants where Tony knew the owner. The grandfather I never met got through the dinner quietly, probably saving his bitter drinking for when he returned home. By that point, he must have given up trying to contain his willful daughter—he certainly couldn't hit her any harder—so he just went along. It looked as if she would be well taken care of.

They were married in February 1948 at a big splash of a wedding with three hundred guests and lots of envelopes filled with cash. The Italian way. The Canzoneri side paid for the big day and my father's sister Lilly was the maid of honor—a role that was full of future irony. My mother was regal in a white satin gown and a high veil that crowned her head. My tall, broad-shouldered father was his most handsome as if he had polished his dark Italian features to come as close as he possibly could to his magnificent English rose. Their massive wedding album was filled with photos of family, guests, and performers that even included a movie-star dog who entertained everyone with tricks. Rita, who had eased my mother's passage that first summer, was at her side again, now as her sister-in-law.

After the wedding, my mother had wanted to live in Manhattan, but the rents were high and, although he had an agent and a producer, none of my father's songs had been released yet. Queens was quiet and more affordable and so close to the city—just three stops on the subway or a short taxi ride—that it was almost as if they were there. They rented the one-bedroom apartment and my mother happily decorated it, paying cash from those wedding envelopes for the Chesterfield sofa, so long that it sat six comfortably, and for the black-and-white marble coffee and side tables with carved wood bases imported from Italy. That first apartment was intended to be temporary, so whatever it was filled with could easily be moved to the next. She didn't know then that they would never leave.

After quitting her Wall Street job shortly before they got married, my mother dabbled instead in modeling. Too voluptuous for fashion runways, she mostly did corporate work and catalog shoots. When they went out to dinner every night at the trendiest spots, including the Latin Quarter, the Lexington Hotel's Hawaiian Room, and the Copa, people were always stopping by their table offering her some bait to audition for dance productions or the next modeling gig. But she never seemed to pursue all that much beyond her role as my father's muse. It must have been enough for her then.

My mother always had a way of dismissing what was worrying her so she could carry on. When she was around ten, *Gone with the Wind* came out, and she saw herself in the heroine, Scarlett O'Hara. No matter that Scarlett was also conniving and manipulative; she was beautiful and strong. Scarlett's famous, "I'll think about it tomorrow" line became my mother's own. When they were out at night surrounded by the biggest names in New York, she told herself that she'd think tomorrow about how few of my father's musical or nightclub efforts amounted to anything; about how there was less money coming in from their share of the resort.

Rita also knew that things in the Canzoneri family were going south. Tony had been a high-paid fighter, and when that part of his life was over, nothing else had been as lucrative. In addition to attaching his name to New York City nightclubs, he had tried getting into show business in a vaudeville skit, acting in a movie, *Ringside,* and in a Broadway comedy that opened and closed over an eleven-day span. "Small potatoes," Rita told my mother. At my parents' wedding, Rita's hair was dyed blond, and her process of inching out of her marriage was already underway. When Rita finally up and left Tony a few years later to go to Los Angeles and start over, she also left behind her daughter, Denise, ensconced with her grandmother in that Upper West Side apartment. Tony wasn't about to live with Rita's mother, so he moved in with my parents for a few years in Queens until I came along and commandeered the converted bedroom.

With Rita gone, my mother became her public stand-in. While my father worked as a maître d' at one club or another when he could, she would make appearances on Tony's arm. Celebrity columns like Walter Winchell's would report on Tony's whereabouts with his beautiful sister-in-law Dotty. Even with my father struggling financially, the glamorous pre–red carpet, pre-selfie world continued to open up for her.

As it turns out, she needed the distraction. Those words I would eavesdrop on years later at the pool—"I lost the baby"— were spoken by my mother about this period in her life. When I heard her unmistakable voice say them, it was as if an electric current had shot through me in the water. Nearly in tears after spending the rest of that afternoon imagining what had happened, I confessed what I had overheard. And she didn't hide. "A few years before you, Debbie, I had a miscarriage at the end of my sixth month. No one knew why. It was a boy we were going to name George after your grandfather." A boy to carry on the Canzoneri name and inherit the Sicilian authority that made powerful people listen.

I hugged her but said nothing. I was full of my own grief, pain encapsulated and swallowed. I had almost had a brother. A wiser older brother who I could have looked up to and loved. And who would have loved me. The idea that I had been so close to something I longed for—to have another person like me in my corner and at my side—was devastating. The shadow of my phantom brother remained with me and must have hung heavy over my mother as well. In those early years of marriage, it's possible that she needed the "I'll think about it tomorrow" distraction of Tony's presence and his jet-setter circles to help her recover.

My father must have needed healing too. But his escape was always chasing big dreams that were hard to catch. As the youngest in that famous family, the scion of a dominant man who could have been more Don than father, he felt he had to make his mark. His father certainly didn't know what to do with this creative musical performer, this warm and affable baby of the bunch. Full of pride and the pressures of legacy, my father believed that success—both for him and for my mother—needed to be through something big, something out of the ordinary. Those pressures continued to increase, even after his father died. More than ever, he was on a mission to prove something to someone.

Although he did have an extraordinary wife, there was little else to show for all of my father's efforts. Along with whatever money trickled in from his slice of the hotel's summer season, my father worked at some of the bars and nightclubs that Tony lent his name to—one that lasted awhile was the Tony Canzoneri Paddock Bar on Broadway near Times Square. In between, my father peddled his songs and tried to sell-in other creative ventures. One, *The Mirror*, a movie that promised to be "the most bizarre love story ever told," had my father as associate producer. Although it never made it to the big screen, it must have added a little excitement for a few years. Another was the Seven Arts restaurant—a hub for food and artistry in the heart of Manhattan. That one actually came to life, and he was a part of it for a short time until it dissolved. Then he had his own bar, then a specialty bakery, then . . . so many ventures with his music in between, but so little return.

When I express my love for you, do you hear me good?
No one can do to me the things you do, do you hear me good?
I'm mad about you, so wild about you
You have me in a crazy frame of mind, oh I love your kind
Do you hear me good?
I've saved you my love and all I've dreamed of
What more can I do but give my life for you?
Baby, do you hear me? Do you hear me good?

At some point, my mother stopped listening and turned away.

Origins

I could never imagine my mother as a young girl searching to find herself as I once did. Her identity seemed a strong, consistent, and forever thing. It was as if she had sprouted fully formed like Athena from Zeus's head, born a grown woman dressed in armor. In truth, something impenetrable did stand between her and the rest of us. When she was older, it was armor as fashion to distinguish—and maybe even to disguise—herself. But when she was little, she needed an invisible scute—like the shell of a turtle or an armadillo—to protect the softness that had to be underneath. A shield to battle her way out of where she didn't belong. To survive.

Born at the start of the threadbare Depression years, her childhood was shaped not only by poverty but by people made bitter and unrepentant by its darkness. Only two photographs remain of her during that time, and they make me wonder who she was when it all began. Both photos reveal a six- or seven-year-old girl, her impatient young face in a fiercely determined pout. But it wasn't really a little girl's face: the adult her can be seen beneath the surface, especially around the chiseled nose. Her arms weren't visible, but one could imagine that they were planted on her hips as she challenged whoever took the picture.

She was dressed in overalls—*overalls!*—that were dusty from playing in Maine's rich summer dirt. Her life, I now realize, was as divided between city and country as my own; between light and dark, hopeful and hopeless. New England's Winterport, Maine, was her summer escape and a tie to her WASP roots—the place where her sea-captain grandfather still lived and her mother and aunt had been raised. That side of the family offered refuge from her poor city apartment where her father often terrorized its other inhabitants. In contrast, he was a man with no family at all—as if he too had sprouted fully formed, miserable and alone after he ate whoever made him.

There was never any money, and her parents fell into their defeated roles, my grandfather caught up in the struggle and unfairness of his poverty. All the blame, it seemed, lay outside of himself and was more important than the destitution. Such uncharitable thoughts found their way into her parents' constant fights. Their one-sided arguments all had the same theme—he would remind his wife that she was lower than low, an entirely worthless good-for-nothing, just in case she had any memories left of a finer life before him. True to her WASP heritage, my grandmother maintained a certain stoicism and took the verbal and sometimes physical blows with total passivity. Only her eyes blinked behind the granny-style glasses so attached to her face it seemed as though she slept in them. Once she actually had gone blind for a year after a childhood illness that left her, as she often reminded, "very weak in the eyes." Perhaps not seeing clearly weakened her in other ways as well.

As she got older, my mother intervened when they fought, equally irate at both parents. Her towheaded, cherubic younger brothers who shared a room—Bobby, fifteen months younger, and Dickie, nine years her junior—were ineffective; only she dared to try to subdue her father. When he'd finally fall into a snoring, drunken sleep, she'd rail at her mother for allowing it all.

The irony of her mother's situation infuriated her even more—Margaret was descended from a prominent WASP line that stretched back almost two hundred years. Her father, Harry, on the other hand, had nothing and no one and yet he controlled everything. My mother decided early on that she wanted to be on his side of the rope.

Their claustrophobic dwelling at the northern tip of New York City was as dark and isolating as the Depression itself. Located behind the storage room in the apartment building's cement basement, with the laundry and boiler rooms clanging on either side, it felt to my mother as though she was on some horrible submarine, going nowhere. Just endlessly floating under the water, never coming up for air, never feeling the sun. There were no windows to view the outside world and few mirrors to reflect oneself—just meager food, patched clothes, peeling walls, and alcohol. When she came home after school or at dinnertime, her parents were always there as if fixed in their places. Her mother's pallor announced how infrequently she left the apartment, and her father only went out when a tenant called to have him fix something. He'd then run his hands over his greasy hair, rinse his scotch-mouth in the kitchen sink, and begin ranting about the people who were able to afford actual apartments as if doing so would make his own lot better.

My mother spent as little time at home as possible. Apart from school, the next best place was Judy's house—my mother's friend-for-life from the moment they met at the age of twelve. Almost as beautiful, Judy also excelled in school and was an early bloomer too—boys were in pursuit by the time they were fourteen. They were both selective, however, because they could be. My mother was typically aloof, but when she was fifteen, one classmate sparked something in her with his falling-down earnest love. But both she and Judy agreed that he was too local and would never amount to anything. My mother needed someone with potential and Judy's doting mother and sister concurred. They were a tight-knit Jewish family, and my mother basked in their loving support for one another and for her. They emphasized learning over beauty in a home that beckoned with wonderful cooking smells and a table that you actually wanted to gather around.

But it was my mother's annual two-week trip to Maine that was both her greatest escape and her safest harbor. Her grandfather, Captain Joshua Thayer, paid for the family excursion that included everyone but her father. The two men hated one another, and every year as the family packed for their retreat, there was a scene. Once my mother—in a rare moment of candor about her father—told me, "He'd get so mad over how happy we were to be leaving that when we were packing, he'd sometimes push me to the floor like he was jealous or something. Or he'd smack me. But," she added quickly, "he never really meant it. He loved me more than anyone. He probably had been drinking a little." At that moment, she spoke exactly like a young girl, one who had to explain away something that wasn't quite right.

But when their little family stepped off the train in Maine, all her worries disappeared. For two weeks there was only familial warmth, the scent of salt air, and the creaking sounds of boats on their moorings. And the captain, called Papa by all, was joined by her mother's sister, Aunt Belle, known as Tante—she preferred the French word for aunt and everyone obliged. Tante was fourteen years older than my grandmother, and the age span between them was attributed to Papa's long years at sea. His wife had died six years before my mother came along, and no one really talked about her too much. It was as if she were a woman from history who had just disappeared, lost in the shadow of her charismatic husband.

Papa was a self-made man whose seafaring adventures befitted a character in a novel by Rudyard Kipling or Robert Louis Stevenson. A favorite pastime of my mother and her brothers was to explore the anchored schooner that Papa had sailed to China. As soon as they arrived, they would clamor to walk the deck with him and discover everything that was below. My mother loved to feel the boat rocking beneath her as she stood on the bow, her arms spread wide. Her grandfather's piercing blue eyes and angled face were so like her own, and she loved it when he told her how much she looked like him. "Cut from my handsome image, you are, much more than my own two daughters," he'd tease.

Margaret—also known as Fuzzy—was the only grandparent I ever knew. In my parents' enormous wedding album, she looked just as I knew her throughout my youth. Old before her time, she could have been seventy when she was merely forty-nine. Born in 1899 just days before the new century, it was as if she were clinging to an old world, with a certain out-of-place ditziness that had earned her the nickname. In other words, she was the complete opposite of my mother in looks, attitude, and behavior. You could find my mother in me if you looked hard enough, but they were two women who bore absolutely no resemblance to one another. When I was growing up, my mother dismissed everything about her mother, distancing herself to prevent contamination, as if Fuzzy were a sick patient. She looked after her as she got older, but it was an obligation, and my mother never seemed to experience any true pleasure or comfort in her company.

One Sunday morning when I was about seven, Fuzzy dropped off a big manila folder when she picked me up. "We'll look through this when we get back from church," she said. "Mommy will love to see what's inside." Fuzzy would move around the corner from us years later, but back then she had to take the bus from Manhattan for our Sunday prayers—the subway would have been faster, but it was too dark and steep given her eyesight.

The doorbell always rang precisely at 9:30 a.m. and I would be ready for our ten-block walk to the 10:00 a.m. service at our Community Methodist church. Fuzzy's roots were actually Episcopalian, but we had to make do with another Protestant church because it was the only one within walking distance. She always made sensible decisions like that, just like her comfortable, but unattractive, shoes and practical dresses.

At that age, I went to Sunday school downstairs while she sat alone upstairs in the church pew. "Your granddaughter has a lot of questions," I once overheard the woman who taught the class say to her sternly. It made me think that this tendency of mine might be a bad thing, although I had thought the opposite was true. Occasionally, they let the children participate in the adult service—I loved being up in the cool, peaceful stone structure as small cubes of bread and thimbles of juice were shared. In those quiet moments, I would will my questions away. Maybe they were there because I knew that our religious routine was not of my mother's design.

When we arrived home after church that Sunday, my mother was in a flowing, feathery-collared robe tied loosely at the waist, her cheeks full of color. She didn't have any of her Max Factor makeup on yet because it was too early. Just her rosy, flawless glow as if she had been walking outside in the cold. "Dotty dear," Fuzzy said, producing the folder. "Look what I found. All about Papa."

"Papa." My mother smiled. She took the folder from her mother and emptied it onto the dining room table, revealing newspaper clippings, papers, and pictures that told the life of the famous merchant seaman.

He had died right before my parents' wedding when he was eighty-nine, but five years prior when my mother was thirteen, there had been a scare that rocked the state of Maine—Captain Thayer was either dead or lost in the woods after his fishing boat had capsized on a lake. The newspapers predicted that even if he had made it ashore, no man could survive in that dense wilderness without food or water, let alone one his age.

My mother had returned to Maine with Fuzzy and her brothers in preparation for the inevitable funeral, but after a week, Papa had walked out of the woods. A miracle. The family rushed to the farmhouse where he had emerged, and when my mother first saw him, this redwood of a man was wrapped in a plaid blanket and giving an interview. She stood in the back and watched as he made everyone laugh. "I've been up in the Klondike and sailed all over the world, but I don't know when I've had a week as disagreeable as this one," he declared. "Ate only roots and strawberry leaves for seven days. And then came to this farmhouse where they were kind enough to give me some warm milk." He paused and then quipped, "But no smoke yet." As he looked around, he spotted my mother. "There she is." He called out, "Come here, granddaughter, and show these fine people how beautiful you are."

My mother blushed, full of love for him, and for the spotlight he had shared with her. When she joined him up front, he whispered that thoughts of her had kept him going; that as he made his way through the wilderness, he had been writing her a letter in his mind to explain life. How it was full of uncertainty and unknowns; how most of the time you don't know where you're going and have to trust yourself to get there, how only what's inside of you can get you out of the dark places. Every summer, Papa had warned my mother not to get too "citified" because "only nature lets you find your way." He was always telling her things like that—in truth, she wasn't too sure exactly what he meant. But when he encouraged her to find her own path and told her that she was strong like him, not weak like Fuzzy, she did understand. And she took it to heart.

Periodically, my mother returned to Maine as an adult, and when she decided to share her summer sanctuary with me, we took an overnight train there together a few times to visit Tante and her husband. Tante was a formidable woman who had worked at a chic department store and had married late, after a long and independent spinsterhood. Like me, my mother had an aunt who she loved. Unlike me, she listened more to her aunt than her mother. Like Aunt Lena and Aunt Lilly, Tante had no children of her own, and she satisfied any longing through my mother, taking a great interest in her beautiful niece, and in return, my mother latched on to her as her family's female role model. When we took these trips, Fuzzy was left behind in New York.

The overnight train was a marvel to me. Not quite as luxurious and mysterious as the ones in films or novels—but exciting all the same because my mother and I slept in the same compartment and moved through space and time together. We always boarded in the late afternoon, had dinner in the dining car, and then retreated to our very snug quarters. Before I could climb up to the narrow top bunk, we had to navigate the tight squeeze of the cabin, twisting our bodies just to get around each other. The train fittingly rolled into Maine as the sun came up, heralding the new day and place. But on one trip when I was still seven, I woke to feel spreading nausea joined by pain in my stomach just minutes after I opened my eyes. I didn't say anything at first, praying that everything would pass. But by the time we got to Tante's house, both sensations were overwhelming and unstoppable.

I panicked. I didn't want my mother to see me this way, vile and needing her to deal with one of the most disgusting and disagreeable jobs of motherhood. I ached for my aunts to spare me the awkwardness of the fumbling between the two of us—me trying to contain whatever I could, and my mother trying to care for me. I was so sorry, so mad at myself for ruining everything. I lay in bed at Tante's house for several days, but when I recovered enough to join everyone, nothing felt right. I hated the way the milk tasted, and Tante couldn't understand, insisting that the milk tasted exactly the same as it did in New York. But it didn't; it was revolting. I couldn't get comfortable in their house after being so sick and unsettled. Every part of me felt like I didn't belong and I wanted desperately to go home.

My mother, however, was like visiting royalty, perpetually poised in a receiving line as countless neighbors and relatives dropped by. Night after night, I lay in bed trying to sleep while the chatter and laughter of the guests below filled my ears. It was worse than all those nights at the resort—here I was the only one on the second floor, and no one would come if I screamed. Instead, I'd crawl out of bed and sit at the top of the stairs each bedtime, listening to their conversations and feeling proud that I hadn't cried.

Fuzzy died when I was twenty, two weeks after a fall she had when she was in her seventies. My mother's sadness was contained; a relatively brief Maine squall requiring a little leaf raking and cleanup afterward to get on with things. It was as if my mother was almost relieved in some way; as if she had carried this adoring, sweet, and submissive woman long enough.

Even though I had always felt that there might be more to Fuzzy, I followed my mother's lead after her death and made her a fond memory just as quickly. Before we could completely move on, however, we had a job to do: disassemble her apartment to make way for the next tenant. Like a story Papa would tell, it turned out to be a two-day journey into unknown territory.

My mother was nostalgic and talkative as we sorted through the markers of Fuzzy's life, from old-lady shifts with snaps down the front to austere photographs of a plain young girl who looked even then as if she would always struggle to make others smile.

"I never understood why she was such a little mouse," my mother said. "Until we went back to Maine for Papa's real funeral right before I got married. What an eye-opener."

She told me that after the reading of the will that left my grandmother and her sister the family home in Winterport, as well as an unusual property—Bare Island off the coast of Maine—my mother, Fuzzy, and Tante went out to dinner. "Tante told her that she should leave my father and move back to Winterport now that they had the house."

From everything I knew about my grandfather and how my mother and her brothers had longed to escape, it was almost inconceivable that my grandmother would not have followed her sister's advice.

"But Fuzzy said no, that she couldn't leave me and uproot my brothers. Tante kept insisting in that high-pitched way she had. She told Fuzzy to stop making excuses for once in her life. To stand up for herself and end the abuse.

"I finally asked Tante right in front of Fuzzy," my mother said, "to tell me why she was such a doormat. And Tante spilled the beans at the table."

It seems that before my grandparents met, Fuzzy had become quite taken with a young man, and in her naïveté, thought that he felt the same. At the time, she was almost thirty, but still a sweet, unknowing little sparrow. "One night, he got her drunk," my mother said. "Of course, I was shocked. Not once had I ever seen her take a sip of alcohol. They thought at the time that he must have spiked her drink. A month later she found out she was pregnant."

My mouth hung open. "Fuzzy?" I asked in disbelief, thinking of her squinty distaste as she told me how men only wanted one thing, of how her eyes fluttered with each repeated warning. And now here it was, the root of it all, a revelation that had probably been strong enough to rock the whole table all those years ago.

"I couldn't believe that she ever had sex at all, let alone this," my mother continued. "Anyway, she told the man, hoping for the best, but he quickly disappeared, never to be heard from again. They could never tell Papa, so Tante created a ruse and told him they had to get away for a few months to help Fuzzy recover from the breakup. She planned to find a doctor in New York who took care of these sorts of things on the side, but Fuzzy wanted to have the baby."

"Did she?" I asked on the edge of my seat and wondering if there could possibly be a clone of my mother out there somewhere.

"I'm getting to that. They went out one night after they'd arrived in Manhattan and she met my father," my mother went on. "It moved too quickly, and before Tante could quash it, they eloped. It was as if Fuzzy had found the answer to her prayers."

"A husband?" I ventured.

"Can you imagine? She was so ashamed and felt so unworthy that she married the first person who would have her."

I stared at my mother—her empathy for Fuzzy was usually low, but at this moment, her eyes were uncharacteristically sympathetic.

"And then Fuzzy made another mistake," my mother continued. "She told my father she was pregnant right *after* they were married. A very dangerous thing to do with anyone, Debbie, let alone a man like him. He lorded her scandal over her for the rest of her life." •

Until that reveal from Tante, my mother had never fully understood all the times that her father had slung words at Fuzzy—slut, tramp, whore—words that had made absolutely no sense, given my grandmother's chaste demeanor. My mother had never paid any attention to their meaning, just assuming he'd shout anything to hurt and diminish her.

"She lost the baby soon after," my mother added, shaking her head. "All for naught."

"She probably said it was God's will," I guessed.

"Exactly," my mother agreed. "Tante told her that she took all of my father's 'crapola' because she believed she deserved it. It was like a living penance she created for herself."

Hearing the story now, I was every bit as shocked as my mother had been all those years before. The Sunday conversations we'd had on our walks to and from church now made sense; the fearful wisdom had been drawn from her own experience. The rules of her day had made her feel unworthy, and she lived accordingly, accepting her fate—a fall from grace and upper-class gentility to menial domesticity, poverty, and abuse because of misguided shame. Fuzzy never got up the courage to leave her tormenter, but a few years after that revelatory trip to Maine, she was finally rid of him. He died from natural causes two years after he walked his stunning daughter down the aisle.

Strangely, given how the family had suffered at his hands, whenever my mother mentioned her father while I was growing up, it wasn't in a critical way. She never lamented her miserable upbringing or talked about his mean streak. Most of the time, when she brought him up, she even sounded admiring. "He was strong," she recalled. "He had all the power." And sometimes she would even say, "I took after him, Debbie."

What little I knew about what their life was really like came from her two brothers, not her. The elder, Bobby—the brother she disliked because she felt he was weak just like their mother—was the most talkative. He did take after his father in one way, though; he grew up to be an alcoholic too. Not a mean one, just a sad, passive one who drank every night and cursed his life. Once a talented athlete, he had lost his shot at pro baseball when he was drafted into the Korean War. He was a man who lived in the past, who let his childhood obstacles weaken rather than strengthen him, and my mother hated that about him. Like the local fifteen-year-old suitor who'd had no potential, Bobby was, to her, just another neighborhood guy who was content to hang out at the corner bar.

But when he was drunk, every childhood trauma came spilling out—the beatings, the verbal cruelty, the desperate and constant poverty. His harsh recollections were seconded by Dickie—the kid brother she adored, and who grew to be a rule-breaking, street-smart guy. Nothing either of them said ever really lined up with the fragments my mother shared. I didn't realize back then that maybe she'd had to paint a different picture for herself to get by.

As we continued going through Fuzzy's belongings, I found a framed picture of my grandparents that had been taken at my parents' wedding. They both looked so old, and on top of that, he looked ill. "Mom," I asked, "how did your father die?"

"He had some sort of disease. Too much iron in the blood."

"Too much iron? Seems appropriate," I quipped, "since he was always hitting everyone."

Silence. I reached for more things on a top closet shelf. A large packing envelope was stashed so far back that I almost missed it. I pulled it down and saw it was marked "Harry Adams" in big block letters. I started scanning the contents, and something immediately caught my eye. "Mom, a.k.a. means also known as, doesn't it?"

My mother rushed to my side so fast that she almost tripped over a pile of clothes. "Give me that, Debbie."

I held on to the papers I had already started reading. "What's going on?" I insisted.

"Oh, here we go. I don't want to talk about this now," she snapped.

I couldn't stop myself. "This says that your father's last name really wasn't Adams. It was Stockton?"

"Apparently," she said impatiently. "That's what all the evidence showed."

"What evidence? These letters?" I moved away from her and kept flipping through what seemed to be a stack of military correspondence.

My mother took a deep breath and rubbed a spot in the middle of her forehead. "When Fuzzy filed for his VA benefit after he died, we found out that he wasn't who he said he was." She paused and regained her composure a bit. "They told us that Harry Adams didn't exist. That he was really a man named Robert Stockton." Her voice trailed off.

"What?!" My eyes scanned the papers incredulously. "It says here he was married to someone else first. In Tennessee?"

"Actually," she said sharply, "he was never divorced."

"So, he was a bigamist? They were never legally married? This is crazy!" I shrieked.

"Well, yes. Despite living together for over twenty years and having three children, they were never actually married," my mother admitted. "There was no common-law marriage then."

My mind was reeling. My poor simpering grandmother, who had resigned herself to years of shame and abuse for the sake of being a married woman, had in fact never been married at all. I looked at my mother. "So that also means you're illegitimate?"

"If you want to look at it conventionally," she answered.

"My grandfather was a total fraud," I said, dumbfounded. "And you never told me?"

"I never told anybody. Not you. Not even your father." Her voice was tight; three short staccato sentences.

"Why wouldn't you have told Daddy?"

"Enough!" she said. "I don't know. I just didn't."

"But you were my age when he died! Only twenty! It must have turned everything upside down. How did it affect you?"

"How did it affect me?" She stared incredulously. "I didn't let it."

"That can't be possible," I said simply.

"It is," my mother replied.

"Maybe being filled with guilt was what made him miserable," I posited. Silence. "Is there more family I don't know about?"

"I never bothered to find out."

"You really don't know if you have half sisters or brothers in Tennessee?" My only-child longings again stepped forward. Why had she not chosen to find out more? Did she feel superior to whoever else might have been in his life? Or was she worried that there might be another daughter he loved more—or was more beautiful— than her? I had just written a college essay on the scandalous

Les Liaisons Dangereuses, which, among other things, planted the notion of dissembling. The art of concealing one's true feelings or motives in society; of constantly wearing a disguise or element of deceit wrapped around one's neck like a scarf. I watched her closely now as I tried to interpret what she really felt.

"Debbie, it made no difference."

"No difference? Really, Mom. I can't believe that. I wouldn't know what to think if I found out now that you were not Dorothy Canzoneri, but . . . Mary Smith. If all your details were untrue; if you were a forged person."

"He was who he was. I wasn't about to let strangers into my life." She was adamant as if the shock of the revelation had hardened her so she could never be hurt like that again.

But I couldn't get over how everyone had suffered at the hands of a man who was fighting some private war that only he knew about. "What would you have said to him if you'd found out while he was alive?"

My mother looked at me, silent. She moved the tips of her fingers together as if she were considering the thread count of a sheet or the weight of a feather in her hands. Finally, she said, "I think I would have laughed in his face. And then slammed the door."

Our conversation slammed shut as well, so I had to let it go—after I told my father. He was surprised but didn't seem particularly unsettled that she had never told him as if he were used to things being withheld.

I knew that despite my mother's professed indifference, an illusion such as this one had to have affected the way she saw herself. She always seemed like the most secure, confident, and courageous of women, but to battle through this discovery at only twenty years old would have required her armor to be firmly in place. It was one more truth for her to tamp down, one that threatened to derail her image of who she was or who she wanted to be. Her resilience formed a barrier like a moat around her until she was like Bare Island—a fortress protecting dark, ugly secrets and keeping people out.

And keeping what shouldn't be revealed inside. My mother was free from Harry Adams a.k.a. Robert Stockton the moment she found out the truth about who he really was and decided to tell no one. If it stayed a secret, it couldn't touch her. She put him on a shelf and left him there. Until all those years later, I found him.

Reversals

Early on in my parents' marriage, my mother added a rounded curio cabinet and tucked it into an empty corner of the living room. Painted pale green, the carved wood piece held her most precious items on its tiered, circular glass shelves. Two antique vases—one, a Japanese Satsuma of rich rust, told a visual story of a foreign land; the other Chinese one had embossed gold dots around a very somber royal couple. The vases joined a porcelain panther and a free-form dancer with arms raised. And, on the uppermost shelf, a highly prized Japanese gem tree.

Teardrop jade stones—somewhat darker than the shade that would later set the gorilla on fire—were held together by threaded wire, forming a mosaic of fibers and gems as intricate as a coral reef. The jade tree was placed right underneath the spotlight hidden in the dome. She would often glance at it as she walked by, captivated by its uniqueness—since no two were ever alike—and by its resilience and permanence. Unlike one in nature, it existed on its own, its independent, solid structure needing nothing more. Never would it shed its leaves or wither away. Perfect for a woman like my mother who hated the decline of anything.

While the tree and its beauty endured, much around my parents' marriage crumbled in their first seven years together. In addition to the sorrow of the late miscarriage, their financial situation continued to worsen. When they got married, Uncle Tony's last fight—a high-profile thriller at Madison Square Garden—had already taken place nearly a decade before. Everyone still knew his name, but his celebrity was on the wane, and this began to affect the resort. The regulars thinned slowly at first, a hardly noticeable change, but each year there were fewer reservations as the hotel became a second or third choice, or as vacationers decided to book for only a week or two instead of the whole summer. Unbeknownst to my mother, some corners had already been cut by the time she appeared on the scene. After my Sicilian grandfather got sick, he had quietly sold some of the vast acreages. By the time he died the year before my parents' wedding, my father's mother had turned over all the decisions to her sons—four brothers with four different, expensive lives, plus a mother and two sisters to support. Soon there weren't enough old-time and new guests to earn even half of the same profit. Nothing was adding up.

My mother began to help in a new way. Her best subjects had always been history and math, and her calculating skills had been sharpened in the Wall Street pool. She worked on the resort's books, putting everything in organized perspective for the Canzoneri brothers and herself. Each year it became clearer that what had started as her gateway to a better life was leading instead to an uncertain future. The years were washing over the hotel like water eroding rock, slowly changing it into something no one expected. My mother took charge, forcing the Canzoneris' hand by demanding a group sit-down—a mediation that would have made her Sicilian father-in-law proud. She brought clarity, which led to acceptance that the resort would have to be sold and ultimately, to the process of unloading the property.

At the same time, my father had a song, "I'm Gonna Break in a New Moon," that gave them some hope. It seemed about to hit, just like some of the others were supposed to. It had been recorded, and its words were clever and catchy and held the promise of a new cycle. The song ended with the lines:

Saturday's Child

I wanna start like a new love, like you and I have just met
Then we'll break in a new moon we will never ever forget.

He might have hoped to begin again with her and with the song, but eventually, it joined the others in a pile of vinyl that somehow never made it through the music matrix to the radio. Just when my father received the unfortunate news that the song would not be the hit he envisioned, one of the clubs where he had been working shut down. He didn't tell my mother right away—there was no point in worrying her. And another work opportunity at a nightclub had come along. It was only a three-month gig, but maybe that would change. If not, he thought briefly about getting a commercial real estate license, but at that point, he clung to his inner artist, pouring all his energy into different creative paths.

My mother's occasional modeling—less a real job than something glamorous to talk about—was not enough to sustain them. Despite their financial instability, she continued to turn down more offers than she accepted, from being in a Ziegfeld Follies–type revue as the prime end dancer to the motherlode— an invitation to Hollywood for a screen test before I was born. I never understood why she chose not to step up when a dream had unfolded before her. "I just didn't," was all she'd say.

Whenever we watched the movies she loved, I couldn't fail to notice that there was always a star who resembled her. "You're even more beautiful, Mommy," I would chirp. "But even if you weren't the star, it would have been so much fun just to be in a movie."

"Maybe, maybe not," was as forthcoming as she'd be.

Was it fear of rejection that held her back? Or that she might end up a little fish in a big pond when she lived the opposite scenario right where she was? Still, her dabblings did lead to one magazine shoot of her I cherish with equal parts amusement and sentiment—the cover of a detective magazine shouting in big, bold type, "The Waterfront Gangs Want My Blood." Not quite *Vogue*, but a cover nonetheless. Her startled eyes in the image, her hand alongside open red lips, her throat encircled by a four-strand pearl choker, all reinforced—at least to me—that she could never quite escape the underworld. Her sophisticated seductiveness was a perfect prototype for just the kind of woman a gang would chase, or a big strong man would want to rescue.

The year before I was born and six years into my parents' marriage, the Canzoneri brothers finally accepted an offer and sold the hotel, along with whatever land was left. My mother was so instrumental in all the dealings that her signature was on the closing paperwork. The hotel was rechristened San-Catri Lodge by the next owner—Annette's father and a family friend, Frank. He owned a successful steel manufacturing plant and felt he could turn around the resort. He got it for much less than anyone would have expected because of its decline, and that meant that my mother and father's share of the sale ultimately was not much of anything at all.

I made my first appearance at San-Catri when I was two weeks old in the mid-1950s, and it was this second incarnation of the resort that provided the backdrop for my idyllic summers. Each season after that, we were always the special guests, the heirs of the founder. But once it was sold, my father no longer had any desire to join my mother and me there—when his last name wasn't on the sign, something shifted for him.

And shifted for the hotel as well. Without the Canzoneri name attached, San-Catri attracted the more straight-and-narrow guests who I grew up with—mainstream Italian families where the men had real jobs. Nothing too fancy, most of their livings were of the regular sort while those who made big money began to vacation in more far-flung locales. If there was any leftover illicit behavior from those Canzoneri days that preceded me, it was more like a fell-off-the-back-of-a-truck kind of guy who supplied cigarette cartons and silk shirts. "Debbie, take this. Give it to your mother for me." Unlike the Canzoneri Country Club's heyday, at San-Catri, you didn't really need a position of power as an entry card—what counted was that you were good-looking and could dance well, tell an entertaining story, hold your liquor, and, of course, sing upon request no matter how off-key.

My mother didn't stay the whole summer when I was born, arriving at the beginning of August for a month to recover. She had plenty of helping hands up there, which was a good thing. Our first week at home together had been relatively easy—Fuzzy stayed and took care of most things for her daughter and son-in-law and me. But my mother was on her own for the second week, meeting the daily chores of life with a newborn firsthand.

The country relieved some of those demands for a few weeks, but by the time she returned to Queens after Labor Day and struggled to get through the next few months, she realized that any vision that she'd had of maternal bliss was not in line with the reality. She was slipping into the chore-after-chore domesticity that she despised. The stooped, stale life of her own mother that she had sworn would never be hers.

Her new world tightened around her and, just as she had realized in the orchard that picking apples was not for her, she knew that taking care of a baby was not for her either. The unending duties were a far cry from what she had imagined her life would be. Coupled with a string of further financial setbacks, both her marriage and motherhood became a stranglehold, a pearl choker gone awry.

A pair of sisters-in-law, Lena and Lilly, were her solution. "If they come and stay with us they'll have a place to live," she told my father. "They can take care of Debbie and the house."

"In this apartment? All of us?" my father asked, worried about the dynamics.

"We're not going to be in Jackson Heights forever, right, Jay? That's what you keep telling me."

"We'll be out of here before you know it. Something big is brewing." The promises piled up, dimming my mother's rays of hope.

"Well, if at least one of them doesn't come to care for Debbie, I can't take this job."

Our financial saving grace had fallen right into her lap, and she used it to sway my father. While she had been at the hotel in August, the new owner, Frank, knew that she'd done the Canzoneri bookkeeping and had offered her a job. My mother had a good relationship with him from the sale and from his time as a guest—he did a mean Cha-cha—and now he told her more about his business, Franchet Metal Craft. The manufacturing plant minutes from our apartment in Queens was growing, and he needed someone like her. The job would be convenient, an attribute my mother always loved. In addition to being a short drive, it would be traffic-free—everyone from Queens was headed toward the city, but she would be traveling in the other direction. And she was used to driving; in fact, she did all the driving in our family. When my father had been a performing arts freshman at Syracuse University, antics during a blizzard had claimed his left eye when a snowball-turned-ice-ball hit him in the face. His glass eye looked normal—she hadn't even noticed that it wasn't real right away—but that accident forever made him a passenger in my mother's life. She would always have to hold the wheel, and she handled it as well as she handled everything. But sometimes I could feel her frustration course through me as the years went on.

One New Year's Eve, the three of us were headed out to their friend's party all dressed up. I slid in the back, and she huffed as she arranged her voluminous dress behind the wheel, sighing as her high heel found the best angle on the pedals. I so wanted to help her, but as a child, there was nothing I could do. I was her passenger too. But I sensed how things could erode to become more intolerable over time, despite everyone's best intentions.

My mother had dismissed the job opportunity when she first heard about it in August, but after a few months of full-on motherhood, she took action. Frank got his office manager, and she got her paycheck, even though the job was about as far away from Hollywood as you could get.

Once the sister aunts arrived, my mother happily disconnected from every mundane detail of household life except for paying the bills each month. She went against every single social convention for housewives and mothers of her day, which took a great deal of courage, especially because she owned it—never cowering or hiding her total rejection of domesticity. In fact, it became a part of her persona.

But she didn't have much love for the small, messy office she shared with Frank, filled with nuts and bolts, open metal drawers, carbon paper, and forms. So many forms. She did the reverse commute every day in a used car that had seen shinier days. Despite her distaste for toiling in a factory to make ends meet, she soon was in charge behind a dinged metal desk and a squeaky throne chair. It was a monumental adjustment, a comedown really, as she faced the realities of her life. The only thing that was running smoothly was the house—the decision to have two full-time family members taking care of three people was the charm. Aside from that perfect ratio, nothing was as she had imagined.

The last years of her twenties were spent in a fog of disappointment that grew as the years went on in that same apartment. A hidden sadness that could be touched like some solid, ugly thing you could reach in and pull out from under the water, long tail and all. Even as a child, I understood that my mother didn't belong to the world she was in—a mermaid on dry land; an effete in rent-controlled housing; an extraordinary woman leading an ordinary life. The longer she went on, the more she simmered, running her hands over the worn-away patches of her velvet chair, a patina that held no real charm for her.

Sometimes a carrot would appear to deliver a moment of hope, a dose of excitement to cure what ailed. Whenever my father was on track to close a big deal, she'd allow herself to get swept away—and sweep me along with her. Even though so few of his deals ever came together, maybe this time it would happen. In those moments, the apartment tingled.

But the up note was always short-lived in their drama: the affable, creative man and the woman, originally drawn to those characteristics, whose feelings changed over time. As she had to support everyone and handle everything, her resentment grew. But that was just the top layer. Underneath, it was that she didn't like who she had to become because of the way he was—she didn't like who she was with him. It wasn't the real her. A sad state of affairs that only two people could create, and only one could undo.

The Rules

We didn't have a whistle in our household like the one blown in the *Sound of Music* to line everyone up. Or a bugle, despite everything being as precisely scheduled as the military. Our regimentation just evolved over time. We all existed in my mother's world, governed by her rules for when things should happen and how. A protocol planned around her schedule and needs that made life as predictable as it possibly could be when living with unpredictable, unscripted Dotty.

My mother started her full-time job after negotiating one of those idyllic, nearly part-time schedules: 10:00 a.m. to 4:30 p.m. Monday–Thursday and 10:00 a.m. to 1:30 p.m. on Fridays—a summer shift year-round that put her in the beauty parlor by 2:00 p.m. She insisted on her terms in the same way she bluffed at the poker table, and Franchet Metal Craft's owner, Frank, folded. Once she started her job, she was always on time, but she never walked through that door a minute early or stayed one minute late.

My mother's personal life was just as precisely scheduled. Monday night she'd come home for dinner and stay—*yay!* Tuesday night she went out straight from work with friends. Wednesday night she was sometimes home. Thursday night she went straight out. Friday night she was home for a fish dinner post–beauty parlor, freshening her makeup at the table with a portable mirror before a quick change for a night out with more friends. After our Saturday afternoons together, she went out at night. Sunday she was home, and I would see her after church.

Her absence and waiting for her return was all I ever knew. If she'd been royal, leaving to fulfill a duty to cause and country, it might not have felt so personal. Instead, there was this floating left-behind feeling—that wherever she was going, whoever she was seeing, was more important than me. I'm certain that my mother never intended to cause me pain. Perhaps at the outset, she hadn't planned to turn me over so completely to my aunts, but the circumstances of that arrangement enabled her to take more and more liberties. Relieved of domestic minutiae, almost anyone would appreciate how much easier life becomes. But freeing yourself from the inanimate is so different than escaping the animate child.

But I never kicked up a fuss—if I did, she might not want to spend time with me at all. I just busied myself with something else, like my lineup of Tiny Tears dolls. Their most endearing feature was their magical ability to cry "real tears" after a bottle of water. I gave them a row of pillows first to make them comfortable, and then alternated the brunettes with the strawberry blonds in order of size all the way down to the baby ones. I told them how important they were to me, how each one was enough to fill my heart. It occupied me for hours.

The schedule never varied and we each had designated times for everything, from bathroom visits to bathing to dinners. Weekday mornings were particularly challenging. My aunts had to set their individual alarms extra early to be able to take turns using the single bathroom, put away their cots, and get dressed so they could start everyone's day. Aunt Lilly would wake up first in the living room—if Aunt Lena set her alarm first, as her roommate I would wake up too early, so she got to sleep an extra twenty minutes. When it was Aunt Lena's turn, I got up too but would wait in bed reading until the bathroom was free after she started to prepare breakfast.

"Hurry up, Debbie. Don't dawdle," one of my aunts would say each morning trying to speed me along. "Mommy will be up soon."

I don't think my father ever had an alarm. He either got up on his own or after my mother—once she awoke at 8:00 a.m., the bathroom would be entirely hers for the next hour to properly prepare for her day.

Occasionally, I'd have enough time before Aunt Lilly walked me to school to help my mother choose an outfit and lay it out on the bed for her. My mother had managed to organize her two small closets to fit all her things. They overflowed, but because she was systematic, everything had a place and could easily be found. The closet right outside her bedroom door and across from the bathroom held all her coats and seasonal clothes stored in tightly packed, white zippered bags. They hung above the luggage and boots stored on the floor, and below shelves that held big pocketbooks by size and color, along with accessories like scarves and gloves and evening bags stuffed in hatboxes. The other closet alongside her vanity was filled with work clothes on the left side and evening clothes on the right atop rows of shoes. I pulled out whatever she told me to and put it on the bed, always longing to touch the sleek dresses—fitted silks and satins and brocades waiting on the nighttime side.

There were only two other closets in the whole apartment— my former-dining-room bedroom had none—so all my father's things, along with all of mine, and both my aunts (including Aunt Lilly's portable cot) had to be squeezed into them, alongside our holiday decorations and household files. It could be very hard to find what you needed.

"Bye, Mommy." I had to think about what day of the week it was to know whether to add "See you later," or "See you tomorrow."

"Bye, Debbie. See you soon." She always seemed a little irritated when she was headed to the office. She left at 9:35 a.m. sharp every day (it was a twenty-minute drive, but she needed five minutes to walk to wherever her car was parked on the blocks that surrounded our building). Sometimes when she came back, especially on late evenings, it could take a half hour or more just to find a place to park, forcing her to circle and circle the same blocks, hoping that someone would vacate a spot. Like being lost in the woods, praying that you'd stumble upon the path. That looping search was especially tiring because she had to be the huntress every single time.

As courageous as my mother was going against the norms of the day, she was motivated by a drive to break free from the mundane, not really by any deep desire to work. She hated every second of her job, every day, every year, for over thirty years. Her annoyed tone when she answered the phone—"Franchet Metal Craft"—announced her distaste to everyone. A character actor would have had to practice incredibly hard to do as well. She made no bones about not wanting to be there, but somehow it never seemed to matter to her or to the owner. She never took one step to change jobs, and her stellar work made her indispensable, so no search for a more enthusiastic employee ever transpired.

As soon as I was old enough to talk, she scheduled one daily call to me from the office—a hello that often ended with an abrupt hang-up if the owner or a customer walked in. It was a sudden disconnection that she didn't really mean—pretty much the only office rule she adhered to was no personal phone calls, and I got used to it over time.

As much as she hated it, I loved her "away" place when I was young. My visits to her office were scheduled a few times a year and opened up the wonders of that small world of hers. I knew I didn't want to do what she did when I grew up—my imagination was consumed by daydreams that could not be formed around clanging metal and machines. But I was fascinated by her authority. From the owner to the foreman to the factory piece workers, what she said was indisputable and unquestioned. And her ingenuity—how she could talk about fabrication and specs and metal weights; and how she and her old typewriter had worked out a system to somehow accommodate those long nails between the keys.

The office was the only place that I ever actually saw her doing things besides dressing and putting on makeup. Or rinsing her lingerie and hanging it over the bathroom rod—she was very particular about doing that one intimate task herself. But her moves at work had a sharp edge to them; angry, noisy bursts far from her usual grace. I watched her bang those typewriter keys as she issued purchase orders, and pound the drab olive-green adding machine to do the books. She was always reconciling something on that device. Long white paper streamed from the top in rolled waves as she punched in numbers from column A and column B. She'd close her eyes and sigh—nothing ever seemed to balance out the first time, just as her internal ledger couldn't have either. All her mental and physical assets listed line-after-line in one column could never reconcile with the realities of her life in the other. And my own feeling that I had fallen short too, that I had somehow failed her, was never far.

Of all her many dissatisfactions with work, not one was about leaving me. Even as a child, I knew this with complete certainty. Because I was so well taken care of by my aunts, there was absolutely nothing for her to feel conflicted about. In my mother's view, she'd left me in loving hands and accomplished every mother's intention—to create a positive home atmosphere for her child. I should be happy.

The summer schedule was also organized around that view—she worked every day and went out almost every night, so it was obviously better for me to spend the summers in the country air. There was no guilt, no concern, no agonizing from her. And I must have understood because I fell in line. There was only that persistent, prickly, quiet question of her true attachment.

Her total abandonment of domesticity also extended to me. She never espoused any practical, homespun wisdom, no "A watched pot never boils," or "A stitch in time saves nine." Just the unquestioned edict, "Debbie, you don't need to do chores, you'll have time for all that later. Focus on school." I followed this directive to the letter. And the enabling didn't just come from her. My aunts were like union members, never wanting me to cut in on their turf. Perhaps they felt the need to justify their existence to the queen. "Debbie, let me make you this . . . Debbie, I'll put it away . . . Debbie, I'll do that for you."

So I was raised like a princely boy, completely absolved from "women's work" and life's day-to-day maintenance. Not in a way that made me spoiled—I loved my substitute mothers too much for that. I simply took their daily ministrations for granted. Our apartment was always spotless, the food was always on the table, the clothes were always laundered, folded, and put away. I never experienced the mastery of small tasks that brings young competency and confidence. Later on, at the outset of my independent adult life, I was bereft of practical skills. That would all change, of course, but I once stared at a bed as if it were a science experiment—*how do you get those sheets and the blanket to fold in and come up from under the pillows?* Until that moment at nearly age twenty, the thought of how to make a proper bed—one that required more than the flick of a comforter—had never even crossed my mind.

Back then, it felt that being as exempt as she was made me a part of her club. And I loved nothing more than being a member. On Friday afternoons, Aunt Lilly would always walk me to the beauty parlor on the way home from school so I could watch my mother center stage again in another female universe. I knew all her beauty parlor friends, the women who tuned in as she talked to them and the hairdresser orchestrating her high-maintenance hair—washed, set with rollers, teased, and sprayed. Her finished look was an artisanal crown, a headdress that was hers alone.

The style changed only slightly with trends—some years a little longer, some with a slight pullback instead of a side-swoop. But never any roll-out-of-bed-blowout "fad." I turned to magazines at the salon for ideas as I tried to manage my curly and frizzy Sicilian inheritance, but she ignored all outside advice. To her, there was no higher hair authority who could dictate anything better than drying under those massive helmets atop leather chairs; no trendsetter who knew more than she did about the right look for her.

One Friday, Aunt Lilly picked me up from fourth grade and dropped me off at the salon for the whole afternoon so she could bring my mother's furs to storage. It was "touch-up" day—an every-three-weeks happening that I knew kept her away longer.

But that day, I got a firsthand look as I held on to the padded armrest of her chair. Her hairdresser first made neat, thin rows all over her head like a farmer about to plant seeds—in brown earth—then began to brush a smelly red mush down each line. I stared at her exposed roots. It took me a second, maybe ten, maybe more, to process the enormity of what had been hidden underneath all the while.

"Your hair . . . your hair isn't really red?" I stuttered.

My mother looked at me strangely, part amusement—as if she couldn't believe I didn't know—and part something else. Sorrow over some lost innocence? Concern that I would never see her a certain way again?

"I was meant to be a redhead, Debbie," was all she finally said.

The truth looped in my mind as if what had been revealed needed repetition to fully sink in. *Mommy's hair is really brown like mine.* It was an ordinary brown, in fact, not even close to my rich, bittersweet chocolate brown. But then, I didn't realize the warmth of my own natural color. It just seemed like more evidence that the parts of us that were the same weren't up to par. I looked down at our hands. At least she wouldn't change her finger if she could—both our pinkies were undeniably beautiful.

Not all Fridays were as full of revelation as that one, but they all were the prelude to our weekends, and late Saturday afternoons when we came home after shopping and before she went out, or rainy Sundays, were the best. That was our movie-watching time on the TV's handful of channels available then. I'd turn the knob on the console until we found an adventure movie. "Stop! This is it!" she'd say. A jungle or high-seas epic would do, but most often it was a western. "I love the wild in the west," she'd say every time as she teased, "I think I was a chieftain's daughter in a past life."

Most of the movies she loved terrified me. I'd be tucked into the corner of the big sofa, and she'd be in her green velvet club chair, slightly behind my side of the couch. During the action, I'd hear her gasp at something or murmur, "So exciting," and I knew to look away. I tried to watch but spent most of the time just peering through my fingers.

Sometimes, as I got a little older, I had a strange reaction when a movie was on. It started slowly and became more frequent until it happened all the time. It was another sort of prickly sensation, a feeling that came in waves rising inside me when I heard my mother even lightly chewing a piece of gum behind my ear. Or twirling her teased hair on a finger while she watched, winding it tightly and then pressing the end to make a little noise that sounded like brittle straw. Repetitive sounds, once heard, were all I could focus on. *What is wrong with me and why am I so sensitive?* But I stayed dutifully quiet about it when I was young. Sometimes the sound was so disturbing that it forced my hand and I actually had to step away from time with her, leaving the room until she stopped.

I finally whispered my dilemma to Aunt Lena when I tiptoed away from the sound. But she was setting up the buffet table for the annual routine that was my father's birthday and must have been distracted because she didn't even understand what I was saying. "Just pay attention to the TV," was all she offered as she added the cakes to the table. His birthday required two because it didn't belong to just him either. On January sixteenth, it was also our half birthdays—actually, his fell exactly on my July day, but my mother and I continued our joint ritual. Aunt Lilly and I made all the decorations while Aunt Lena whipped up my father's favorite lasagna and the dessert—one full round cake for him and a half for my mother and me to share.

"I know I say this every year, but you really don't seem like a Cancer at all, Dotty," one of their friends at the little party remarked.

"I really am more like a Leo." She smiled. I didn't like the sign for our month—Cancer—either and didn't much care for the crab that was its symbol. People would always comment in the summer too about her having more of a lion's personality than the sensitive, soulful nature of the crab. I had to try my hardest to hide the upset that fell over me whenever I heard her response. It felt as if she was saying that she really wasn't like me at all.

"Mommy, someone said at school that 'Moon Child' is another name for our sign," I offered. "We could say that instead of Cancer." I liked Moon Child better anyway because that's what I felt like.

"That may be, Debbie, but they're right. I feel more like a Leo. Maybe I'm on the cusp or something."

I pushed the conversation out of my head by deciding that astrology couldn't possibly be real anyway, and we blew out the candles.

Our annual routines always included holiday schedules. The one task that my mother never assigned to others was buying presents for me. She had a generosity of spirit when it came to gift-giving that, of course, always earned her my delight and appreciation. But sometimes, as Christmas approached and I helped her dress in the mornings or at night, I would spy wrapped presents in shopping bags hidden in the closets. If they weren't wrapped, I looked away, not wanting to spoil my surprise.

Not all of the gifts could be wrapped. One Easter I found six little chicks in the kitchen chirping and scampering around in a low box. I'm not sure she had completely thought that one through—I was devastated when they got too big for their habitat and we had to give my babies away. I begged to drive them to San-Catri so I could see them in the summer, but my father put the box in the backseat, and my mother took them to work with her one day. I tried not to think about what became of them. There were also two poodle puppies at different Christmases, one gray and one black. My aunts took care of the feeding and walking, and my mother and I took care of the petting and playing.

Christmas brought joy to the apartment, and everyone seemed happier most of the time. I would catch glimpses of my mother entering, bags and boxes under each arm. If she knew I had seen her, she'd say, "Santa will bring presents too, but some come from Mommy and Daddy." I'd usually be decorating the house with Aunt Lilly, putting up the fake evergreen tree that we pulled—with great effort—from the back of the hall closet. When I was very young, it was a silvery white tree. "So chic," my mother pronounced. And so, it was.

One year, my mother gifted me seven Russian and seven

Japanese nesting dolls. They were hand-painted in each country and brought to America, she said. That they came from far away and were intricately made didn't matter to me all that much. It was what these two wooden women unfolded.

The Russian doll was ornate, a blond celestial being in an elaborate headdress of berry vines and jewel-toned flowers. The Japanese doll had black bangs with hair pulled into a tiny carved bun set on top. Delicate and reserved, her hands folded into a blue-and-gold kimono, like a graceful, wise queen of light. Each held smaller and smaller versions inside—and some sort of promise for me.

I ignored all my other presents that year. Aunt Lilly sat alongside me, picking up the pieces of discarded wrapping paper as she read the card tucked into the tissue around the Russian doll: "Matryoshka. It means motherhood and family," she told me.

I pointed to the card, which had more written on it. "What does that word say?" I knew that she wasn't telling me everything, that she was leaving out things I shouldn't know. Sometimes, Aunt Lilly would be tight-lipped over something she couldn't voice. Like when we'd been decorating the tree a few weeks before. I had just moved the needle to play Alvin and the Chipmunks' "Christmas Don't Be Late" for the hundredth time. My mother had said something as she was leaving that I couldn't hear even though my head was angled toward them. Aunt Lilly's lips turned toward each other to form a thin line. She said nothing in return, just nodded, but carried some disapproval with her for hours. After a while, I just switched the record to "Silent Night" because when I missed the high notes, I could make her smile.

"That word?" Aunt Lilly asked. "It says fertility. Um, it means lots of babies."

I twisted each doll carefully at the middle to reveal the next and the next and the next. All the sizes split in half to reveal a smaller one. The faces were the same, but as the dolls got tinier, there was a sacrifice of intricate detail—headdresses became less heavy, outfits less defined, so each piece was the same yet different. I could play with them for hours. I gave them all different personalities; I'd group the middle ones so they could tell stories to inspire the younger ones who vanished into the ones more grown, all the while getting closer and closer to the largest, most distant one. And all of them adored the baby, perfectly formed at the end of the row. Pure and whole and carved from one solid piece, she waited to bloom.

The Secret

My mother had a flair for making magic happen. Or so it seemed. She was always full of surprises, and that's just the way things were. One weekday when I was around eight, she had called from work to say that I should come outside in twenty minutes and wait for her in front of our building. A few minutes ahead of schedule, my eyes were on the far corner where she would turn onto our one-way street. Suddenly there she was, rolling down the block and honking behind the wheel of a beautiful, sleek rusty-red number that matched her hair. She pulled up alongside me, and I ran over to her window, breathless.

"Mommy, I love it! Drive around the block again and again!"

"It's a Caprice Classic, Debbie. The best car in the world." My mother always deemed everything she had "the best"—which was either her ego talking or simply her way of coping with the reality of what she lacked.

I struggled with the door handle a bit and slid in. However much my mother might have wanted to be driven, she was always the one driving. Of her many friends, she was the only one who would drive on parkways, through tunnels, and over bridges. Her courageousness anointed her not just my father's, but everyone's designated driver before the term was ever coined.

"Light me a cigarette, helper." She smiled and motioned to the lighter's raised top. "Just press it and watch what happens. This one works, not like the one in our other car."

I flipped the gold buckle of her new black alligator bag and reached inside for the Benson & Hedges. It was a fresh pack, but I knew how many times she tamped down the top before pulling the silver edges back on three sides, so I did it for her, just as she would. Then I lifted a thin cigarette, feeling sophisticated as I held it in the air between my own index and middle fingers. I jumped at the lighter's pop, the end now red-hot and menacing, and touched the tip to it, drawn by the sizzle and overjoyed to be doing something so grown-up so perfectly. She took it from me, holding it just as I had, and inhaled. The trail of smoke pulled to the left window, which she always opened with the same thin crack to let in fresh air. Her hand resting on the wheel in between drags made a rich still life, she the model and me, the observant artist. We sped off, and from that day on I remained her copilot, responsible for tolls and cigarettes wherever we went. I made sure she never had to ask for either.

She pressed on the horn. "Idiot! Cut right in front of me. Did you see that?"

I nodded. Except for the muffled arguments that she had with my father a few nights a week, the only time I ever heard her yell was when she drove. Aggression that might have been slightly subdued in other circumstances appeared when she was fully in control of the means to get her where she wanted to go.

"It's such a beautiful car, Mommy. How did we get this?"

"I saved."

I wanted to believe that this was true, that all those hours at the factory had really provided enough for this car, and for some of the other things that occasionally popped up, like furs and jewelry. But what I wanted to believe even more—what I wished for—was that it all came instead from my father. That he would be the one to relieve her burdens, to give her the luxuries she deserved, and the money to care for us all. So that things would tip more in his favor and he wouldn't be dangling in midair.

At some point in my early childhood, it became clear that one job was no longer enough for my mother. She was just past thirty, and at the peak of her glamour. My father's various lines in the water continued to attract only nibbles, so the financial pressures remained on her, and what she was earning wasn't really enough to sustain us. It happened that someone knew the owner of a great nightclub that needed a hatcheck girl where my mother could work one or two nights a week and make as much as she did in a week at her day job. Lured by the atmosphere, she jumped at the chance. Dressing up like the star of *Gilda* must have felt much closer to Hollywood than machinery parts. She filed for the necessary hatcheck license and got it as easily as she got the job.

Stepping into that nightclub brought her back to the woman she had been when she first walked into the Canzoneri Country Club. She was herself again, an elegant shining star. With the same low-lighting and long wood bar—but with heavy maroon draperies and brass sconces—the nightclub served Italian food on platters and drinks in oversized glasses. Tables were arranged around a small dance floor and a stage for live music. It was an upgrade from the hotel's cocktail lounge, but not as fancy as the Manhattan nightclubs she had been to with Tony and my father. It bordered Queens and Long Island, and it drew a predominately male clientele of regulars—loud, smoky gatherings of friends out for the night, along with some couples and larger mixed groups where the women and men seemed a bit too flashy and celebratory to be married. It was convenient to her day job—she would bring her dress to Franchet Metal Craft, then change at the nightclub when she got there around the 5:00 p.m. set-up time for the dinner crowd. But the most important part about the place was that she felt renewed—even though she had already put in a full day, she was never tired once she was there.

On the second night of the first week at her new job, he walked in.

"You must be new here. I could never forget that face."

She stared at him, feeling. Just feeling.

"You're a good dancer. I can tell," he continued.

Her beauty had made her an object of admiration her whole life, so she was used to diffusing the unwanted attentions of men. But she knew in an instant that she had no such intention with him.

"You know what they say about women who dance well?" she asked, mixing her words with a sly smile.

"No, sweetheart," he answered. "Tell me. Waddah they say?"

Still staring up at his face, she was astounded by just how incredible he smelled, a scent so enticing it left her unbalanced. As ruggedly handsome as someone so well-groomed could be, he was about an inch taller than she was with her heels on, with deep blue eyes and lots of dark hair. A combination that some would call Black Irish, but she had no doubt that he was Italian. The whole place was. His eagerness was palpable. She artfully waited a beat, saying nothing.

"Come on now." He leaned in. "I really wanna know. What about women who are good dancers?"

She gave a slow smile, followed by a wink. "They say their feet hurt."

He laughed. "You sure got it goin' on, don't you? I'm Dom." He handed her his black cashmere coat, lightly touching her hand. "But sweetheart, you can call me anything you damn well please. Just be sure to call me."

She wasn't certain who he was—or who he was to her— but she had never felt anything like the chemistry between them before. Trapped behind the coat check's half door, the club came alive for her when he walked in. The two nights she spent there became the highlight of her week. She anticipated his arrival, their banter, watching him, becoming more and more feverish as the weeks went on. She thought of him first thing in the morning and the last thing at night, and daydreamed scenarios in between. Dom, it was all about Dom. He became her world, her drug.

At home, she started to smile more, for real. The persistent disappointment faded. There was no time for that; an undeniable energy was coursing through her. It came from him, even from thoughts of him, and it lifted her higher. One night, she leaned on the coat check's half door ledge and stole glances as he ate, imagining him slowly trailing his mouth along her neck, from the base of her collarbone to her left ear. She heard her own sharp inhale.

It was a rich fantasy. But for all the banter, nothing happened between them for almost two years. She was, after all, married (however unhappily at that point), and any step forward would be irreversible. There was a reluctance in him as well. Not because he was married—that concern was not part of his code—but because he knew that she was it for him. The one. He was afraid of the weakness that came from handing over such power to another person, afraid that somehow she could ruin him, make him lose his edge. So apart from flirting, the romance just cooked on high heat inside of them for the time being as they got to know one another. It was an emotional affair, in today's vernacular.

One night, Dom had had enough of the teasing, and he made the club owner an offer no one would refuse. He trotted in a replacement hatcheck girl whose salary he had agreed to pay for a year.

"You're free," he told my mother. "Now get out from behind there and come sit at my table."

"Dom, I need the money."

"You're free, and you're mine. Don't worry. I'll take care of it." She shivered as he slipped a black mink stole around her shoulders. *At last,* she thought, the satin lining cool against her skin. And so their story began, a compartmentalized, rationed, double-life existence that continued for the rest of her life.

At the time, I think I sensed the shift in her but didn't know the root of it until I was an adult. Then, it just felt like there was always something I didn't know. Before Dom, she was almost always upbeat when we were alone, working hard to spare me the strain that she constantly had to face down. But looking back, during those early years with Dom, she was at her best, her most compelling self. I could tell that something was pumping through her veins that made life even more of an adventure. Maybe my father had closed a deal, I hoped, and she didn't have to worry anymore.

But I could also feel that something more than the usual was distracting her—when we had our time together, she was sometimes living in her own head, smiling over nothing in particular. At those moments when I felt her slipping away, I would become even more full of ideas for things we could do. "Debbie, you can't be entertained all the time," she'd say when my need to fill our hours together became too much for her.

Apart from the car, which was too big not to discuss, my mother would never flash the other accessories she was acquiring. I'd often just stumble across something in our apartment that wasn't there before. A new ivory and opal ring or diamond-encrusted watch would appear in her vanity drawer; a lynx hat would suddenly be in a box on the top shelf of her closet when it got colder; a new fur-trimmed suit or sequined dress had taken its place in an otherwise-familiar row.

"When did you get this, Mommy?"

"Do you like it? It's beautiful, isn't it?" She always gave soft nonanswers worthy of a politician.

I couldn't know the source of all the material tokens then. Or that Dom and my mother would never be without each other again, except for one blip.

When I was eleven, she trusted me with a secret.

"We're going to move," she whispered. "The two of us."

My heart skipped. "Where, Mommy, where?"

"To a house in Jamaica Estates. We're going to look at it today. But just say we're going shopping. It's our secret, you understand?"

"Yes, Mommy." I would never have betrayed her. But the implications of what she said began to set in. "But what about Aunt Lena and Aunt Lilly?" I frowned.

"They can't come with us. But you're big now. You'll only miss them for a while. Fuzzy will come with us."

Grandma? I guess I loved her and she did call me sweetie pie and came for dinner some Wednesday nights and, of course, took me to church on Sundays—but she couldn't compare to my aunts. Besides, as with so many people, there didn't seem to be enough room for me in her heart because it was so full of my mother. She still wrote little ditty *Miss Dotty Jane* songs about her but never wrote a new one for me; she'd just put my name into my mother's songs. Maybe she was too tired from her hard life. Or maybe, it was her weak eyes that made it difficult for her to see me clearly.

On my inner scale, though, the secret news still tipped more toward positive—something was going to change to bring me and my mother closer together.

"And Daddy?" I whispered. The balance could tip back.

"He'll stay here with your aunts. They'll take good care of him."

I swallowed, trying to not let anything show on my face, trying to cover the upset I felt over losing all of the other members of my club. I just told myself that she was right, they would take good care of him, and at that moment, I pushed all the other uncertain thoughts away.

I remember little of the house in Jamaica Estates except that it seemed enormous in comparison to our apartment, with lots of shuttered windows, and a big bedroom for me with a tree outside that I instantly loved. A week went by, then two, then a month. I asked a few times—when I was sure we were alone—what was happening with the house, but sorrow that I had never seen before had fallen over her. She spent more time alone in her bedroom and when she ventured into the living room, she sunk low in her chair, mummified by a heavy quilt to keep the cold at bay. In her orbit, we were all at a loss, my father, aunts, and me. It was as if her planet had pulled away from the sun, floating further and further until darkness fell upon the house. None of us could handle things without her, and no one would dare to intervene. I soon knew to stop asking.

My mother never spoke of the house again, and the memory slipped away from me. But when thoughts of it, and her despair, suddenly resurfaced after she died, I turned to Annette for more details about that time. Members of my mother's inner circle had filled in many blanks about her life with Dom since her passing, but Annette was my most trusted resource. Our close connection had only strengthened through the years, and she continued to occupy a critical space between my mother and me, always full of insight about us both.

"Your mother was pregnant then," she told me. "It was Dom's child."

"Pregnant?!" I raised my hand as if to stop oncoming traffic.

"Yes. And she felt that this was the time to move out."

"And into the relationship she wanted?" I asked.

Annette nodded. "But I don't want to make it sound easy. She didn't want to hurt your father. I remember her telling me that it was possible to love two men."

I sat stunned, trying to digest what Annette was saying.

"She gave Dom an ultimatum, and he agreed," she continued. "He was buying the house she took you to visit. It was around the corner from my parents—they actually helped her find it."

"But . . ." I was reeling. "We never moved. And there was no baby."

"In the end, I guess his unwritten code won out. He couldn't go through with leaving his wife. So then . . ." I held my breath.

"My mother went with your mother to have an abortion," Annette revealed. "It was still illegal then, but they got connected to a good doctor. And she left Dom right after that."

My hands folded together over my mouth. Once again, it felt like my loss too—another almost-sibling who could have been by my side. I thought back to that time, how it had seemed like she was receding. She went out less and ate too much ice cream every night. When my father would soft-shoe around, I'd catch the harsh glances she'd throw his way—*Don't say a word I despise you* looks that shared her disillusionment with their situation lest he be unaware. The unhappiness in that apartment then was thick and viscous, choking me. I could only read between the lines to try to figure out where it came from. *Was it my father? Or did I do something?* I'm sure I found a way to take responsibility for at least part of her sorrow since I never would have guessed the truth. Just as the illusionist at the hotel had warned me, I couldn't see it because I didn't know it was there.

"But even if he had stayed married," I asked Annette, "why wouldn't she have compromised and still had the baby? Found some middle ground where they went on as they were? She would have had a house and him and another child."

Annette laughed. "Your mother wasn't a middle ground person! I guess she wouldn't leave your father to publicly be a mistress. She would only do it if she were Dom's legal wife."

"It's hard to accept that she bowed to such convention when her life was built around so many unconventional circumstances."

"I think it was about status more than convention," Annette said. "To leave a marriage and end up a goomar must not have felt right when she could have had it all."

"And maybe it wouldn't have been right to bring me into a situation like that?" I ventured. "Maybe she didn't compromise for my sake?" The thought caught me by surprise and immediately made me feel ungrateful. Whatever hurt I had felt through the years, perhaps she had shouldered an even more devastating hurt because she was looking out for me.

"That could be," Annette said. "I doubt she would have put you in a situation like that. And what would your father have done then? To divorce so she could marry someone else would have been one thing. But I can't imagine him letting you leave his house if she had compromised. And she wouldn't have left you behind."

She wouldn't have left me behind. Perhaps it was possible that she had put me first. But then, a roiling seasickness overtook me. If it were true, I had stood in her way. I was the one who ruined her life and bore the responsibility for taking her down.

Before those dark months, I had never once seen her cry. I recalled walking into her room one Tuesday night not realizing that she was home and finding her sobbing at her vanity. I froze, not knowing what to do next. She looked up and saw me standing there. "I'll be fine," she said. "Don't worry, Debbie." But it took a long time for her to be fine again. My mother had failed—she had lost. Her power had been a delusion, and now she was defeated and betrayed. It must have been unbearable for her.

"I'd never seen her so upset," Annette recalled. "And furious at the same time. But then she was even more miserable without him. It was like nothing could replace him."

Perhaps she had sacrificed for me, I thought, but there was no way for one child to be enough to fill all her holes and patch the wreckage.

"She was so independent," I reflected. "I wish she could have just bought her own damn house."

"But she was dependent too. We all were then. Not like you, Debbie—you can take care of yourself. If she had been born into your generation, the rules would have been different. She would have gone to college. She could have been anything."

I was silent, then nodded in agreement. "When did they get back together?"

"It was almost a year—about ten months, I think. He was just as miserable. I can't remember who reached out first. But they were never apart again."

So she had stayed with my father, Dom stayed with his wife, and they stayed together. She was as much the other woman as Dom was the other man. Even though things had not gone the way she wanted them to in their arrangement, she was never second place in this complex triangle. Somehow, she remained ever after, first to both.

My mother was a woman of secrets. Not because she was ashamed or apologetic—not in the slightest—but perhaps because she knew the heartbreak embedded in some of her choices and wanted something else for me. Maybe she knew I was built for another kind of life. She had to know how closely intertwined with her I was, how I danced around her being. I told her everything but she selectively withheld, always keeping that cool distance between me and her own reality. Could aloofness have been a way of sparing me, a way of ensuring that I didn't follow in her footsteps? I wonder if she ever realized, though, that her coolness could be mistaken for something else.

Only recently have I also wondered how the magnitude of her father's own secret influenced her. It turns out that they were actually quite a bit alike, both shape-shifters who transformed themselves to survive. Although she didn't change her name, she had two different lives, just as he did. It's possible that for my mother, her father's own deception even gave her quiet permission to straddle two worlds. "I am like him."

And it made me think—*Am I like her?* Maybe if she had made such an enormous sacrifice for my sake, she really did know me after all. Maybe she knew that she and her father were of one kind and that I was a sensitive other. Her secretiveness—over her father's second life, over the details of her own duality—now seemed to be practically maternal. My mother did, in fact, understand my emotional nature; she knew I wanted to be just like her, but that I never would have been able to handle her life as she did. So it was best to keep some things quiet.

Betwixt & Between

Like any flower struggling to emerge beneath an imposing shade tree, I was slow to appear. It took me awhile—quite a while—to come into my own. An invisible step-by-step process of discovering myself as I progressed up the line of Russian dolls; of finding my way out of the shadows and into the sun. My mother had matured young; at fifteen she knew her own mind and, if not exactly what she wanted out of life, definitely what she did not. In a way, she had formed isometrically, tensing and flexing in opposition to the parents from whom she was trying to break free. A kind of resistance-based strength training that lengthened and stretched her. In contrast, my own progress was slight and slug-like early on—I formed while fervently running toward something with no wish to escape or pursue a separate self.

For most of my childhood, I lived in my own daydreaming head, trying to sugar-plum my way into my mother's heart, flitting around her and deciphering her every move. My naturally intuitive nature—honed razor sharp at her feet—helped me to thrive in the gray uncertainty of her love. When I look at old photos, I can peer into my own eyes and see a shy knowingness, an unquantifiable strength of spirit and tenderness of heart. But I also see tension and caution—a little girl who had to take in everything;

to first observe and make sure that there was ground beneath her feet before she took a next step.

I had friends, but they all came with the safety net of family ties; the offspring of my mother's friends became my own pack. They, as well as a small group of classmates—all of them also only children, I now realize—were the circled wagons I kept around me. Elementary school had opened the door to sniper girls, the ones I tiptoed around, sensing that they were lying in wait for some cruel opportunity. I was gentle and vulnerable and exposed, insulated in such a way that it seemed impossible I would ever stand and survive on my own.

My idealized version of my mother had such an influence on me that it was as if I were the weaker Siamese twin, grown out of some awkward place on her side and bouncing along for the ride. Living in her shadow, I felt bewildered and uncomfortable, like being in a skin that never fit. I had no notion of who I was apart from her. This left me proud but also secretly pained because I realized the truth very early on—that while I was many things, I was not *that*. The knowledge that I somehow might not be enough for the rest of the world too was something else to worry over, another secret to withhold so my mother wouldn't be disappointed. I couldn't bear to reinforce what I felt she must already know— that I was born from her but was not *of* her. That I was a mixed breed not nearly as perfect as the purebred.

Because I spent so much time chasing adults, I developed no childish silliness or sibling-banter ease; no tolerance for the roughness of youth, for the shoulder push or blurted criticism. My otherness in the eyes of children my age—mixed with early height and lankiness and a massive, unruly head of hair—fingered me as one to prey upon and bestowed a new dimension to my loneliness. Dreaded glasses were added to that list when, in fifth grade, I failed my eye exam. My mother's perfect blue eyes saw everything clearly, but I was pronounced nearsighted, an odd affliction that sort of creeps its way in and makes you feel lost when you might not be. You think your sight is the way sight is, not realizing that others benefit from a sharpness you lack. It distorts what lies beyond your immediate purview—the vast unseen—which might not be scary at all.

A pair of tortoiseshell cat's-eye specs brought clarity, but I knew their potential for humiliation. After we carefully selected them together one Saturday, my mother and I passed a sophisticated shoe store for women and children. She saw nothing for herself, but her eye was drawn to a pair in the window that was apparently calling my name. Bright orange patent leather slip-ons, topped with an enormous shiny flower at the toe. "Oooh," she said. "Look at those, Debbie. Fabulous." And they were. But it was a different time in the mid-1960s. There were hippies on TV, but ten-year-olds in Queens were supposed to conform rather than stand out with wild self-expression. She was ahead of the curve with her vision but unfortunately couldn't see how wrong those shoes might be for a shy fifth grader's schoolyard. "Wear them on the first day you wear your glasses," she instructed. "They'll distract everyone!" I got on board with her idea, hopeful for her little sleight of hand.

The next day at school, a doom drumbeat started in the line waiting to go into the building, kicked off by my nemesis—a popular blond who made me goose-bumped and hair-on-end afraid. All the other kids followed.

"You know you look like a clown, right?"

"Orange shoes! How stupid!"

"Now you're a four-eyes. Where'd you get those glasses?"

"You're a joke."

"Ugly glasses and ugly shoes!"

I don't remember much else beyond holding back tears all day. It was a Tuesday, so I didn't see my mother that night, and by the time she came in late the next evening, I had swallowed it all. Except for one little sprout trying to push its way up from the dirt—the notion that my mother's judgment might not be foolproof. Not wrong, never wrong, but maybe just slightly off. It wasn't a consolation by any means, but something to ponder one day.

I had stayed up and wandered into the bathroom as my mother slathered on her thick white cold cream to remove her makeup. A nightly routine. "How did everyone like the shoes and glasses?" she asked.

"They all thought the shoes were so special," I told her. "But it might take a little longer for everyone to get used to the glasses." The lie about the shoes made me feel even worse, so I tried to include some shred of what really happened. But I couldn't, just couldn't, tell the whole truth—that it all had come down on me because, I was certain, it was my fault.

Identity is a fragile thing at age ten, easily shaken and stirred. I never realized until much later that perhaps—just *perhaps*—I was a tad obsessed with my mother. And obsession is not a fragile thing at all. It is consuming and enormous, yearning and possessive. It plants seeds of doubt. It distracts from everything else, most notably from oneself.

In the years that followed, my focus remained on her, and even as I approached my teens, I still loved the fantasy of watching a glamorous mother dress. I'd pick out jewelry from her vanity's top drawer asking her, "Yes or no?" as I modeled a towering pearl-crested pinkie ring or the golden globe for her index finger or the bamboo bangle or any of her many other baubles. The evening's dress waited on the satin bedspread, an arms-outstretched costume ready to be worn. Her accoutrements were spread wide across her vanity, a treasure trove of transformation. And her makeup process was always my opportunity to talk.

"Mommy, I think I like someone in my class," I confided one night. Always a romantic full of longing, I was almost twelve when I tentatively broached the topic.

"Really? That's nice, but it won't last long."

I had just finished scribbling his name all over four pages buried deep in my notebook, with a Mrs. in front of each one to see how my new married name would look. But there went that.

"Remember, Debbie," she continued. "What you like now, you won't like at fourteen, and it keeps on that way. For sure, what you like at eighteen you won't like at twenty-five. You change."

She seemed so certain. I dared a follow-up, eyes down. "How do you know?"

"I know," she said, holding tight to her secret font of knowledge. "And what you like at twenty-five you won't like at thirty-five," she went on.

She was thirty-six, so I assumed she must really know. Was she secretly telling me something about my father? Was that why she suddenly seemed sad?

"I think he likes me too," I continued. Then, before losing courage, I rushed to add, "Even though I don't look like you." I stared at her tiny pearl of an ear as she faced the mirror. So perfectly formed; closely coiled like a translucent shell that I could trace with my finger.

"Debbie, you don't need to look like me. You're more the Natalie Wood type. Just as pretty, only different." She stopped tweezing and half stood to pat my hair for extra measure. The spot she touched ached from the gigantic pink plastic rollers I had slept in the night before; a new method to tame its nature.

That reassurance planted itself lightly, a temporary aloe vera for my burn. We had once seen *West Side Story* and Natalie was undeniably beautiful. Still, I knew from my own mirror and incessant adult comments that I looked more like my father. And I was pretty sure my mother didn't feel too strongly about him. Somewhere in my young brain, beauty and love had gotten tangled up; I was never able to shake the feeling that if only I looked more like my mother, she would love me more. That was the disclosure I could never say out loud.

"And don't worry about your ears. When you're grown, we can pin them back." She knew I thought my ears were too big in comparison to her flawless ones and pronounced her easy solution as she sat to apply her second lipstick. Two were needed to achieve just the right tone of cabernet meets rosé.

With my ears pinned, I wondered, *would I still be able to hear her secrets when she was ready to tell me?* So much confounded me in my sheltered, lonely girl world. Without siblings, there was no sounding board, no other person to test out a theory or give feedback on what was real; to tell me if my perception of what was true actually was.

Maybe my lack of a Greek chorus was why I was so drawn to the myths I'd read over and over, searching for clues. In my little corner, there was no moral to the story, no neat reconciliation that led to an *Ah, I've got it* feeling that explained everything. When I was younger, I was particularly attracted to mother-driven tales like Bambi and Dumbo. I always wished for a feather like the one that helped the elephant let go of the fear and take a leap. Such a feather might have helped me see where she ended and I began, might have encouraged the flexing of my own muscles sooner or introduced me earlier to the resilience deep inside.

Back then it was hard to find my strengths and even harder to hide my perceived weaknesses. In my junior high years, I only excelled in English, and everything else felt like hard labor to make sure I lived up to her. After a particularly grueling day, Aunt Lilly was in the living room with me while I was bent over a textbook I didn't want to read.

"Do you remember that old nursery rhyme about the days of the week?" I asked her, unsure of why it had suddenly popped into my head.

"Yes, of course," she answered, and began:

Monday's child is fair of face
Tuesday's child is full of grace
Wednesday's child is full of woe
Thursday's child has far to go
Friday's child is loving and giving
Saturday's child works hard for a living
And the child that is born on the Sabbath day
Is bonny and blithe, and good and gay.

Aunt Lilly paused. "You were born on a Saturday, Debbie."

That felt true to me. I was used to feeling like I had to work for things. "So, Mommy was out on a Friday night when I was born?" I asked. The Dotty-lore story of my birth had her rushed to the hospital at 2:30 a.m., uncertain if it was actually labor or if she had just mixed too many drinks with baked clams.

"That's right, you sure interrupted her party," Aunt Lilly smiled. "Mommy wanted your name to start with a D to be like hers, but do you know what Deborah really means?" Not waiting for my answer, she continued, "A prophetess. Someone full of wisdom, a seer of truths. So even though you have to work hard, think about how all of it will be for good one day."

I hugged that thought tightly, and in those areas where I did excel, I began to step into them more, gaining confidence. I found that I had a way of enlivening the class, of asking pointed questions, often humorously, to share a perspective that others might not have thought about. When my eighth-grade class discussed *Romeo & Juliet* and how it was the ultimate treatise on love, I offered a different opinion. "If Juliet were unattractive or had no front tooth, Romeo would have moved on. Their story only proves the superficiality of love." Afterward, my middle-aged male teacher, who always brought my grandmother's cautions to mind, warned that young women could be too clever—and if they were, they would never get a boyfriend. His authoritative words slammed against my emerging verbal acuity and creativity. They made me wonder if my mother's version of a desirable woman was really the one true path—and if it was, what then did that mean for me? It took the rest of the school year for me to recover.

My slow braise continued into high school—those non-idyllic years where I remained an outside observer. But one simple event cracked open my world when I became a sophomore: joining the newspaper and yearbook clubs provided the excitement of shared experience and collective collaboration in a way that the classroom never did. I made more friends, and we bonded over our love of writing. This new sphere felt safe and supportive, like a hammock of sorts, and I began to have more trust in myself and what I had to say.

As the resort dimmed in my teenage years, I no longer spent the entire summer there with Aunt Lena. Even though I still enjoyed our visits, my mother and I began to split our free time in the summer between the country and the ocean. Her close friend Candy had a cabana in the Rockaways, and we integrated ourselves into that scene (once again, minus my father), which was filled with grown-up party animals always ready for a good time. Candy's daughter—my friend MaryEllen—and I ran free with all the other progeny, while the adults got progressively more and more drunk. When Dotty was in the house, the party got better—she and her pool looks were a hit there too, even though she didn't drink nearly as much as the others. She had to drive us, after all.

I loved the beach club, a sandy kingdom of untamed wind and free spirits. Its social structure was similar to that of the hotel, split between adult and young adult tribes. Before the cabana, I had never even seen the ocean and certainly didn't expect it to be almost as magical for me as upstate New York. But the rhythmic and predictable waves, the shifting ebb-and-flow of it all seemed to offer another type of reassurance. I loved the invisible power that salt water had to keep you afloat, as well as upend you, so different from the controlled experience of the pool. The ocean was wild and uninhibited, and sometimes I gave myself over to it as if no one was watching. Not entirely, given the undertow, but close enough to feel free. I never ventured out too far, just a bit past the cresting waves so the rise would lift rather than flatten me. And so I could still see what was coming. The only downside to the new landscape was that it brought out the absolute worst in my coarse hair. I was five feet seven by the time I was thirteen and around one hundred pounds—a gangly body that seemed to be all legs with a hair halo that did not go well with surf, wind, and humidity. Despite the rollers and wrapping and blowing, it sprang up and out near the sea, an embarrassment impossible to hide.

As we drove to and from the beach, alone in the car, my mother and I would talk, especially on the return trip. In comparison to the hotel's lounge where adults drank between dances and songs, the cabana club was more of a pressure cooker where alcohol was the main attraction each weekend. Maybe because they only had two days to really live it up, the adults all attacked it with a gusto that I had never seen before. They started drinking at lunch and were stumbling and slurring by dinner. Then the arguments would start, filled with accusations and disappointments. One woman literally fell down every time we were there—how she never injured herself more seriously was a mystery, but why she kept repeating the scene was even more so.

"It was extra crazy tonight," I offered late one evening as we were driving home. "You know the woman in the next row who comes by? The sweet one? We did shell crafts in her cabana at lunch, and she made us all sandwiches shaped like cookie-cutter stars," I continued. "Then later I saw her scream at her daughter. She was practically choking."

"Really? That's rich. She's always doing something to prove she's the great mother. Caught in the act! Nobody could be that perfect." My mother laughed.

I had been drawn to the pre-drunk version of this woman. Whenever I saw her with her daughter, she was extra tuned-in—they seemed so close, and she routinely dropped everything to arrange her day around her offspring.

"She's far from perfect," my mother went on. "All that sweet let-me-do-everything-with-you is an act. When she drinks, the truth comes out . . . she really hates it all."

A shattered image of maternal perfection. *Was there really no such thing?* I wondered. "Why do they drink so much? Aren't they embarrassed?" I asked.

"Maybe not. Everyone else is drunk too."

"I'm glad not you."

"I wouldn't allow myself to lose control," my mother reassured me. "I know when to stop."

"I'm never going to be like that."

"I hope not, Debbie." She paused. "Never lose control." My mother was silent for a moment. "You know why I never went to Hollywood?"

I sat up straighter. This was an answer that I had always wanted to hear. "Why?"

"Because to get, I would have to give. I found out that they just wanted to use me. And nobody uses me, Debbie. Nobody."

I flushed with admiration. "I knew there had to be a good reason. I'm really proud of you."

"It's not so easy being a grown-up," she said lightly.

"It's not so easy being a kid!" I glanced at her smiling profile while she drove. "What's the hardest part?"

"I guess it's the difference between what you want and what you get," my mother said.

I didn't add that I completely understood. For a moment, I was going to ask her if she'd gotten what she wanted, but I already knew the answer. I just hoped, as always, that her disappointment wasn't with me. One thing I was sure of was that she was more than the life she was living. A half life would be bad for anyone, but it was especially so for someone who naturally had so much. It made me worried too. If someone like her could end up with such a life, what chance was there for me?

And yet, despite my awkwardness and uncertainty, there were times when I began to feel something shifting and tugging on me, the way the moon pulls on the tide. Nothing as dramatic as waves, just water lapping at the shore with little foamy bubbles full of promise. Maybe distance had something to do with it, a separation from the safe comfort of the resort, or maybe it was just small awakenings from experiences that were entirely my own. But I could feel something new and natural within me being spun, something innate, that might weave itself into fine cloth, eventually.

Mothers & Daughters

Certain moments or special occasions mark passages that create breathing room for change, and sixteen was just such a year for me. In keeping with tradition, I celebrated that birthday at San-Catri with a weekend extravaganza that enlivened the fading resort with an influx of my mother's close circle of friends. My circle had widened a bit, but many of my friends still stemmed from hers—so even though it was my party, it was really hers too. As always, I adored my mother's friends, embracing their differences as if each of them represented a distinct aspect of her. Their daughters completed the generational cycle bringing us all together. Like a night sky with big and little evening stars, there was something infinite and soothing for me in such a gathering, something real that could actually be observed.

The resort still felt like coming home—it remained our place. The hotel had been spruced up for that weekend, and the cavorting around the pool with the same loop of crooners in the background made it feel fully alive once more. Everyone had arrived by early Saturday morning, so the festivities were well underway that afternoon as my city friends, and hers, mixed with the regular San-Catri summer visitors.

"I'm glad *they* all have such a nice time up here," my mother whispered to me, as we watched them enjoying the water and each other.

"Don't you?" I leaned toward her, sensing some misalignment.

"Me?" she answered. "God no. Not for a long time. How many years can you do the same thing?"

I felt stung. "Even when I was younger?"

"Even then," she said softly. "Even then."

The notion that she had been restless all those years since I was little shook me. I had thought that she was as happy as I was, that the resort meant as much to her as it did to me. It was her history, her life. It was a magical, madcap place that we shared— she was its star, adored by everyone—how could she have wanted to be anywhere else? "But then why have we been coming every year since I was born?"

"For you, Debbie. I come for you. You're the one who's so happy here."

I let her words sink in. The thought that I had been out of step with her feelings about the resort for so long was crushing. But it also shocked me that I had the power to make her do something that she didn't want to do. I wished I had a vial of truth serum in my pool bag to slip in her drink. Then I'd know once and for all where I really stood, what she really felt.

Amid the buzzing in my head, I heard a friend calling my name from the pool. I went over to the deep end and sat on the chipping concrete near her float. The sounds around me seemed muted as if I had sat too close to speakers or had been out in the cold for too long. I dangled my feet and pushed the water around. "If only my mother were like yours," my friend commented as we watched her holding court amongst a group of invitees. When everyone compared their mothers to mine, the consensus seemed to be that theirs fell short in some way. I had the most glamorous one, the most fun one, the one everyone wanted for themselves.

We also had the mother-daughter relationship envied by adults. Many of my mother's friends would say, "You two never fight. I wish I were as close to my daughter." Or, "You two love spending time together—you're always out shopping." Or to me, "You always want to be with your mother. I feel like I have to force my daughter to spend time with me."

But the other mothers and daughters all had something in their relationship that I couldn't quite grasp. Something that was more a feeling or a way of being. An intangible that gave them permission to be imperfect, that made room for rebellion and understood that closeness and connection could live alongside disagreement and petulance. Adolescent rites of passage that were totally unfamiliar to me.

That weekend, I watched both generations with equal determination, wanting to understand the dynamics between them, and why they seemed to differ so much from my own.

Annette, and her mother, the owner's wife, Kitty, were locked in a daily power struggle for dominance without a clear winner. Completely unfiltered, Kitty had an excitable temperament that ensured she would always blurt out whatever thought crossed her mind. Funny, often embarrassing Kitty-isms were quoted in disbelief, and no one took her literally or seriously. When America landed on the moon, guests had squeezed into the card room to watch the historic occasion on the resort's only television— black-and-white and full of static despite the rabbit ears. Everyone had been talking about it for weeks, and all eyes were on the screen while Kitty ran around saying "A moon? What moon? Our moon?" Annette just shook her head and laughed with the rest of us.

But Annette was also on the receiving end of a continuous stream of barked-out orders (which she sidestepped) and criticism that would have devastated me (but that she let slide right off her). I marveled at Annette's lighthearted tune-out, mystified by her back-turning superpower to ignore her mother's impulsive, negative remarks. I could barely withstand Kitty's stinging outbursts when she sometimes reminded me as I'd walk by, "You look nothing like your mother, Debbie." I guessed that Annette's aplomb came from identifying more with her father, Frank—she, like my mother, wanted to be nothing like her maternal example.

There was a kind of competition between Kitty and her daughter for his attention that was totally absent from my own house, where both my father and I chased my mother. At the end of the day, Annette had learned how to survive and just do what she wanted, whether her mother approved of it or not. A behavior that was also foreign to me.

My closest summer friend, Anita, had always been a part of San-Catri since her mother, Mary, was Kitty's sister. The whole family lived in what was once my grandfather's house. Anita was filled with intelligence, creativity, beauty, and the spirit to win no matter what. "I'm going to be a designer," she'd pronounce as she scraped together swatches of leather and lace for looks that would become trends years later. Mary, however, faced a litany of challenges—she was uneducated and poor, with an on-again/off-again relationship with her husband. She had also lost a young daughter to a congenital heart defect and had a disabled son, Anita's fraternal twin. Anita was like an unexpected blossom in a battered bouquet that few would carry. Her mother played a big role in the hotel's zany chaos that pulsed through each day—Mary rang the two bells for breakfast, lunch, and dinner, each peal joined by her free-spirited cock-a-doodle crowing, with a little yodel at the end to make certain no one ever missed a course. When her husband would "take a powder," her song choice in the bar would switch to "One Less Bell to Answer, One Less Egg to Fry," with a big tearful finish. Mary accepted her life and loved her prize daughter, and Anita loved her too, in a way that accepted her mother's limitations and made no excuses for them.

Day two of my birthday weekend was no different for Anita than any other. She had to do hard labor at the resort to earn her family's keep, bussing the dining room tables at each meal, toting boxes, and crates of food, and cleaning the bar each morning. As the one with no assigned chores, I was always foot-stomping mad on Anita's behalf. I usually helped her in the bar to speed up the process of erasing the remnants of the night before, but nothing could really ease her burdens all that much. Her lot was very different from mine, and you could not find a mother more opposite to my own than Mary. And yet, when she and her daughter danced together and cared for one another; when they picked up what the other could not do, there was a unity that drew you into the goodness of them both.

Anita's cousin Cathy, another one of my summer crew, also had that bond. Cathy was the only one in her family who didn't know she was adopted. Her mother, Josie, withheld that fact from her—but after a hard life marked by abuse, Josie was so grateful to have a daughter who was bright and lovely that she cherished every moment and was afraid to admit the truth. They had a simple life together, and the loving bond between them was like a blood pact as if Josie had promised to live for her daughter and Cathy had pledged her fidelity in return. One might say that Josie had little else in her life so of course, she gave everything to her daughter, but that would be dismissive of all that they had together.

Two of my mother's friends had been deeply wounded by their mothers—and both were my favorites from her circle, although, at the time, I didn't examine why. Arline's mother had committed suicide, and Candy's mother had died giving birth to her. Both of these women had only daughters who, as they grew older, fought with them fiercely. These were completely normal tugs-of-war, but since I never fought with my own mother, I found it startling and daring in a way that I could never be. Nevertheless, Arline and her daughter—my friend Gina—were also the closest companions and confidants. To make up for what she lacked from her own mother, nurturing Arline had poured everything into Gina, who thrived. When Gina became a teenager, and the fights began, I felt how secure she was, never worried that her mother would turn on her because of her behavior. Arline's tending had raised a smart, independent daughter who wanted to free herself and begin her own life, ready to take on the world.

Cabana club Candy and her daughter MaryEllen were like loving lightning rods for each other. One or both of them seemed to always be crying. Her own mother's absence from birth had left a wound too gaping for Candy to bear, so she drank a lot to ease the pain of that loss and life's other disappointments—and Mary-Ellen hated it. She would confront her, often and bluntly, with the truth. As sensitive and emotional as MaryEllen was, she never hid her anger from her mother. She flung it where it belonged.

Our neighbor Sylvia and her daughter, my friend Melanie, both had a quick intelligence accompanied by a sense of proper exactness and almost aristocratic politeness. Sylvia had been a child during the Holocaust and had lost many close family members. There was a deep-seated need in her that must have gone unmet, and she was always traveling back to Europe for short respites alone. Melanie resented her mother's absences and could—and frequently did—tell her mother how she felt in a cool, controlled sort of way. Secrets lived in their house too. Years later, and only after Sylvia's death, Melanie learned of her mother's affairs during those trips. Her reaction was the opposite of what would be my nonjudgmental stance when I learned the same—Melanie was full of a fury that put the blame for many of their problems squarely on her mother's behavior. No blurred lines and root causes—her mother was wrong, and that was nonnegotiable.

I watched them all, stupefied by their shouting and upheaval. I thought it was misguided and unnecessary, and a testament to the strength of my own mother-daughter bond. I didn't realize that the calm between my mother and me might not have been the sign of closeness that others perceived it to be. And that I did too.

That summer, my sixteenth birthday brought two milestones. It was the first time my mother and I didn't share a cake, and it was one of the only times my father put his pride aside and joined the festivities at the hotel. That weekend, my mother gave me a ruby ring from them both. Our birthstone. But unbeknownst to her, my father had brought his own special present that he pulled afterward from his pocket—a gold love-knot ring with four tiny diamonds atop. "Just from me to you," he said. I had never before received a separate present from him. Cards yes, and thoughtful notes, but never a gift that he had gone out and bought. I loved it, but there was something about the gesture that felt so odd as if he were trying to tell me something else. What exactly, I wasn't sure. I watched the pleasure on his face and my mother's surprised smile.

"Something good happening, Jay?" she asked.

"Perhaps," my father answered, noncommittal.

Perhaps it means nothing at all, I thought. Just a special present for my sixteenth birthday. Or perhaps . . . it was a sign of something. That night I decided that *perhaps* was the most wonderful word. The most beautiful, versatile word. The perfect answer to absolutely anything because who really knew what was or wasn't going to be? Depending on your tone and whether or not it joined forces with a smile, a side-eye, or even a slight frown, it made you the dealer. You could disguise a yes or a no, convey possibility, feign interest, encourage or discourage gently. It was the ultimate card to have in your deck.

Around 2:00 a.m., the night was coming to a close, and my mother and I stood beside one another leaning on the bar. Everyone had had too much to drink, and my mother's eyes were half-closed, her mouth soft and smudged. She had gained weight—hardly noticeable at first, but over the last several years, her voluptuousness had turned thick and heavy. We never discussed it. Even though she remained enormously beautiful, I hurt for her, certain that she was grappling with marred perfection. She was changing as I was, but for the first time, it was my long and lean frame that was changing for the better.

"Each family is so different," I said, watching my friends on the dance floor. I touched the ring my father had given me, suddenly struck by the prominence of the other fathers, as nearby to their daughters as their mothers. Triangular units that perhaps had more balance than my own seesaw for two.

"That's for sure, but none like us," my mother answered, slurring so slightly that only I would notice. She looked down and saw me twirling the ring and gently closed her hand over mine— and his love knot. *Had the gift really been meant for her?* I wondered.

"That was so nice of Daddy," I said.

"Yes," she answered, revealing nothing.

"And all this was so nice of you," I added quickly. "This weekend for me. Thank you, Mom." Being the source of every-thing material was the role she had fallen into or set up for herself. There was a power in that, I realized then, that she perhaps might not have wanted to share.

Some pinhole of wisdom opened that weekend, and among other things, I voiced out loud to some of the party guests that I had made the decision to major in journalism when I went to college. I felt I had an instinct for discerning the truth behind the news, for how a journalistic approach can move us past illusions and misperceptions—even when they serve a larger purpose—to what is real. But sometimes, illusions need to stay in place for at least a while longer because you're not yet ready to see what's underneath.

Unrequited Love

I heard all about my parents' sister-in-law Rita over the years but met her only once when she flew from Los Angeles to New York to see the daughter she had left behind—my first cousin Denise, who was then thirty-six years old. I was nearly seventeen at the time and could not get the just-released Paul Simon song, "Mother and Child Reunion," out of my mind that whole day leading up to our dinner. Paul had given an interview about his inspiration and although he claimed not to be entirely sure of his song's real meaning, he said that "Mother and Child Reunion" hit him when he saw the famous Chinese dish by the same name on a restaurant menu—a special chicken-and-egg concoction that brought the two ingredients back together. It signified something to me, although, like Paul, I wasn't entirely sure exactly what. But it was still floating in my head as I walked into the Upper West Side restaurant with my mother to join the infamous "Malafemmina" Rita and my cousin.

She was a part of our family history, and now Rita was before me. The four of us had converged at nearly the same time in the small Italian restaurant bursting with the aromas of fresh basil and garlic. My mother and I had arrived together, while Denise and her mother came separately, with Rita being the last to appear.

She had embraced my mother tightly, kissing her on both cheeks, while Denise and I received warm, but more perfunctory hugs.

Even though Rita was in her early sixties, her face was completely unlined, as if she had never worried about anything in her life. Her dyed California-blond hair fell to her shoulders with only a hint of dark roots, and her opaque burgundy lipstick matched the restaurant's ornate, heavy drapes. Apart from the blend of that one color, the feeling from her was not one of belonging. Rita's West Coast reincarnation overshadowed her East Coast past, and she was cloaked in all she had become since being a boxer's wife. To me, her persona now seemed more inclined to a breezy outdoor café, picking at a healthy salad while nodding hello to agents.

Denise and I shared dark hair and eyes and little resemblance to our mothers. But where I had inherited my mother's height, Denise's form was shorter and ample. I had always spent time with Denise growing up and loved that she wanted to be a dancer and an actress—her professional portfolio of headshots and full-length glossy photos made the dream all the more real, although she struggled to coax her body into a performer's ideal thin shape. She adored my mother, and my aunts were her aunts too. As Tony's only child, Denise was special to Lena and Lilly, although they did not have the same closeness to her as they did to me, the child they essentially raised. I looked up to Denise and reveled in her company. But I always felt that she had a wound, an emotional frailty that made her focus inward rather than outward toward me.

I see now that my cousin and I had a common root—we both understood unrequited love, love for larger-than-life mothers who were distant as they charted their own courses. At the time, I didn't recognize the similarities or the underlying emotional pain that bound us together. But Denise had no such shortsightedness. Where her mother was concerned, her emotions were as visible as a raw, unbandaged sore. Denise had never moved past her mother's blatant neglect and never recovered from the shock of her father's death when she was twenty. Uncle Tony had adored his daughter, but he died in a dingy hotel room, alone and broke at fifty-one, five years after leaving my parents' apartment. Headlines shouted of his death from every newspaper, most sportswriters citing a broken heart over losing his wife. Denise's mourning for her father had never ended. He had been her rock, the only parent that she felt ever gave her any love.

I was as excited as my mother to be in Rita's company, and she was living up to all I had imagined. Full of stories about Los Angeles and its creatives—including her second husband, a well-known writer—she was a sophisticated woman of the world. Then the wine came and brought the tears.

"Oh, Denise," Rita chastised. "The night just started, and you're at it already."

"What do you expect?" my cousin whimpered.

"Some things never change." Rita sighed. "What's that line from *All About Eve*? Fasten your seatbelts, you're in for a bumpy night." Rita looked at me and winked as she poured underage me some wine.

"Well, Mother, I haven't seen you in so long, and you've barely said hello."

"We're out with friends. I haven't seen Dotty in ages, and I'm just meeting Debbie." She smiled at me again, winning me over. "Let's not make it about you."

"It's never about me, Mother. Never."

Rita went on, ignoring Denise totally and focusing on me, consciously or unconsciously widening the divide. She wanted to know what interested me in school and what I wanted to study when I went to college. Her crimson lips smiled wide when I said I wanted to be a journalist.

"That's terrific. Brenda Starr, reporter! Just dye your hair red like your mom!"

Rita had nailed me in an instant. Brenda Starr was my one-and-only comic strip idol—the beautiful, glamorous (and coincidentally red-haired) reporter whose career brought adventures and a mysterious boyfriend with an eye patch. That was going to be me.

"And if you go to college in California," she offered, "you can even stay with us."

Rita worked her own breed of seduction that rivaled my mother's, and I loved it. Like two goddesses with magic wands, they had a way of making you feel special and chosen whenever their light shone on you—and then left you hungry for more of that feeling. Before I could answer that I had decided to stay close to home for college, Denise jumped in.

"I could have gone to college too if you hadn't pushed me into being an actress."

"Denise, stop, you're a grown woman. You're embarrassing yourself."

"You mean I'm embarrassing you!"

"That too."

The tables alongside looked over at us, and I smiled limply and shrugged my shoulders.

"You just wanted me to be a star so you'd have something to be proud of. Now I have nothing," Denise said loudly.

I glanced down, embarrassed, and sad for Denise. I knew that her portfolio was from years before and that she hadn't tried out for any parts recently. But I had never thought of her as bereft over an unrealized dream until that night.

"That's your own fault," Rita barked. "Stop blaming me, will you?"

"Why? It's all your fault. All of it!" Denise poured herself another glass and held her head down. I watched a few tears form concentric circles atop the red wine and put my hand on hers but said nothing.

"Now, Denise," my mother intervened. "It's nobody's fault. You have to learn to let the past go and make the best of things. You can't be too sensitive."

"I tried my best with her," Rita said.

"That was trying?" Denise looked up. "You abandoned me! You just left me behind with Grandma and took off."

"Denise," I said, siding with the mother sorority against her. "You had your grandmother, and I had my aunts. It's the same."

"That's right, Denise," Rita said, jumping at my bait. "And look how good Debbie's turning out. She seems your age, and you seem hers." I glanced at my mother and saw pleasure in her eyes.

Denise turned to me, hurt. "It is not the same, Debbie. Not even close. Please! Your mother is nothing like mine. Aunt Dotty, you're nothing like *her*." She glared at Rita. "You don't know how to be a mother at all."

"Hah! Well if I don't know how to be a mother, you sure as hell don't know how to be a daughter," Rita said as she poured another glass. "Debbie knows,"She winked at me again.

"Stop it! This isn't about Debbie. It's about you and me."

"You wonder why I don't come to see you? This is why! Who could stand this?"

"Just admit it. You never loved me," Denise cried.

And so it continued, Denise a fragile little bird with a broken wing, still waiting to be fed. But no food was forthcoming, at least not from Rita. I shifted on the chair's black cushion, crossing and uncrossing my legs. In truth, my cousin spoke words that were also floating somewhere inside of me, words that I tried not to voice even to myself. But instead of drawing them to the surface, Denise's display pushed me to tamp my feelings down further, discrediting them. I was only confused, I told myself, whereas Denise was absolutely convinced. She was a ten on the wound scale while I only hovered around five. They were extreme, and we were not. My mother and I bore no comparison to this bloody mess, so I should just put every worry or feeling of her ambivalence to rest. Denise was floundering, she had clearly been stunted—but I was flourishing. Wasn't I?

In our taxi back to Jackson Heights, my mother and I quietly stared out our individual backseat windows as if the evening had drained everything from us both.

"It's so hard for Rita with Denise," she finally said.

"Yes," was all I answered, unsure of which side I was on, or if there even was a side—it seemed as if it was the whole of them, of who they were together.

Looking back, I'm ashamed to admit that I didn't admire Denise's courage to confront her mother and speak of her pain, however bluntly; that I didn't champion her or have her back in our disaffected daughters sorority of two. Most shameful of all, I didn't feel my cousin's torment because I was too busy seeking Rita's approval and basking in her compliments, often at Denise's expense. Too out-of-touch with my own pain to be empathetic, I used the intensity of her wounds to further deny my own.

That night I was just one more person who made Denise feel wrong and unwanted and unworthy. All I saw was that Rita loved my mother because she was special, and it seemed she felt the same about me, and I clung to that. I let Rita's approval distract me from thinking about how she could have inflicted such a mortal wound upon her daughter; how she was able to float above any accountability or apology. But to look past Rita's slick veneer then would have also meant looking past my own mother's. And I was too in love with her—and with her façade.

Rita and Denise's story dynamics were mythical in proportion. Plain and simple, Rita had broken Denise's heart. I thought of the many myths and fables I had read seeking parallels that would help me understand my own story. The most famous mother-daughter myth is the tale of Demeter and Persephone. The daughter, Persephone, is kidnapped by the god of the underworld, Hades. Demeter, the earth-mother goddess of the harvest, mourns her daughter's absence, bringing on the cold, barren winter. So, a bargain is struck, and Persephone returns to higher ground for several months each year, heralding spring. But below, symbolically at least, Persephone had become a whole woman and been introduced to the darker side of her good girl self. I wondered now what happened if the myth was reversed—if the daughter was Demeter and the mother was Persephone? If the mother was the one spirited away to the underworld and the pure-hearted daughter was left all alone? How would the story change? Denise and I both waited for spring to come with our Persephone mothers—and we had both tried to live as good, nurturing Demeter to compensate. But what happens if the daughter became a Demeter only in opposition to her mother? Would her true self be hiding in wait somewhere underneath?

The Ransom

I always thought that my father was less of an enigma than my
mother. On the surface, he seemed so much more transparent,
but that wasn't actually true. It only felt that way because I never
had to chase him. But this didn't mean that he let himself be
known. Concealing, in fact, ran so deep in his family's Sicilian
blood, that I once overheard him instruct my Aunt Lena—who
had suffered a fall as she was beginning a slip into dementia—not
to reveal the whole truth about her forgetfulness to the doctor.
"Then he would suspect," he told her. It's hard to know the inner
workings of such a protective mind. Hard to know what it was I
didn't know.

Still in my sixteenth year, we had a family incident so bizarre
that there were few buoys to hold on to. As usual, my mother was
the heroine, my father the victim, and I the frightened onlooker
observing it all.

My father had finally earned his commercial real estate sales
license a few years before, convinced that skyscrapers would be
his next path to success. As he worked to build that business, he
had developed a deep network of connections, with quite a few on
the financial side. This time, someone who knew someone knew
someone who needed a loan, and to get it, was willing to put up

a rare coin collection as collateral. Acting as an intermediary and hopeful of securing a fee should a deal happen, my father introduced that someone to someone else who was interested in lending the money.

He then backed away and let the deal take its course. However, it seems that the someone who was lending the money took the coins without ever writing the check. At a loss after a month with no resolution, the irate collection owner concocted a plan to kidnap my father and hold him for ransom. Their scheme kicked off a three-day manhunt that filled my little Queens apartment with the FBI.

On the day that it happened, I arrived home from school, oblivious. My mother surprised me at the door but didn't open it all the way. I was headed to a planned sleepover with a friend, and I was swinging by to get my bag. Packed by my aunt, it was right by the door for her to hand to me.

"Mom, what are you doing here? Are you sick?" She was never home midday, so I pushed on the door to come inside and see what was wrong.

"Not at all. See you tomorrow!" my mother said, sounding falsely bright as she held firm to keep it only slightly ajar. "I have to go now. All's well."

When I arrived at my friend Diana's house around the corner, I stood at her front door not remembering the steps I took to get there. The strange exchange with my mother had completely disoriented me, pulling me into a current of rushing worry.

I was surprised again when Diana's mother, Marina—a first-generation, gentle Greek woman who loved the myths of her ancestors as much as I did—opened the door. I hadn't expected her to be there—she had been absent for several months to care for her own ailing mother in Greece.

"Come in, come in. Welcome," Marina said as she turned away from the door, ready to dash so she wouldn't intrude. Theirs was a quiet house with just the two of them, and even when Marina was there, it seemed as if she walked on air so we wouldn't feel her presence. As an independent second-generation daughter, Diana accepted her mother's solitude when she was at home, and her long stretches away when she was not—it seemed all part of a life led between two countries.

Diana came up behind her mother, and we settled into the bright living room while Marina presented us with stuffed grape leaves and pastitsio. Normally, she would have left at that point, but maybe because she had just returned home, Marina lingered.

"Something feels wrong," I blurted out to the two of them. "Upside down, really. My mother wouldn't even let me in." I could feel the color draining from my face.

Marina put her arms around my shoulders, and Diana quickly reassured, "But your mother is there, you saw her. It's nothing, it's all fine." She moved to the record player and put on a Jim Croce album as her mother gave me a final pat, then retreated to her room.

Diana's sure-footedness, a trait that had only increased as she spent more time without her mother, was always calming. Of all my friends, Diana was the only one with divorced parents, and although she frequently saw her loving father, she was often on her own. I borrowed her certainty and lost myself in the music and our plans for the next night with two more friends.

The phone rang in the morning as Marina was preparing us a late breakfast. She spoke in hushed tones and after hanging up, turned to me. "Your mother would like you to come home right now."

So it was true, something was wrong. I jumped up and put on what I had been wearing the day before, shoving everything I could grab into my bag. Diana was right alongside me as we ran to my apartment.

My mother met us at the door, not even giving me a chance to use my key. Unlike the day before, she now looked worn down as she pulled me in by one arm. "Debbie, I need you here." Everything else faded for me, and I stepped inside as I heard her gently turn Diana away. "I'm sorry, sweetheart. No company today. Debbie will call you soon."

Out of the corner of my eye, I caught a glimpse of Aunt Lilly pulling at her hair and my Aunt Lena banging her head on the wall. Not a good sign. The last time I had seen that was when her brother Tony had died alone in his hotel room when I was five.

Then I saw the men in black. Everywhere.

"Debbie, your father is missing," my mother said as she took my shoulders in her hands. "Everyone is doing their best to find him," she quickly explained.

"Missing? Like he went to the store and didn't come back?" I asked, surrounded by strangers and utterly confused.

"He was kidnapped, young lady," a man in a black suit who was standing next to my mother said. "But he's alive, and we're going to find him and bring him home."

My mouth was agape as I just stood there, trying to take it all in. "Who would want to kidnap my father?" I finally asked everyone and no one—they had all moved on, and I was swept into the wall-to-wall crowd. The realization that my father was gone and might be killed slowly and painfully sunk in as I saw what was unfolding in our apartment. I stood back, trying not to cry or trip over the cables and black wires crisscrossing everywhere. Horrified and trembling, I watched my mother in action.

As always, she was something to behold—calm, cool, full of tears on cue when talking to the kidnappers and when not, full of ideas to track my father's whereabouts through some connections. It was 1971 and wiretapping was still a cumbersome process. Someone needed to be on the phone for a very long time to have the hope of tracing the call, something the kidnappers seemed wise to. They limited the length of time my father would be placed on the line to plea for the ransom. The FBI needed all the help it could get.

My mother, for her part, needed all of the backbone, ingenuity, tenacity, authority, and haughtiness instilled in her by those who had formed her, and that she had cultivated over the years on her own. I could see that she was actually helping the FBI—apparently, she was rounding up information as to where my father might be from different sources of her own.

"Ma'am, any word?" another FBI agent asked her.

In addition to the tap on our line that would hopefully trace the location of the kidnappers, my mother had convinced the FBI that some connections she had could help locate my father in those pre-cell phone days. She needed access to one untraceable line, or at least that's what I made out from the whispers—a special line that allowed her to contact and be contacted by people who didn't want to be traced themselves. Without that, she wouldn't be able to put the word out or get feedback freely. Maybe it was a technique my grandfather had heard when he mediated disputes at the resort or one that Dom suggested when she looped him in. Whatever inspired her request, she said it and they did it. She became part of the information gathering, canvassing her network for word on the street. She didn't have to name names, just help track my father down.

I didn't know who Dom was at the time or that he could not be in a room full of FBI agents. But I sensed that there was someone in the background, or on the end of that untraceable line, who was important to my mother. Her breathless appreciation when that other line rang told me that there was a card she was playing that I hadn't known about. When I look back, I think how strange it was that Dom was operating in parallel, tapping his own covert network of spies who might have leads on the kidnappers and where they took my father. The lover was helping to rescue the husband. Why? Because she asked him to. My irresistible Persephone mother, my detective magazine moll. Whether country or city, she could never quite escape her underworld.

"Nothing specific, yet," she reported. "But they've definitely taken him somewhere in upstate New York. As you suspect." The agent nodded with an upward curl of his lip. I don't want to trivialize the severity of the crisis, but I knew as I watched that at least three of those FBI men had, in their limited exposure, developed a thing for her stunning forty-one-year-old self.

When our tapped line rang about once an hour, everything stopped. The FBI was usually ready after three rings, and an agent would signal to my mother to answer. The kidnapper's angry, accented voice came through the phone in the hushed room.

"Listen to me," my mother said. "I am getting the money. You can't expect that much so fast."

One FBI agent or another would pull his fingers apart as if there were a string in his hands, indicating that she needed to play for time. So, she would stretch the conversation, asking them questions and making her own demands.

"No," she said. "I promised I wouldn't call the police and I didn't."

If I hadn't been so upset, it would have been a funny thing for her to say given everything going on around us. She lied so coolly and convincingly, and I was proud of her.

"You sound like the sort of person who means what he says, and I understand that because I am too," my mother continued. "I'm doing exactly as you say because I need him to come home. His daughter needs him to come home."

I did need him back. I had never thought about losing my father before, and the precariousness of his situation slammed into me at that moment. The minutes were ticking by and in a matter of hours I could be fatherless. I squeezed my crying eyes shut and held a tissue over my face to not make any noise.

"Now don't go back on what you promised me," she commanded. "You agreed that every time you called, you would put my husband on the phone. I need to know he's all right. Put him on now."

She got a thumbs-up from the FBI and another hand signal to stretch.

"Jay? Jay? Are you OK? Yes, Jay, tell them I'm getting them the money. I'm draining all our accounts. And a check from that deal you just closed came," my mother added.

My father knew that we didn't have the $200,000 ransom, knew that he hadn't closed any deal, and knew that we were lucky if the one account we did have had 1 percent of the ransom amount in it. But what he couldn't know was if she really had called the police, if he would ultimately be rescued before his kidnappers got fed up waiting for money that wasn't there.

"Jay, the bank is helping me speed up the process, so the check clears by tomorrow or the next day. Tell them. Jay . . . ?"

The kidnapper pulled the phone back. "Look," my mother said, repeating what she had just told my father. "If the check can't be cleared that fast, the bank is going to give me a loan. The money is coming. We have it. Don't worry. And don't hurt . . ." Then the call ended abruptly like all the others.

"They hung up too soon, ma'am. Just a few minutes more next time," the FBI agent said.

My mother's eyes were red-rimmed and moist as if she too had just realized that this man, my father—who had been in her life for almost as long as she could remember—could really disappear.

And so it went for another thirty or so hours, my mother and her sources working in tandem with law enforcement to save my father. I don't remember sleeping, but I do remember feeling strangely reassured that she wouldn't let anything bad happen to him. Even if she didn't fully love the whole man as I did, she had to love the wonderful parts of him. The part that was a poet who wrote songs. The part that worked so hard for so little. The part that wanted a creative life and then gave up what he loved to chase pots of gold.

I turned inward, away from the bustling and back to memories of my father and me while I waited. Navigating the wires, I made my way to his chair in the corner of the living room. The hours were agonizing. I thought only of him and our wobbly life together as he gave his love, but most of the time, not much else.

He had been sitting in that chair recently when we had watched the Miss America pageant—he and I took it very seriously each year, critiquing, voting, and predicting the winner. Years before, when I was little, he'd sing the "Here She Comes" theme song while I pranced victorious, even though I knew that only my mother could be crowned. But this last time, as I searched in a drawer for the pads and pens we'd need as armchair judges, I had come across a business card that said he was the manager of the Seven Arts Restaurant.

"What's this, Dad?"

He rubbed his finger over the card as if it were braille, even though it wasn't embossed. "Something I tried before you were born," he said. "It was a restaurant inside a beautiful building that taught the seven fine arts."

I had never thought of the arts grouped as a whole, and only writing and painting came to mind. "Seven?"

"Architecture, sculpture, music, painting, literature, dance, and theatre," he quickly rattled off. "The restaurant was like a hub in a dramatic arts center in the city. It was something I'd wanted to do since I left Syracuse."

I thought of how his dream of being a music major had ended with the loss of his eye. I wasn't sure why that meant he couldn't go back to school, but it felt too personal to ask. "How did it go?" I asked tentatively.

"Just one of those good ideas that never made it. But you have to keep trying."

As with most fathers in that day, he had very little to say about my upbringing or the rules governing what I did. In fact, I actually spent less time with him than I did with my mother. And like my aunts, when he was home, he was eclipsed by her presence. But he always tried to teach me something, to implant a guiding thought.

A few months before the kidnapping, after we had returned from my sixteenth birthday bash in the country, he gave me the second part of my special gift—a night out together. He was hell-bent on opening my eyes to the underside of life so I would never make a misstep. To do this, he arranged a trip to Times Square near midnight.

"Take a good look around, Debbie. Let it sink in." We walked in silence through a world I had never known existed. Lights turned night into day on bustling Seventh Avenue, but there was little illumination on the side streets he made us walk down. I held his hand, petrified, as I avoided men and some women in tatters, their faces dirty and vacant as they slumped against buildings. I didn't want to hold my nose, so it was impossible not to breathe in the stench.

"Look at these junkies," he told me. "Bums in the street. One puff on a marijuana cigarette and you could end up here. I've seen it happen too many times."

We walked for about an hour, and I never felt closer to him than I did that night. It wasn't just those sights that later kept me from indulging like so many people I knew at school, it was the care and concern he had for my well-being. That night, I believed that I could see through to his essence. And I knew that my father loved me.

He did want the best for us. The deal that my mother had referred to on the phone—the one that never happened—was either the sale of a Manhattan office building or the raising of the Andrea Doria sunken ship, I forget. He had been talking to us about it for months; it was such a sure thing, he promised that we were going to get a big house on Long Island. The possibility had animated the three of us as my mother drove to the dreamy suburb of Manhasset to look at houses every weekend.

I let myself believe. There had been other such moments, but this time it felt so real. And I was ready for an outward change, something that would shift my circumstances and shake things up.

"Let's park here," my father said, two pages of written directions in hand. Both my parents had handwriting full of similar flourishes and oversized first letters, but I could see that this time, he had written down all the flower-named streets and rights and lefts that had brought us here. This was his mission. We stood across from a stunning long ranch set high on a sloping manicured half acre. Three adventurers discovering the territory we would soon mark for ourselves.

"Jay. It's perfect. We wouldn't have to do a thing," my mother said, her hand on his arm.

I fell in love with the house even from a distance, even before I saw what was beyond the white cedar shakes and black shutters. Whatever was inside had to be beautiful.

My father crossed the street for a better view. A friend of his told me years later that he believed my father could have accomplished anything, if only he had been able to see better for more of his life. I was struck, never fully realizing how many years he had suffered and was hindered. Ironically, sight—and perhaps those adjuncts, foresight and hindsight—were both physical limitations and limiting beliefs that afflicted him. What I never knew was that the sight in his right eye, his good eye, had been worsening for a long time. He finally had a cataract operation right before we started looking for houses. I came home from school one day, and there he was on a chair in the dark. He pulled me onto his lap and cried in my shoulder. "Debbie, I can see. I can see!"

So, things were looking up all around, and the three of us smiled at each other, and at the real estate agent who was showing us the house.

"The only downside is that it doesn't have a basement," the agent said.

"Oh, that's OK," my mother answered. "I wouldn't go down there if there were one—I hate basements."

The realtor knew she had a sale as my parents shook her hand, and I dreamed of my life within new walls, ones that I'd helped choose. That search for our perfect nest was one of the happiest experiences we ever had as a unit; we'd found our beauty, and all was in motion to close. And then . . . nothing happened. It all fell apart when my father's deal crumbled. I was devastated when the vision died. It felt as if I was always going somewhere but could never quite get there.

My mother must have felt the same way then and for all the years leading up to it. It was the give-and-take of him, both exhausting and heartbreaking. But now, all I wanted was to have him back home.

My father was ultimately rescued when the FBI, after all their hard work—and a few clues provided on the side by my mother—tracked the location and then stormed the premises. My father was handcuffed to a chair, a gag in his mouth. A little bruised, hungry, and very tired, he was escorted home from upstate New York. All his statements were taken in our apartment which, by that time, looked like a police station anyway.

When he returned, our building was full of reporters and photographers—he later complained when the *Daily News* described him as "the balding Canzoneri"—and as soon as he walked in, my mother and I rushed over to him. She kissed him on the mouth, something I rarely ever saw. We both threw our arms around him and stood there for quite a while, the three of us clinging to one another, holding on like we had just found something we would never give up. I felt complete.

As I look back at this moment within the context of our lives, I realize that there's a story within the story here, one that I keep building on the more I learn, one that lends itself more to song than narrative because it's not so literal. Any kidnapping holds hostage something that is not yours. My father willingly gave his heart to my mother, and she held it hostage without even trying. She couldn't help that no ransom was ever possible. She had his heart and kept him tethered to her until the day he died. He loved her still, even as he wilted in her grasp. Maybe I'll write the lyrics and put this story to music one day in his honor.

The Bloom

I launched into my college search knowing that I would join the newspaper before I even registered for any classes. I surrendered to the writing dream and, although my parents and aunts cheered me on, I selected a college like a novice at a horse race—one who places bets by what feels right, like a name or a color, versus any intimate knowledge of the contenders or stats. It's stunning to me now, but I never even considered going away or thought of leaving home to be on my own. I just completely ruled it out, attributing it to some arbitrary certainty that dorm life wasn't for me. The truth was that leaving felt like quicksand at the end of a mossy, wild-branched path. It was too soon to leave her. I was nowhere near ready. I would stay close.

I did all of my own research, a massive college directory in hand. It was so heavy that I had to invent a feet-together yoga position to be able to balance it in my lap while I flipped through. I narrowed it down to colleges within a daily commuting distance and ripped those pages out. The other crucial requirement was a good journalism program, although I have no idea how I determined which ones were good or not. Also, the school had to be affordable since my mother had to find the money to pay for it.

The winner was Long Island University's Brooklyn campus, but its commuting distance meant there was one more thing my mother had to fund—a car. I saved everything I could from my after-school job at the elegant British emporium Arnold Constable, which was at the time the US's oldest department store. Two or three days after school, I would take the subway to Manhattan with my friend and fellow part-timer Diana to join the distinctly proper staff behind the beauty counters and in the fashion aisles. I loved everything about the job—it was more than just the feeling of having my own money, it was having all the answers to the perfunctory question, "How may I help you?" That simple ask revealed each female customer's predicament and story, and I was the one to guide her on her quest.

I had just earned my driver's license when my meager bankroll joined my mother's larger stash to acquire what I envisioned as the only car for me—a Mustang. This dream vehicle called to me as a real-world incarnation of my plastic country toys, a motorized horse that would take me to and from college along the always-congested Brooklyn-Queens Expressway. The lure wasn't the "stallion" properties of the car so much as its "mare" attributes—I fell in love with its beauty, not its speed; with its style and design, not its roaring engine. The mare of it meant freedom, and I would be holding the reins.

While we searched for a Mustang old enough to be affordable, my mother taught me to drive in her latest Chevrolet—still considered by her to be the best car brand in the world. By now, her rust Caprice Classic had been replaced by an icy-blue Impala that matched her eyes. She was clearly not as comfortable sitting in the passenger seat, fearful that her novice daughter was behind her wheel. But I was an eager driver in spite of her foot always pressing down on a phantom brake and her right hand clutching the armrest.

"Always drive in the middle lane, Debbie," she advised on our parkway test runs after I had managed the city blocks well. "The middle is easier."

"I thought you were a fast-line driver," I teased, both hands on the wheel.

"I am, but it's harder when you have a barrier on your left."
She paused as if to let the line sink in. "And in the right lane, you
have to worry about cars getting on the highway. The middle gives
you the most freedom. Room to maneuver."

I had never thought of her as a middle ground person, but
as I drove, I suddenly saw how no boundaries on either side really
did afford more options. You were less constrained in the middle
than on either side's extremes.

One day, I navigated the Impala to another used car dealership, and there it was—my Mustang spirit animal, a classic 1969
two-door whose headlights were pointing straight at me. But with
a cardboard sign on the windshield announcing its $3,000 price,
we were $750 short. My mother and I slowly walked around the
white Mustang on opposite sides while the lot's flags snapped in
the breeze.

"Is this the one you want, Debbie?" she asked when we met
at the front.

"This is the one," I whispered as the salesman walked toward
us. "But it's still too expensive." She had my $250 from Arnold
Constable combined with her $2,000 buried deep and divided
between three envelopes in her tightly held bag.

"Can I help you?" the middle-aged salesman said. I saw my
mother glance at the windshield, and then at one of his middle
shirt buttons pulled taut by his girth to reveal some flesh.

"I think we can help each other," she answered, smiling.
"I've noticed this car on the lot for quite some time."

Had she? I wondered. The dealership wasn't on her normal
route. I leaned on the car, watching.

"Not that long, ma'am," he said.

"Long enough to mark it down at least once already." My
mother smiled, pointing to another cardboard edge underneath
the $3,000 sign. "My daughter loves it, and I'm prepared to buy
it, but we'll have to take our chances. If we don't find another one
in the meantime, we'll see what the price is next week," she added,
taking one step closer to him before she turned.

"What do you need it to be?" he asked quickly. "I'm the owner."

"Good. I only deal with owners," she answered. "I need it to be $2,250. All in."

He squirmed. "Way too low. I couldn't . . ."

My mother put up her hand to stop him, smiling wider. "I understand. You're running a business. But we both know that this is an old used car with problems I'll discover when a mechanic takes a look. I have $2,250—in cash, right now—and I'm prepared to buy it with no inspection." She reached out for his hand. "Yes?" she asked.

The owner stared at her for a few seconds while I held my breath. Then he took her hand and folded his cards, and I had my dream car, albeit one with quite a few issues that we would have discovered with a proper look under the hood. But then its imperfections would have stood in the way of that Mustang's perfectness for me. I had no clue about what an older vehicle might need beyond gas—no knowledge of oil gauges or power steering fluid or maintenance of any kind—but I always got where I was going on the way to earning my higher degree, despite the occasional stall. And I did so in Dotty-esque style.

College was territory unfamiliar to my mother, the first major rite of passage of mine that she had not experienced. And I too entered an entirely new space—one that had no knowledge of who my mother was. No one knew of her beauty or style or smarts; no one had heard snippets of Dotty lore. It was just me meeting new people, standing tall with grace and genuineness all my own. The only person who could bring my mother into the conversation was me. One might think that as I tasted my own separate power for the first time, I might keep quiet about her, but I did not. Like a parent bragging about an exceptional child as a reflection of oneself, I carried her with me into college, pulling her out in stories I shared with my new peers. However unconscious it might have been, it was usury, certain as I was that her very being enhanced my own specialness.

Still, I did feel the sweetness of having my own identity—as well as the joy of contributing to and producing the grand endeavor that was the weekly college newspaper, *Seawanhaka*. And slowly, the petals began to bloom. For me, that paper was accordion-like, unfolding to open my world wider and wider. My days began and ended with its community of writers and editors. I felt like I belonged from the start and loved everything about the weekly pace and late nights at the printer, thriving by being part of something larger than myself. I jumped in as a freshman and never left. It gave me influence and recognition and thrills, which included interviewing professors and earning their respect. Being empowered to ask tough questions and articulate the answers for a wider audience put me right into my element.

It also put me right into the arms of a fellow journalism major and newspaper staffer, Bob. We spent every day hanging in the dusty *Seawanhaka* office, two glorious rooms of creaky desks and old typewriters, he the sports editor and me the news reporter. Bob was almost three years older, but only a year ahead in school, having had to work full-time first to afford college. We started as friends for over a year, full of poking banter as we ate cheeseburgers and played our parts to meet the deadlines and publish each week's edition. It was like a classic movie that my mother and I would watch, full of snappy dialogue and starring a female lead who was breaking new ground for women in unfamiliar territory. Bob was incredibly brilliant—a critical thinker and contrarian—who was more seasoned and, it seemed to me, could do everything well. Better than me, I thought, but that was the way things were supposed to be. So secure in who he was, he never conformed to anyone or anything, and his mindset made him the opposite of a flatterer. When he gave a compliment, he meant it, and he didn't give them often. Something about that attracted me too—I never had been drawn to easy conquests or constant professions of love. Part of his appeal was knowing that I needed to work for it. But the real pull between us was the chemistry of cleverness. He could make me laugh and, at the same time, made me feel understood. Slowly, even when we both dated other people tied to the newspaper, we were becoming central to each other.

Replaying it all like a movie in my head makes me smile, so obvious and inevitable was it that we would fall in love. And the first person I wanted to share it all with was my mother. I never worried that she would fear to lose her only daughter, or that she would feel sidelined by my affections for someone else. Instead, it was as if my first big romance put my mother and me on equal footing at last—finally, we were both in on the conversation around the pool, speaking the same language now that I too was fully adored and desired. And almost as if she knew that my relationship with Bob was the real thing, there was no longer any counsel that feelings changed, or that I would change, as the years went on. My mother just nodded when I shared my certainty that no man could ever know me or love me as much as Bob did, that I would always be the center of his universe. She allowed herself to be swept up along with me, perhaps even somewhat relieved that I had found what had always come so easily to her.

I wanted to share the resort with Bob so he could understand its importance to me, but when we visited, I struggled to conjure the magic of what it had once been given the dilapidation in front of him. No longer a thriving vacation destination—my sixteenth birthday weekend had indeed been its last gasp—the hotel was now open only to family and close friends, and only rarely. Most of the rooms had been converted into apartments for local renters, which meant people who couldn't afford to live anywhere else. But as we stood in my grandfather's house, looking out over the open field toward the empty pool, he took my hand. And when he did, I felt he realized everything it had meant to me.

Bob seemed to know and understand my mother too. Although we never really talked about it then, a part of him saw through us both, right to my need to please her and hers to be pleased. Maybe because he had grown up with a mother who also had a maternal wound, something had already been illuminated in his own childhood. He grasped who my mother and I were together, but I never doubted that he was in my corner, and mine alone.

Bob graduated, and in my senior year I became Editor in Chief—the first female student to hold that title—and 75 percent of my tuition was absorbed by the university in return for the heavy workload I assumed in addition to my classes. I earned my keep through my passion, and I was exceedingly proud when I received a special wood and brass plaque in recognition at graduation. My mother's favorite line on the plaque was that I, "as Editor in Chief, demonstrated that the spirit and independence of John Peter Zenger still lives and flourishes." She loved the comparison to the famous Zenger who had come to the colonies from Europe and established freedom of the press.

But my favorite line on it was more personal: "A neophyte journalist, she has demonstrated her mettle and won her spurs." I read it over and over. I still felt uncertain about the future, sometimes convinced that no one would ever want to hire me, but those words simply meant that I was recognized for boldness. I had won on my own. However haphazardly I had made my college choice, it had been the right door to walk through. The course of my life had changed as much as my mother's had with her first pick of an apple.

Those years of independence and self-discovery were marred only by a few goodbyes during my college days. With me grown and out of the house so often, my aunts moved back upstate to be closer to their two other brothers and began a slow withering. These two women, who had given me everything they had, who rescued and broadened me by balancing my mother's ways with their own grounded-ness, were ushered from my life without fanfare. Each stage of their dismissal and decline was a wrenching upset. But like the resort changing over time, the needs of our little household had also morphed. "Debbie, it's time," my mother pronounced one day toward the end of my freshman year. She must have looked at the two older women and seen that unless changes were made, she would end up as their caretakers rather than the other way around.

First Lilly went with many tears and promises to visit and write. I remember feeling stirring indignation at the unfairness of it and of my loss at my mother's hand. But other than my tears, there was little that I could do. In my junior year, Lena joined her sister, first in an apartment funded by Social Security and then in a nursing home nearby as dementia fully took hold. When I visited, she no longer knew who I was.

When my parents and I were fully on our own, we were a trio of compromised and incapacitated souls unable to care for themselves. Only my mother's drawers and closets were neat—everything else was a mess, and we could barely feed ourselves, ordering in every meal. Our house of cards had met a dust storm, and we were done in by life's details, as perplexed over laundry as we were about the mechanics of vacuum cleaner bags and sweeping floors. It was also around this time that Fuzzy died, and I uncovered the secret of my grandfather's true identity—just as my mother had done when she was twenty—which only added to the maelstrom.

I missed these three women so much—each of them had shaped me in ways that were now bursting into full bloom—but my college comings and goings and my burgeoning relationship kept me preoccupied and looking ahead. When Bob proposed right after I graduated, all the wedding preparations gave us new focus—my mother had to spring into action to fund her daughter's wedding as convention dictated. And she did willingly, envisioning an affair for more than two hundred people at Terrace on the Park, an elegant remnant of the old World's Fair.

We had to take one break, though, from our planning for a weeklong mother-daughter trip back to Maine. We were off to try to reclaim lost treasure in the setting of my mother's childhood summers. The inheritance of Bare Island hadn't stayed in the family for too long: Fuzzy's elder sister, Tante, had acted on her own and decided that she didn't want to pay the taxes on the property (a few hundred dollars a year) and sold the entire island for a mere $25,000 soon after Papa's death. For someone who was always full of advice, that was one of her worst decisions—what the island is worth today could have sustained generations.

Now, however, it seemed that the sale had not been handled properly. Fuzzy, a half owner and, as always, a passive player, had not been consulted at the time by her sister. The present owner who was selling discovered that he did not have a clear title. Dreams of reclaiming the island floated around us for a little while and after much legal back and forth, we went off to Maine as the hopeful, rightful heirs. At the very least, we thought there might be a settlement; at the very best, we'd get it back. We had a lawyer, a claim, and Klondike spirit in our blood.

My mother and I shared a room with double beds in a quaint New England inn—"A little too quaint," my mother pronounced. We also shared a carafe of rosé and lobster every night we were there and a hangover every morning. She was wistful, almost vulnerable, after the day's meetings and visiting her family's old haunts. I was too—I could sense a change between us, a subtle shift as more balls were amassing on my side of the court. Finding love, graduating from college, and beginning the hunt for my first job were all reinforcing who I was. She seemed proud as I left our apartment each day, toting the portfolio full of my college news-paper articles under my arm. Sometimes my mother would even walk me to the door, looking hopeful. "Good luck today," she'd call out before locking the double bolts behind me. I wondered if the tables had turned without my noticing and she had begun to see herself in me; if she wished for a second chance now that the world seemed to be full of choices. One thing I knew for certain as that child born on Saturday, was that by doing and accomplishing, I was leveling some private playing field.

One evening in Maine, wanting to let the wine work itself through before bed, I wrote a poem after she fell asleep. Poetry was never my milieu, but I suddenly felt pulled to express a feeling and turn it inside out to see if it was true. Coming back to Winterport had made me wistful too, and highlights of prior trips when I was young circled around in my memory—especially one particular conversation about change that I had overheard between Tante and my mother. It had reached my ears as I sat at the top of the stairs one night, still too anxious to fall asleep on my own.

"How are you progressing with your troubles, Dotty dear?" Tante had asked her.

My mother's voice was low, made up of indistinguishable words strung together in a late-night confession to someone she trusted.

"You should talk to a lawyer," Tante continued loudly. Living in an echoing house that had never been filled with children who required discretion, she had spoken as if no one else was there. "You could get a separation for two or three, maybe even five years, and then dump your hanger-on."

More hushed whispers from my mother and when I heard her chair move, I ran back to our room, fearful of being discovered but also worried that my mother might not have needed any extra encouragement. I wondered how long I had carried that concern with me or if I had managed to tell myself that somehow, I had misheard. The returning memory made me think about all the gray within choices that are not clearly black and white, like whether to leave something or someone. Nothing ultimately did change between her and my father, but I could feel that much was changing between us now.

On our last night in Maine, after our efforts to reclaim the island had proven unsuccessful—my mother's share was a token settlement that barely covered the cost of our trip—I pulled out the paper as we polished off the carafe.

"OK," I swallowed. "Here goes." And I read:

Warmed air tempts the buds
Waiting, teased, below the surface
For the moment to be seen.

"I like it," she encouraged. "What's it called?"

"Right now, *Renewal*," I told her. "But I'm not sure." I went on to read the second verse:

They rejoice in their freedom
They smell their own sweetness
And turn toward the sun.

"Very visual, Debbie. I can see it."

"Can you feel it?"

"Yes, that too," she said.

I paused to sip and then continued:

The light becomes their world
Chasing blinding slivers
Never glancing below
They resist the thunder
Ignore rain's relief
Unforgiving rays sap them.

"Mmmnn," she offered.

Winds unsettle their hold
Mist clouds their vision
Darkness frightens them.

"Where's the renewal part?" my mother asked.

"Well, I guess in what comes next," I answered. "The cycle repeats."

"I liked it better before. Time passes, but it's depressing." I read the last lines:

Grips loosen as the sun recedes
Common lifelines fade
Falling, falling, one by one.

"Enough," she said. "More wine."

Innocence and wisdom meet
Knowing is renewal after the fall.

I paused. "That's it, the last line."

"What is this about? Really?" she asked.

"I'm not sure. How forces can change our nature or how experience makes us see more clearly. Maybe it's a little about us," I added tentatively. "It just sort of came out."

"Well, let's put it back," she said, staring straight at me and through me at the same time.

"It makes you sad?"

"It makes me think about things I don't want to think about. That's what it does."

"About getting older?" *Or about us?*

"Well, I'm still young. But yes, I guess so. When you have all this"—she gestured at herself, head to waist—"you never want it to slip away."

"Mom, you'll always be spectacular," I reassured her, but my words felt hollow. I couldn't add that the poem revealed my own fear of one season giving way to the next. My mother was indeed changing and, it seemed, could weaken just as I was strengthening. I wanted no part of the inevitable. Her creeping menopausal heaviness of twenty or so pounds made her more lethargic at times, too. Almost a little jaded, as if she had seen it all and might not be too excited about what was to come. These slight shifts harkened other ones that could diminish her, especially if her world remained the same while mine broadened. If only there were a way for her to always be as luminous as she had been. I might once have yearned for a more balanced scale, but one where I would inch up to her level, not one where she would come down to me. She was the ground upon which I was built. A scale that could eventually tip in my favor was as foreign as it was frightening.

"When you get older, Debbie, you'll understand. Change is hard," my mother offered.

"Even positive change," was all I said in reply.

My lifetime of near invisibility under the majestic tree that was my mother had made only small steps possible when I was younger. But invisibility had also carried a power with it that I was only just beginning to understand—it had freed me to develop a rich inner world outside of anyone's reach; an interior life that was alive and churning under a placid, pleasing surface. I was starting to realize that my unusual childhood had sharpened fine powers that would be assets and made me strong well beyond what I imagined myself to be. There was no resisting the external forces that were now pushing me to blossom like a hothouse orchid that, when it finally opens, is beautiful and lasting after so much waiting in the dark.

Acceleration

How true it is that the first time for anything is the most memorable. Although steps into the unknown may send shivers down the spine of any debut, all first experiences also carry the tingle of the new and the promise of possibility. Usually. As my mother and I finessed and finished plans for my wedding, we were, as always, sailing on calm seas. We picked out dresses—mine and hers—place settings, and flower arrangements, and agreed on a hundred other decisions as if we shared the same mind. Unlike Rita and Denise's constant battling, my mother and I were still known for never arguing. So, I was caught completely off guard by our first fight, radioactive in its fury.

One would think that—since there had never been any other arguments—it would be easy to remember every single facet. But, in fact, for years I blocked out the entire incident from my memory like an amnesia victim. It had never happened. Then as time passed, it reappeared. First, as a vague impression—*didn't we have a fight about something?* Then slowly, the memory came back, but the edges of it were blurred, and the middle singed away like a melted old photograph that had come too close to a flame. I could feel it, I could see it, but I had no idea what it was about or what had been said. Until one day, I realized that I had actually uttered the word "No."

It was just before my bridal shower. I was twenty-two and, I guess, flexing too much independence. My mother could be teased. Loved it, in fact, when you poked fun at her eccentricities—her long presses on the horn and drive-by cursing; her empty threats to take her business from her favorite department store if something was amiss at the register; her feeding of our little poodle Suzi on her lap at the dinner table until the pet turned into a vicious beast that terrorized the rest of us. But true defiance was another matter.

I know we were in the midst of planning the shower. I know she wanted something that I adamantly did not. I know she was furious. I know that I ran to the bathroom and locked the door. I know she came after me banging on the other side and screaming things, saying things that I cannot remember. All her pent-up rage, all her unbalanced ledgers, all her disappointments rolled into those forgotten words spewing as she pounded.

"OPEN THIS DOOR!"

She had just put up new wallpaper, diverting attention from the bathroom's old-fashioned yellow tiles with a bold animals-in-the-jungle print. Trapped between cheetahs and lions and elephants, I stood with my hands on the locked door as it shook, slipping down to the floor with no way to escape. That door became the great divide between us, holding back the rushing river of her life's injustices. On each of its sides was a different truth, but hers was the only one that mattered. At that moment, the door was the only protection from what I had spent my whole life avoiding, and now it was all coming at me—spears of words and rage aimed at my ungrateful, unworthy soul. One single misstep and now here it was, unleashed. I'd misspoken, and I lost whatever love she had for me. Gone. Irrevocable. Just like that. Such a flimsy thing love is.

After the memory returned to me, I'd think about it before falling sleep hoping that I'd retrieve some new strand in the morning. Whatever had been blocked for all those years because it was too painful, I felt ready for now. The texture of what had happened that day deepened, a bit, in the months that followed. What she was wearing—a zippered paisley caftan of browns and greens.

That she had slippers on, the kind with no backs and a little marabou topper. She had put them on carefully because I had done her toenails earlier. For years, she paid me for a pedicure every month—a full one, from foot bath to callous removal to toenail cutting and filing, then finished off with a massage and the polish that always matched her nails. It sounds subservient, but I was a willing participant. It was an intimate game, and I held the control console in my hand. We laughed if the water I carried in was too hot or too cold—*did I do that on purpose?*—if the massage was too short; if I playfully bossed her around, placing her feet where I wanted them to go.

But even though I tried to summon more details of the argument, there were few. I know that I also heard my father's muffled voice on the other side of the bathroom door, sounding as shocked as I was. He had dared to intercede on my behalf. Then my mother turned on him instead, perhaps realizing that there was no good way out of the situation with me. I huddled behind the door, horrified, listening as I tried to hear and not hear. *What was going to happen? How far was she willing to go?* My father continued to take the heat in the hallway as they backed away and into their room. I opened the door then and ran past them and out of the apartment. I think. I might have walked for hours, crushed that a lifetime of careful sidesteps had vanished, that the moment I'd always feared had finally happened: the moment she revealed how she really felt about me.

That day, it all seemed irreparable, unrecoverable. But somehow, we mended. I also don't remember just how we patched the wound, but I'm certain she never said she was sorry—those words were not a part of her language. And I'm certain I must have, my apology a part of the unspoken terms of the détente. But no matter. I do remember I could breathe again.

And I needed to breathe deeply for the other firsts of that time, all hash marks on a yardstick that tracked my progression to independence. Especially work, since the hunt for the perfect job as a journalist was a long one. It's amazing to me now that I never gave any thought to the root of my fascination with Brenda

Starr—the redheaded, adventurous girl reporter who took over the news desk and got every story. Years of reading her comics had worked on my subconscious, convincing me that journalism was a way I could channel my mother in a career that suited my own talents. It was almost as if my mother had a spin-off character in Brenda, made in her own image and adored by millions. As I played with my Brenda Starr paper doll as a child, transforming her with one outfit after another, and when I read of all her daring adventures in the Sunday funnies, the first seeds of my desire to be a writer were planted.

But the root of my adoration recently became clear when I stumbled on an old interview with Brenda's creator, Dale Messick, a pioneering newspaper cartoonist (who took on a pseudonym because her real name, Dalia, revealed her gender). Hoping to give her character the widest appeal, Dale had made a conscious decision to make Brenda look like the actress Rita Hayworth—a.k.a. my mother's doppelganger. Brenda was who, I imagined, I'd be when I went off to my office, a routine that my mother's daily trips to Franchet Metal Craft had prepped me for. As always, the goal was: see her, be her.

What I hadn't realized when I was very young, however, was that work was a call my mother had really never intended to heed. Her apple-picking start was more an escape than a desire, and her view on work was ambivalent at best. The post-WWII era was a gray zone for women and work, a fact that was especially ironic given their help while the men were away. A career was not a must-have for her personal fulfillment (or for most of the women coming of age in those years, no matter how smart). Or maybe it was less about the cultural backdrop and more about how she was built. Whatever the reason, she never relied on a traditional job to define her, preferring to define herself.

Growing up as part of a new generation, I had the opposite expectation—that I would do it all. There was no question that I was going to have a career, so work and motherhood, when it arrived further down the road, would be wrapped up together in that neat I-can-have-it-all package.

My initial goal on the path to becoming Brenda was as simple as not starting out in an entry-level secretarial job. I was determined that I would not type for someone else. But despite that full portfolio under my arm, I soon discovered that there were no Brenda-in-training roles at newspapers unless I moved far away from New York—which, of course, was out of the question. So I expanded my search to magazine editorial (highly competitive and you still had to start as a secretary), corporate communications newsletters, and any other job where writing was involved. I searched for several months and the further away I got from newspapers, the less passionate I became. Nothing was extraordinary. In fact, everything was quite ordinary.

My very first job—a brief stint—was as a production assistant at an advertising agency that serviced magazines. It was the first non-secretarial offer I'd received, so I just took it. During my first week, I realized that the content they produced was on the circulation side of the magazine business rather than editorial—I was working on direct mail subscription offers, and not even writing them. I had just started out, and I already felt like a failure. Only later did I realize that the job actually taught me an enormous amount about marketing and the business of magazines, something that would later separate me from the pack.

I found that first job while I was engaged and shortly after I started, Bob and I began the search for our perfect first apartment. We looked in more upscale areas in Queens close to the city like Forest Hills, even though the rents were lower and apartments bigger in my old Jackson Heights neighborhood. This was my big move up and out, and I wanted no part of the old haunts. But one day, Bob said he wanted to compare a new Jackson Heights listing to the ones we had seen. I resisted, especially when I learned that the building was literally a forty-five-second walk around the block from my childhood apartment—but once inside, I was overcome. The apartment was beautiful, with parquet floors leading to a step-down living room with grand casement windows. Although it seemed like some intentional daughter-mother master plan, this time, it truly wasn't. Perhaps the universe just felt that my moon still needed to orbit her sun. At the very least, I had turned the corner.

Bob and I began to furnish the space that we would move into after the wedding and our lives as married adults officially began. I remained somewhat unprepared to assume responsibility for the tedious details of life. That unmade bed I had once stared at as if it were a science experiment was at the house of my very traditional mother-in-law. I knew there was no choice but to make it properly in the morning, however baffled I was. It was Bob, very amused, who showed me how. My non-domesticity set his mother's hair on fire, and I not-so-secretly enjoyed being the outlier, the college graduate who was choosing a career over her son's care and feeding.

In the beginning, there was absolutely no conflict between my commitments to work and home. I figured out how to do the least amount possible to clean the apartment and fill it with food— takeout four nights a week, dinner out on the rest, milk and juice in the fridge, shared light dusting once a week, floor vacuuming once every two weeks—and we were happy. We were a modern team, and it was easy to balance. I'd inherited a love of furniture and fabrics from my mother, so decorating was my domain. Never a packaged set of anything—just hand-selected, beautiful items paired together. Unexpected wallpaper in our kitchen; an unusual color combination in our living room; a modern oval white marble dining table paired with chestnut Chippendale-like chairs. I took such pleasure in these inanimate objects—and far less pleasure in cleaning them, my other inheritance. To this day, laundry, which seems to be the biggest, most repetitive waste of time ever, makes me feel as anxious as an intruder banging on the door. My mother was onto something with her housework edict: getting bogged down in all those details held women back for centuries.

I was relatively free from the mundane at home, but work was a drudgery of its own. My feeling for that first job just couldn't compare to the love I'd had for the college newspaper, and the experience didn't line up with what I had envisioned. It wasn't that the work was so bad, really, it was just that I had no passion for it. I was in turmoil thinking *what the hell am I doing here?*—a sentiment that was all too familiar to my mother. I never got to the point of answering the phone the way she did, but there were certainly days when I felt like it. I understood something I hadn't before about the every-day-ness of it all, the monotony of doing something that doesn't inspire you while not being able to see exactly how to break free.

A year later, though, things picked up a bit when I left to work for *New York Magazine*, one of the agency's clients. I was on the business side again, not editorial, but it was still publishing, and it contained a good enough dose of glamour for my mother—and me—to be proud. It was nationally known and well-respected for its features and fashion, and as the ultimate resource for what to do, read, watch, and buy. At the time, the magazine had its own three-story brick building on the east side of Manhattan, and I was charmed by being so close to the bustle I had dreamed about. There was a new role model there—I watched the female publisher from afar, a tall, cool, gorgeous blond who was decisive and determined as she made her way up through the ranks of men.

After two years, the skills that I had tripped into on the circulation side whipped up demand for me as business began to shift toward one-to-one marketing, and I accepted an offer from another magazine company, Times Mirror, to be a subscription director. After another two years, I went to work for the magazine division of CBS to be circulation director of multiple titles. But although I loved the milieu of magazines and there seemed to be a bright future ahead, work was still just a way to occupy my days and earn a living as a young married. It didn't really speak to my heart or make me wake up in the middle of the night with my head full of inspiration and ambition.

What I did dream about, however, were babies.

Lullabies

When I finally had my first child, I was flattened and thunderstruck and crazy in love. A son. A miracle. Richard. And the same rapture happened two more times—my daughter Elizabeth, was born nearly four years later, and my second son, Edward, arrived almost five years after that. Birth was my ultimate creative act, my own brood of Russian dolls.

Ahh, though, that first time. Your brain knows you're having a baby, your body knows, and you know, and yet it is still impossible to truly comprehend what it all means until that new individual comes out of you and into your arms. The moment my first pregnancy was confirmed, the seismic shift from one person to two happened, and literal navel-gazing began. The definition of such a gaze is the self-indulgent or excessive contemplation of oneself. For me, however, the contemplative indulgence was not of self, it was of the actual inner child.

I willingly bought into the whole motherhood bundle—all the virtue, all the sacrifice, all the standards. Each flutter I felt held an inexpressible mystery. I read everything I could find about every second of fetal development. The visible proof that someone was really in there was endlessly fascinating in the last trimester— I would sit around just waiting for the baby to move, trying to feel who he or she was. This was in the days before parents could easily know the gender and my mind ping-ponged between the two possibilities—my dreams would whisper *boy* but when I was awake, the idea that I could birth someone of the opposite gender felt inconceivable. Being female was all I knew, I had been surrounded by throngs of women my entire life, so I was sure it must be a girl.

I scheduled my maternity leave carefully to maximize time at home after the birth, but the baby was not in any hurry. I had stopped work a week before my due date, and now I was a week overdue—*two weeks of my leave wasted, and nothing had happened!* I was restless and still waiting on a hot summer day, holed up in our apartment's only air-conditioned room with swollen ankles propped on a bed pillow. I flipped to Phil Donahue's afternoon talk show—his clever balance of both eccentric and serious guests was the only thing I connected with on daytime TV.

While staring at his silvery hair on-screen, the first labor twinge hit—a very minor, but clearly new, sensation. I stood and paced as I waited for the next, which predictably reared about ten minutes later. Then another and another. *I can handle this*, I thought as I called Bob—*this is it!*—the moment I had been waiting for my whole life! Excitement mixed with utter terror as the twinges began to turn sharper in the few hours before Bob got home. But even at five minutes apart, the manageable early labor gave me confidence—if it were any indication of what was to come, I was going to survive.

One thing about those first few hours had completely startled and amused me—despite absorbing all possible fetal facts, despite the Lamaze classes, the videos, and the countless birth stories from other women, I had completely misperceived where the pain actually was. With each contraction, I had expected that the pain would fill my entire, enormous pregnancy belly as it tightened all around—a vast circumference in an unbearable body grip. Nothing I had ever read, saw, or heard specifically mentioned one truth—that all the pain was really concentrated in a thin line above the pubic area like a ferocious, gnawing menstrual cramp. *I can handle this,* I believed. There was something about the pain being tucked away in just one little spot that resonated with me, encouraged me in a way. I felt I could brace myself for it and keep it in its place. As day turned to night and night turned into the early morning hours, it became clear just how one tiny area of unresolvable pain can spiral out of control and completely take you over. By then, I had been transferred to the hospital's crisp aluminum brightness and had surrendered to an unending cycle of ripping agonies that were a minute long and two minutes apart. And no drugs—not that I didn't beg for them. Fully monitored with sticky patches and wires inside and out, it seemed that when I had a contraction, the baby's heart rate and oxygen level slowed. Any drug to relieve my distress could potentially increase the baby's, so too bad. I had to find my own way through. My first true lesson in motherhood came before he even appeared—*sacrifice*.

But the second Richard was born at almost dawn the next day, all the pain just stopped. No sleep, no matter—I floated high, radiating with happiness, and everything else melted away. I stared into fresh eyes so like my own, open and curious from the start. His dark hair surrounded a face that reflected mine, and as I enveloped him, I made silent promises to be the most loving, best mother ever. Both sets of grandparents rushed to the hospital, and the ecstasy of unveiling the next generation to my mother and father both inflated and conflated me. *Look at what I have done!* This, I immediately realized, was a different kind of love. One that had lain in wait for years, hopeful. Redemptive love. Healing love. Love that also sated my own need to be held close in a mother-child embrace.

At the time, a progressive trend was the option to have the baby in the room with you for extra bonding. Immediate hand-raise from me—*yes, please!* There were no "chores" in his ministrations, only opportunities to be amazed. Every bottle, diaper, and soiled burping cloth were little gifts from him to me and me to him. My purpose was in his tiny twisting body, swaddled and then not, his freed arms reaching up for connection. I felt fluent in his language of soft murmurs and babbles. Richard knew me, and I knew him—his face, his moves, his scent. Mine.

Aunt Lilly immediately came down from upstate New York to help during my first week home, taking charge of all the excess things rather than of him. She knew I would not delegate that role. I would care for him, and she would care for everything else. My mother also visited her new gift of a grandson every day, but it was Aunt Lilly who helped me get my bearings.

After sacrifice, the second awareness of motherhood hit me during my first week home. I should have had an inkling that returning to work might be problematic for me given how consumed I had been by the pregnancy. Now, just staring at him was a day brilliantly spent, and it began to dawn on me how work was going to totally interfere with the type of mother I wanted to be, that I felt destined to be. I wanted the maternity leave to go on forever as a new inner conflict began to take hold. As the little girl who had been delicately consigned to others, I did not have the desire—or perhaps the courage—to neatly separate myself from him. What I craved was to be *the one,* the knowing earth mother totally in step with her offspring, the always-present being that no one ever could or should replace. I feared the consequences of delegation and absence because of my own experience. And I feared losing something that I had just gained—the euphoria that omnipotence bestows.

I felt like I was the queen of the world, irreplaceable, as if no one could do what I did with him, know what I knew about him. Going back to work meant learning that "only me" was an illusion. It was a motherhood lesson that I wanted to forestall. But it wasn't cool in the 1980s to be just a mother. Yet it was equally uncool to be a full-time working mother—a paradox of the transitioning times that was just as confusing as everything that I was feeling. It felt unbearable to even think about separating, but I knew I couldn't just give up my job. Whether it was the fulfillment of something I needed to prove or the financial reality of the new two-career household norm, I wasn't sure. A little of each, perhaps.

Then, when Richard was ten days old, a third truth about motherhood reached up and grabbed me by the throat. Despite my elation after birth, the postpartum period brought a different kind of strain. Not hormonal blues, though. Instead, it was like the opening of an unaddressed wound, one that had been lying dormant since I was young. I stared at Richard as he slept and burst into tears, thinking that I should never have had him, for if anything ever happened to him, I had basically signed my own death sentence.

And as soon as I had that realization, it hit me head-on: *my mother never felt this way about me.* Giving birth made my own childhood a deeper shade of gray. Becoming a mother sent me down a funnel back to my own. I felt like a little girl again, crying when no one was looking and grasping for something I couldn't quite reach.

As those first weeks went on, I also witnessed my mother's complete devotion to him—her immersion and tenderness—and it gnawed at the edges of that hole in me. She took to grandmothering in ways that pleased and unexpectedly rattled me. Consumed with her new grandson, she anointed herself "Nano"—grandma would never do—and visited every day, laser-focused on her "poo-boy." It was exactly what I had been so hungry for as a child. To see them together brought happiness as well as a resurgence of my deepest fear—that I had somehow been a disappointment, someone she couldn't fully love.

I'd heard other grandmothers say that their grandchildren were the loves of their lives and their securely attached daughters never flinched, never worried that something unconditional might have skipped a generation. I quickly needed reasons—excuses really—to explain why my own mother had turned into a poster child for grandmothers when she was not at all typical for mothers. Very rationally, I determined that she was just in a different phase of life with more time on her hands—it was believable enough to help me run from thoughts that tormented me so I could bury the knot in my heart once more.

At the half point of my maternity leave, I began to search for the nanny who would take the reins from me. *How can you even interview someone for this?* I wondered. Sometimes, I would sink to the floor as Richard slept, feeling impossibly torn. I ultimately chose a warm and loving woman, and when my leave finally ended eight weeks later, I rejoined the working world. But the moment I left, I only wanted to return. I burst through the door each evening knowing that at least another half day's work lay ahead of me—and I was already exhausted—but none of that mattered. When I arrived home, it was all about him. My life's dance around my mother had conditioned me to focus on the target, so I was an expert.

I realized that I had entered another space that she had never occupied—hands-on versus hands-off motherhood. For me—unlike for her—any time away from home only meant time not spent with my child, my priority. He was the new being on a pedestal that I revolved around, and I wanted nothing to interfere. I wouldn't even go out for dinner with Bob until after Richard fell asleep—how could I be gone all day and then come home only to leave him again? No means no. Demeter I would be.

I was determined to be the spotlight that made Richard feel that he came before anything else. Every night closed with a lullaby—the song my Aunt Lena used to sing at the resort, "Till There Was You." The verses of that sentimental classic—all about love and finally understanding its meaning—spoke the truth of the world he had gifted me.

But having a family came at a price for me, and my love was packaged neatly with conflict and guilt. After I returned to CBS Magazines, those two came barreling in, taking up permanent residence in my head as they made themselves quite comfortable. To pile on the pressure, we moved to the suburbs when Richard was turning a year old. The suburbs were a middle lane for me between country and city extremes but added a longer commute and property to the list of things to be cared for. Having only previously known apartments, I had a call-the-super mentality, and the realities of a house were a shock that upped the ante on drudgery and demands.

No longer living just around the corner, my mother and father would come for the weekend bearing little presents. And even though my universe had changed dramatically, my mother still had certain center stage expectations. Unfamiliar as she was with the daily tasks that ate up so much of my time, she often grew frustrated when my mothering responsibilities kept her waiting if she was ready to go out and shop or have lunch. I could feel her impatience burning through me. Often, as I stood at the sink or did some other repetitive task, I'd close my eyes and use my Lamaze breathing techniques, the only move that could counter the constriction in my chest that I felt from her unspoken disapproval. She was waiting for me, and she definitely preferred it the other way around.

I needed that breathing technique at my job too once I returned. I managed to juggle it all, and as the months rolled on, I was eventually promoted to be the executive overseeing the circulation of seven of our national magazines. What my bosses didn't know was that I was certain of one thing—I couldn't go on working full-time. At that point, Richard was three, and I was still torn from living the having-it-all, doing-it-all myth. It was a decision I never thought I'd make, but once I did, my answer to any new opportunity was that I'd only be interested if it was less than five days a week.

And then, a new role manifested that changed my life. Another magazine company wanted a senior person but didn't have the budget to afford one. They made me an offer for a three-day-a-week job. An unequivocal yes set me racing to resign my current role, citing a lifestyle change. But the next day my company countered with the same three-day offer, so I stayed. I took a prorated pay cut but kept my job and made it all work.

There were many reasons they carved this out just for me, all wonderful and validating to hear. But I learned later that one of the behind-the-scenes forces had been a powerful former marine who ran the largest of my magazines. He tortured everyone including the CEO whenever he was unhappy with his assigned business staff. I was the first circulation director that he was pleased with, so management was timid about upsetting his apple cart. When they consulted him, he said, "She can make chicken salad out of chicken shit. I'd do anything to keep her if I were you."

I realize now that I helped pave a new way by being one of the first female executives to earn a flexible schedule. Being talented gave me leverage, more power than I knew it was possible to have, and I became a work-life balance pioneer. Now I recognize how I had consciously designed my own life and made it happen. But all I saw then was how the new balance happily shifted my world, even though in reality I had to integrate work seven days a week to pull it all off.

And I had a secret. I was pregnant with Elizabeth. This second time around, my dreams whispered that the wonder contained within me was a girl. When the twinges of labor came, I was prepared. Since becoming a mother, I had completely scrapped my philosophy of non-domesticity—I was now in the groove, able to dish savory recipes and cleaning hacks with anyone. I made us an early dinner, prepared all meals for the next few days, and got Richard's clothes and playdates in humming order until it became too difficult to hide my escalating labor. I would never want him to see me in distress.

Ironically, as with Richard's delivery, drugs that I had pleaded for once I got to the hospital were withheld. Overdue again by exactly one week, my regular doctor was away when I went into labor, and his replacement seemed reluctant to interfere with a normally progressing delivery. He kept stalling me—another half hour and he'd give it to me, then another, and another—until it was too late. But all the suffering fell away as I looked into my daughter's big brown eyes and she into mine. As perfectly and delicately formed as an English rosebud, she lived up to the first of many nicknames that sprouted from me—Elizabethan. When Richard came to visit his new sister in the hospital—carrying a single red rose as he walked down the hallway—my heart nearly shattered with joy and gratitude. I instantly created another pedestal.

When I went back to work after that maternity leave, conflict and guilt had redecorated their rooms, but I was ready. Especially because of my three-day schedule, I knew I could tuck them away in their place. I had arranged it so the nanny only came to the house on the three days I went to work, and on the other days when I was home, there was no one but me overseeing every need and delivering every hug. Exactly what I had longed for when I was younger.

What I didn't know then was that I would be able to keep the three-days-in-the-office arrangement for the next twelve years, making up ground and getting promotions despite my schedule. Ultimately, I made up all I had sacrificed. But at the beginning, I only knew that stepping back and taking less—but having more— was the right balance for me.

As the years went by, I let work carry me along and up. I went with the flow and took what came my way, never asking if the job I was doing was really what my heart wanted to work on. I never thought that the demands of the corporate world might not have been in line with my more creative side. What mattered most was the schedule—on this point, I was just like my mother. Convenience and flexibility were the keys. Titles and raises were side benefits, not necessarily the goal itself. But whatever I was promoted into, success followed. As the person who once thought no one would hire me, I learned that there had never been anything to fear.

At home, blessed with a boy and a girl, I could have easily been done. But, I needed more children, at least a third. When Elizabeth was nearly two years old, I had an unexpected miscarriage right at the beginning of my fourth month.

"When it happens at this point," the doctor said, "It's for the best. It's usually a misfire—the fetus wasn't forming properly."

The notion of something abnormal growing inside me was every bit as unsettling as the miscarriage itself. It took months for me to get it out of my head, but by the next year I had chalked it up to the one strike that almost everyone has. It was out of the way, over and done with, and I was pregnant again the following year. And then, at the very same point, I had another miscarriage. Completely shaken, it seemed like a clear sign that my body was betraying me, and more children might be impossible. I decided to try one last time the following year—Bob and I agreed that if it ended with a third strike, we would be done. No more babies.

But the third attempt was the charm, and as Edward was added to our brood, I knew immediately that three was my perfect number and my limit—balanced with work, there could be no stretching beyond that. But there could have been no grander finale or homage to maleness than Edward—all ten pounds and three ounces of him. On the opposite end of the size spectrum from his petite sister, and the other end of the temperament scale from his calm older brother, no child could have been more original and surprising. Almost born in a supermarket, Edward roared into the world, someone with a big footprint, destined to make his presence known. I was rushed to the hospital nearly ready to deliver him. In the chaos, and especially because they suddenly realized the baby was very large, there was no opportunity for any drug, despite my pleas.

The irony of the same situation happening three times really hit me afterward. It was as if birth and motherhood were some sort of test for me, an initiation that required me to demonstrate just how hard I would work for each of these children. I was Saturday's child once more, and the three I birthed led like little stepping stones straight to my door—Richard born on Wednesday, Elizabeth on Thursday, and Edward on Friday.

Elizabeth's May birth always fell near Mother's Day and tied her to that holiday, so much so that over time everyone assumed she had actually been born on the day. When Elizabeth was two, her May fourteenth birthday actually fell right on Mother's Day, as it would continue to do in cycles. While she was growing up, we always gathered with circles of aunts, uncles, and cousins on that Sunday, and each year she was celebrated with all of the mothers in the room. At some point, in the collective consciousness of family myths, everyone came to believe that she had indeed been delivered on Mother's Day as a special gift to me. It made perfect sense given our close connection, and so it was.

In addition to singing my aunt's "Till There Was You" to her and to her brothers every night, I was always making up little verses when they were little. I had my own creation, "I'm So Happy to Be Home with You"—a special song for the two days that I was off from work. But their favorite was my ever-changing "I Am a Little . . . " fill-in-the-blank series. For Richard, it was "I Am a Little Elf," for Elizabeth, "I Am a Little Doll," and for Edward, "I Am a Little Bull:"

I am a little bull
I fight and fight and fight
Give me that to pull
I am always in the right
No food can make me full
Every no means I might
I am a little bull
And everyone's delight . . .

And on and on each of the rhymes went, little litanies celebrating the uniqueness of three individuals that further bound their hearts to mine and to each other.

My mother never understood my need to do it all with them, but she seemed proud. Everything I was doing reflected well on her. At home, her grandchildren were thriving. At work, I advanced. I was particularly good at being part of a team, of being someone's second, of anticipating what was needed—all attributes that get rewarded in the workplace.

Soon, I had even acquired an a.k.a. of my own at the office, bestowed by a CEO after an arduous client meeting that even he feared to attend. A grueling three hours of posturing and negotiating ultimately led to deeper understanding and a victory for us, while all of the other executives around the table left pleased by the outcome as well.

"You know who you are? Our velvet hammer," my CEO pronounced. "You can make anything happen, and no one ever gets mad." I wasn't sure initially how I felt about that, but the alias stuck to me and, over time, I realized just how true it was.

My accomplishments gave my mother conversational fodder for her weekly beauty parlor ritual still firmly in place after so many years. Sometimes, before we moved to the suburbs, I'd stop in on the walk home from the subway and catch her under the dryer passing a note to her circle about some success of mine. Doses of any maternal pride still made me giddy, as if little boxes of sugar cubes had arrived on my doorstep. Although there were achievements for her to brag about in those notes while she lived—I had risen to a VP level at the time—there were more ahead that neither one of us would have imagined, and only one of us got to see.

Poker Face

"**D**ebbie, I'm sure it's nothing, don't get upset. It's just a little lump," my mother said, cupping a left breast so ample it was full of places to hide. "Come with me to the appointment."

I hated everything about the word lump. The spongy feel of it, the awful, lowly sound of it. And its real meaning—a lump is a sneaky revolution, misguided cells conspiring and amassing power while you sleep. *Let's stick together and take over.* A lump is a thief in the dark stealing everything you love. Can there ever be anything benign about that?

My mother had first felt it in the shower several months before. An accidental discovery that she kept secret for months, assuring herself that it couldn't possibly be anything. She was never even sick with a cold. It was a different time then—no annual mammography, no monthly self-exam, no breast cancer awareness month with fundraising year-round. In the 1980s, cancer was an even more frightening word than it is now, hushed and solitary. It sounded like a death sentence.

But when she thought the lump felt bigger, she took a step. We had just celebrated our birthdays a few months before as I tipped over into my thirties, my mother into her mid-fifties—quieter celebrations than in our hotel days, but still ours. Now, we went together with my father to see a surgeon who she declared was "the best doctor in the world." Affiliated with a Queens hospital, he wasn't a breast specialist—a decision that would be unthinkable today—just a general surgeon who had been recommended for the hernia operation my father needed to have. The doctor sent her for her first mammography, and then he examined both the results and her. When my father and I were called in, it was the first time I had ever seen her in one of those lab robes—open to the front and barely covering her cleavage. Both she and the doctor seemed in good spirits.

"We'll need to do a biopsy just as a precaution, but it appears to be nothing," the doctor said. "I'm sure everything will be fine. No need to worry." He hadn't taken his crinkly, smiling eyes off my mother. "Get dressed now, and I'll meet you at the front desk. The nurse will schedule a biopsy in a few weeks. Let's get this over with so you can get back to your life."

My father and I walked out with the doctor. "Come into my office for a moment while she's dressing," he said to us. Once there with the door closed, he continued. "Look, there's no need to trouble her now. She'll know soon enough. There's no doubt it's cancer." My mother's X-ray—that peek inside her magnificent orb—was in full display on a light box behind his desk. "Here," he said, pointing to a large white misshapen mass. "The radiologist and I are 100 percent certain. We'll do a frozen biopsy in the operating room and then do a radical mastectomy while she's still under. There's no need for two procedures. So, let's get the surgery scheduled as soon as possible."

I stood paralyzed alongside my father. The inverse of the good news we heard just seconds before about the woman who meant everything to us both didn't seem real. "Is she going to die?" was all I managed.

"We're all going to die, but let's take care of this and see what we're dealing with. If it hasn't spread to her lymph nodes, the prognosis should be good. If we talk too long, she'll suspect. Just wanted to be sure I told you both. Chin up now," the doctor said as he ushered us out the door.

The false reassurance gifted to my mother by her doctor was a breach of patient rights and information that would never happen today. My father and I were left to absorb the enormous weight of the revelation. We had a secret my mother didn't know, one that had to be hidden while we acted normally. I remembered my mother's poker instructions: "Whether my hand is good or bad, don't let it show on your face, Debbie." I promised myself that I would not, just as I had promised her years before. But this knowledge was almost too heavy for me to bear. I knew that I could only pretend in short bursts while in front of her; that I would break down as soon as she was out of sight.

Scheduling the operation was easy since both of my parents were using the same doctor. My father's hernia was slotted for the following week—we all agreed that it was better to take care of his minor issue first. "This way you'll be recovered, Jay," my mother said, "when I have the biopsy." Even a little nothing procedure might hurt afterward, and she wanted to be sure that he'd be ready to care for her. Hers was scheduled for two weeks after his.

And so, a chain of events began that—at least for me—linked my parents in illness and death more closely than they had actually been linked in life. Even though she was always the main character cast in the starring role, my mother's story could not be told without my father's. The culmination of their individual tales threw my thirties into a blur of chaos and loss as if I were seated on a speeding train, unable to make sense of the landscape that flashed by. All of it made me again afraid of the dark, of unspeakable things that lay in wait.

What wasn't routine at all about my father's simple operation was that, in addition to its numbing sleep, the anesthesia bestowed on him a temporary condition that sometimes visits older men, particularly those who have never been hospitalized. When he went into surgery, he was himself and hopeful about the outcome. My mother had decided not to take a day off now because of her own upcoming procedure, so I was at his side—he and I were both looking beyond his minor hernia like a team in planning mode, knowing what was to come for her.

But all of that disintegrated when he regained consciousness in the recovery room. "Debbie, help me," he whispered, his parched mouth gluing his lips together with thin white strands. "Find my glasses. We have to get out of here."

"Daddy, what's wrong?" Although fully awake, he had a vacant look as he fumbled with his IV wires.

"Debbie, they're trying to kill me. They're holding me here against my will. I have to get out of here."

"Leave the IV alone, Daddy. Everything is fine," I reassured. "You had your hernia operation, and you're in recovery."

But everything was not fine to him. Terrified, he refused the nurse's care and kept begging me to help him break free. He no longer saw me as a daughter but as a getaway accomplice.

"You're trying to give me more poison. Stay away from me," he yelled at the nurse.

I turned to her in a panic of my own. "What's happening to him?"

"It's called 'hospital psychosis.' It's from the anesthesia," she explained as she began moving on to the next bed. "It will work its way out of his system."

"Debbie," he cried, "it hurts so much."

"Dad, it hurts because you just had an operation. She's not poisoning you, she's trying to give you pain medication. Please listen to me."

"That's what they want you to think. I have to find a way out."

He kept rambling crazed phrases, trapped in a bubble of his own making that reality couldn't penetrate. No matter how I reasoned and reassured him, nothing stopped the 007 drama in his head. An hour later, my father was moved into his own room, which served to only escalate his fears.

"Where are you taking me? I'm not going to let you kill me," he yelled as he tried to hop off the gurney even as I held his hand. In his two-person room, the ranting continued. There was another patient in the window bed, but I don't remember ever seeing him, so consumed was I with the drama in front of me.

"Is it possible it could be getting worse?" I asked as I stood at the nurse's station later in the afternoon.

"It shouldn't be. But it's not going to just disappear. It could take a week to resolve or maybe even two."

Two weeks? My temples felt as if they were being squeezed together in some torture device. "I need your help," I begged the nurse. "We have to try again to give him something."

When we walked back into his room together, he was gone. We spotted him limping down the hall dragging his IV pole, holding his side and bumping into walls. Adding to the problem was that he could barely see without the thick black glasses he wore since the cataract operation. An escapee who literally could not find the exit even if it were right in front of him. We chased after him, each of us taking an arm to lead him back to his bed while he screamed, "Help me! Someone help me!"

My mother was displeased when she arrived at the hospital later. "Jay! What is wrong with you? Stop it now!" Even her commands couldn't pierce his delusions. "Debbie, what are we going to do?" she asked. "I can't handle this right now."

And so it went throughout that day and the next. The nurses would round him up from closets where he would hide; once they even found him on another floor trying to convince a patient to escape with him. Arm restraints kicked in temporarily, but they didn't last, and he continued to resist all medication.

The night before we were scheduled to take him home, I was in a fog of worry and despair. How would we cope with my mother's surgery just over a week away? I could only hope that being home would calm him. I left the hospital that second night urging the staff to sedate him so that he would stay in his bed and sleep until I picked him up in the morning.

My phone rang at 6:00 a.m. "Please come to the hospital now," the voice on the other end said.

"First tell me what's happened. Is my father all right?"

"Please just come now. I'm not at liberty to say more."

I arrived at the hospital, nearly choking from panic and fear, to find out that my sixty-nine-year-old father was dead from a freak fall out of the hospital's fourth-story window.

Through a whole series of wild events and poor judgment

calls, the hospital staff had never found a way around his refusal to take the sleeping pill that would have kept him in bed all night. They had done a test to see if he was getting enough oxygen to the brain—and he was—so incredibly, they had deemed him a sane adult who could not be forced. He had gotten all dressed at 2:00 a.m. to try to escape anew. Without his glasses, he had crept into a strange dark room, causing one of the unsuspecting patients to scream. Startled, he picked up a chair and broke the window, looking for a way out. The only nurse on call at that hour reported that she had run toward the commotion just in time to see him walk out of the window as if it were a door on the ground floor. Except that it wasn't.

Alone, I identified his body from behind the glass as if I were picking out someone in a lineup, hidden by a two-way mirror for my own protection. They gingerly pulled the crisp white sheet back very slowly, out of kindness perhaps. My face wet, my hands covering my eyes, I peeked through salty fingers as if I couldn't take in the whole of it all at once. I let in a first glimpse, a little sliver. There he was, and wasn't, nevermore. The distinctly rounded tip of a prominent nose gave him away, purple and raw but unmistakable. He didn't die instantly, they told me. He had lived for twenty minutes, although he wasn't conscious, they said. Thoughts of the fall and final seconds of his incomplete life were only eclipsed by the heartache; by the monstrous absurdity of it all—*how did this happen?* Every promise he had made was now truly and forever broken, smashed along with everything else.

I left the hospital and went to my mother's apartment to break the news that her husband had died. At the time, I didn't think it was strange that the daughter knew, but the wife did not. It was just my job to tell my mother. I wasn't sure if they had tried to call her and she didn't answer the phone. Or if that doctor, in all his misguided benevolence, had said that I was the one in charge, still trying to spare my mother any unpleasantness, even if only for an hour or two. Sputtering in agony and choking on my tears, it was almost impossible for me to see as I drove, his personal effects in a bag beside me.

"It's me," I called after unlocking both deadbolts with my keys—I knew the chain would also be latched to prevent the door from opening more than a crack, but this method of entry would be less startling than ringing the bell so early in the morning. "Mom?" I called a few more times until I heard her slippers clacking toward the door.

"Debbie? Is that you?" she said as she unlatched the chain. Once I caught sight of her, I could barely get the words out. Just two words. "Daddy died." We fell together crying, half in the hallway and half inside, as I tried to explain all that had happened.

Her grieving on that first day seemed like shock mixed with remorse. "Poor Jay, poor Jay, oh my poor Jay." I knew she wished that their life together had been different and that she would miss his caretaking presence now that she was alone. But I also knew that she wouldn't be throwing herself on a funeral pyre anytime soon. She would go on.

I had little opportunity for my own grieving. She was the widow, and I took care of the many funeral details, navigating those first brutal days with Bob. I didn't think at all then about the role I was playing. Why I had been the one conferring with his nurses, why I had gotten the early morning call to come to the hospital, why I had been the one to identify the body. I never asked why so much had fallen to me when certain roles belonged to her. I didn't feel any resentment. I just stepped up and handled it, the copilot, the helper. My mother automatically relieved of minutiae while I was steeped in it. Even though the loss of him might have been even more devastating for me.

Coupled with what I knew was lying ahead for her, everything felt even more traumatic. I grieved for him, but in a context that connected the two of them—*Oh my god I just lost my father, and now I'm going to lose my mother.* I knew these thoughts shortchanged him, sacrificed him at her altar, but that perspective seemed the only possible way I could react.

Writing his eulogy, though, was my time alone with him. In my childhood apartment, I flipped through his papers and files and fragments of a life that had been lived in so many different directions, digging for inspiration that would spark the tribute he deserved. His paisley pajama top steadied me; I tied it around my neck like a cape, close enough so I could inhale him. His song sheets peeked out from a beat-up brown folder, and for the first time, I looked at them as a whole collection, a life's creative work. At some point—maybe due to what the music-buying public wanted or maybe due to his own disillusionment—his lyrics changed from the loving and kissing songs of the early days to sadder songs as he got older. But beneath all my father's lyrics lived a metric pattern of necessary beats. My father could read music—a language of his own—and he had once explained, "Debbie, some beats are strong and emphasized, and some are weak, but they are equal. It's by design because you have to have both. They work together to form a tempo, a rhythm. That's when it gets really interesting. You can create on the fringe of it, and that's how you get something new."

A cousin ultimately read the eulogy that I wrote; writing it had been hard enough. "My father was a man full of hope; a man rich with dreams," it said. "He did not understand that he needn't make a miracle, but he tried harder than anyone to live up to his name and his honor and his expectations for himself. He meant for us to have the best, and we did, for we had him." I heard my mother crying softly in the front row chair next to mine, but I couldn't see her face as he finished reading. My head was in my hands.

Once the funeral was over, I couldn't simply roll up into a ball as I wanted to. I had to roll forward, out from under the weight of the loss and the shock for the sake of my mother. I tucked the pain away as if I were slamming hard on an overstuffed closet. Right on the heels of his death, my mother's gruesome downward spiral began—one that I had my usual VIP seat for—so my father was once again in negative space, overshadowed by the immediate crisis of the insidious thing growing inside her.

But only after I took care of one more thing for my father—a sit-down with the hospital administration after his horrific end the week before. When the hospital had to report his death, they spun into political mode. Their reputation was on the line along with their finances. Malpractice, malfeasance, mal-everything. How could they have allowed this to happen within their walls?

After the burial, the funeral director handed me my father's official death certificate. As I absorbed the enormity of what I saw, any poker face I had left completely dissolved. The sight of such an absurd, insulting, boldly checked box was beyond all reason.

To sidestep any liability, the hospital had told the medical examiner that his death was a suicide—a verdict that made it beyond their control. No facts about their fatal chain of decisions and oversight would then have to be shared. When I confronted them, they even tried to convince me that he had committed suicide, questioning his mental state before the surgery. Their machinations, though, never placed a seed of doubt and brought out the fierce Sicilian in me as I battled to change the pronouncement. In a velvet hammer move, I tried negotiating—I promised not to file suit (even if the hospital were entirely liable, any settlement would have been minimal given his age and the fact that Social Security was his only income)—*if* they admitted it was an accident. Just check that damn box instead! Then there would be no illusion about how he died. But ultimately no mediation, no tactics were successful. I failed him—the powerful forces of protocol and procedure cast a shadow over my father that I could not erase. I shredded all the copies so I would never have to look upon it again.

Especially because of their blatant lie and having to push his death aside so quickly, my father's untimely end always haunted me. Just thinking about the moment of impact when he hit the ground still makes me gasp out loud; any closeness to the edge of something still makes my heart pump wildly. Whenever I thought about the strange delusion that swallowed his final days, I always wondered how much of his imagined imprisonment and escape from nefarious captors tracked back to the kidnapping so many years before. Had the anesthesia reawakened all the terror? Was he intent on escaping to save himself this time?

I recently found a folder from that period of his life that contained all the newspaper clippings about the kidnapping that I had seen when they first appeared. But there were also notes written in his familiar handwriting that I didn't remember seeing at all. It was clear that he had intended to write about his version of the ordeal, perhaps for a book.

"They had their eye on me, but mine was on the window," it began. "I had to get back to my puddie-woos." It was so startling to see his nicknames for my mother and me in writing instead of in the air. He knew that we certainly didn't have the ransom, he wrote, and also knew that no one else could come up with it to free him. As the hours wore on into days, he faced the possibility that he might not be rescued. His last-ditch plan was to stage a bathroom diversion, break the large old wood-framed window with a chair, and jump out, handcuffs and all. Just what he had done in the hospital when he needed to set himself free.

The anesthesia had most certainly taken him back to his own nightmare, the most violating and invasive life-or-death incident he had ever experienced. He was just trying to escape the hospital in the same way—through the window. To get home to us. I knew in my heart that the hospital's posturing on his death certificate was wrong, but holding his words close, I hoped he knew that he was entirely and forever redeemed.

The Appearance

It seemed like an unimaginable, cruel joke, yet here I was again, returning to the scene of the crime days later. As I waited for the hospital elevator, I tried not to think about the morgue below me. There was the same smell of bleach over blood, an antiseptic disguise for what lurked underneath, the gray tiled floors with the blue-striped border, and the same cart of vile food rolling down the hall. I closed my eyes as the elevator passed the fourth floor and tried not to think about the window. *Just think of her. It's all about her now. Save her. Save her.*

It was incredible that we even got there—right after my father's funeral my mother wanted to postpone her surgery. "The doctor said it was nothing. I can't do this now," she cried.

I'm sure the doctor hadn't foreseen how his deception would create such a delicate high-wire act for me—now I had to hide the urgency, but still make her go through with it. "Mom, I know the timing is terrible, but you have to do this. Everything's set, and I called the doctor's office," I lied. "He wouldn't be able to reschedule you anytime soon. It's better this way because you won't even be thinking about it. I can't have this hanging over my head now and neither can you."

"And what's going to happen when I come home?" she resisted. "No one will be there. I just can't handle this now. It's too soon."

"It will be fine, Mom. I'll pick you up after the procedure and you'll just keep staying at my house. We need to be together now anyway."

Ultimately, she relented, so a week later I listened as the doctor told me that the lump was indeed cancerous and they had gone straight to the radical mastectomy they had planned for. As he led me into the recovery room, he added that the operation had gone smoothly and her lymph nodes looked clear.

"Is she awake enough to know she had a mastectomy?" I asked, needing to keep the storyline straight. When my mother and I were together in her room before they brought her into surgery, the doctor had still downplayed the procedure as he prepped her. Reassured, she was upbeat and remained so even when the doctor slipped in a caveat—that they would act aggressively while she was anesthetized if the biopsy revealed something serious. She paid little attention to what sounded like something he was required to say to everyone, something that really didn't apply to her.

"She's groggy, but yes, she knows. I told her it was cancer and although we had to remove her breast, everything was contained, and there's nothing to worry about. We'll know for sure in a few days about the nodes, but it's looking good."

I'd never seen my mother so helpless. Her gown was off her shoulder on the left side and a bandage, wide and thick, wrapped two or three times around her chest. Flat on one side, bountiful on the other.

"Oh, Debbie." Tears rolled down her face. "I didn't expect it to really be cancer."

"I didn't either, but it's completely gone, Mom. The doctor just told me the good news. You'll be fine."

"Oh, but Debbie, look at me. I'm torn apart."

That was the worst of her reaction and self-pity. She bounced back the moment she was transferred to her room, a model patient who never complained about any pain and did absolutely every-thing she was supposed to do to recover. "I have great recuperative powers, you know. I'm going to heal faster than anyone," she promised. *Always the best.*

Every day when I walked in, she was taking a stroll with a nurse, or doing arm exercises against the wall, or using the plastic breathing machine, mouthpiece in and blowing a ball higher and higher to keep her lungs free of post-surgery mucus. After a week, she was set to be released. I stayed and had a hospital dinner with her on her last night there.

"Oh, good news. Debbie," she said, looking down at her food. "You don't need to bother to come back here tomorrow to pick me up."

"But how will you get home?" I asked, confused.

"Dom will take me."

I looked at her, completely baffled. I knew all of her friends, all the women who bubbled up around her, and—I had thought—all the men. And yet, a new name. "Mom, who is Dom? Did you hire him?"

"He's someone I know," she said nonchalantly.

The plan had been for me to pick her up from the hospital and take her home to collect more things, then bring her to our house to recover. But now she had that faraway look that meant she was calculating or reconciling something. I pressed her, "How will you get to my house?"

"There's no point for you to set foot in here again, Debbie. I know you took the day off, but now you'll have extra time to get everything ready—instead of noon, you won't have to get me until 5:00 p.m. When you pick me up at the apartment, you can meet him." She smiled. "And no, I didn't hire him."

"But Mom, who is he? You know this person so well that he would go out of his way to take you home from the hospital?" Something was off. I had felt gutted and restuffed with some for-eign substance that barely allowed me to creep through the days since I first saw the white mass in her mammography—before I knew that my father's funeral would follow right behind. They were our shared misfortunes, but she didn't seem ransacked. In fact, she spoke these words as though none of those things had just happened. In an animated whisper, actually, like she had a secret to share but had instead been sworn to discretion.

"He's a friend," she answered.

"Well, clearly." I smiled, trying to disguise my own ciphering. But I wasn't up to doing my usual interpretive dance. It had been only seven days between my father's burial and her hospital check-in, and all I could muster was a weak agreement. "All right. I'll meet you at the apartment by five and say hello, and then we'll go to my house."

The next afternoon, I used my key to get into the lobby but stopped in front of the door to apartment 1B. I never rang the bell to my childhood home, but for the first time, I knew she wasn't alone and was with a man I didn't know. *Should I just walk in?* I stood there, wondering, then finally pressed the bell. Heavy steps moved toward the door that was always locked with a triple dose of protection—those two security-bolt locks and that heavy brass chain. But the person on the other side simply turned the knob and pulled the unlocked door wide open.

"Nice to meetcha."

Over his left shoulder, I could see my mother sitting in her favorite chair. She was smiling, looking pretty fabulous given all that she'd been through, in a lavender silk caftan loose enough to hide the drain and the fact that one side of her chest had been cut away. "Debbie," she called, "this is Dom."

I stepped inside as an unexpected feeling took hold. A light breeze of a feeling that used to appear whenever my mother came home with a surprise or manifested some new magic. Strangely, some of the heaviness that had been dragging me down these last few weeks suddenly seemed to ease a little. "Well," I said, "nice to meet you too." I stared at him.

"I was . . . ah . . . just leavin. Gotta go. But wanted to meet the kiddo." He grabbed a black leather bomber jacket from the back of the dining chair near the front door. I could tell how butter-soft and expensive it was just from the look of it.

Somehow at that moment, I didn't consider the awkwardness of another man standing in the family home that my father had inhabited just two weeks earlier. In fact, I could barely conceal a grin as I took it all in—the way he spoke like a character in *The Godfather*; his very handsome, cleanly shaven Italian face; his thick, salt-and-pepper pouf neatly gelled; his nails buffed and polished.

What is going on here? I watched his confident swagger-stride as he walked over to kiss her goodbye on the cheek. He whispered something, and she laughed.

"Call ya later, doll."

I closed the door after him and turned to my mother.

"I guess you don't feel the need to lock up when *he's* here," I said playfully.

"I didn't even think about it! I'm glad you met him, Debbie."

"Mom, there is definitely more to this story." I could sense even in those first few minutes that my mother—such a force and presence—was strong enough to bend with Dom. There was some natural male-female dynamic between them that made the walls of that small apartment vibrate with a different energy, one that I had never been witness to growing up.

"What do you mean?" She looked at me, her face leaning to the side, her full, arched eyebrows gathering in feigned confusion.

"We know casual acquaintances don't usually do hospital pickups. And he seems very friendly."

"Oh, that's just the way he is."

"And you seem . . . well . . . sort of upbeat for someone who's just been through so much." He had made her feel better, I could tell. Some sort of pendulum effect between them, a balance that spawned togetherness and enjoyment instead of the separateness and melancholy that I was used to.

"You wouldn't want me to be on the floor, would you?" she asked. "I'm trying to deal with everything the way I always do. What other choice do I have?"

"None," I said. "All I want is for you to heal. And be happy." I eased her into a standing position from the chair and slipped her mink coat over the caftan. "Let's talk about it in the car."

She dozed a little as I drove to the suburbs and then woke with a start. "Dom?"

"No, Mom. Just me. We'll be at my house in fifteen minutes or so."

"I must have been dreaming. I've really been tired since the surgery. I try not to let it show."

"You've been doing great." I put my right hand on top of hers folded together in her lap.

"You know, I think I'm probably going to stay with you for a few months, Debbie. To recover. And get through the holidays. The second I stepped back into that apartment, I realized that I'm not ready to be alone there yet. I need time."

"I was sort of expecting that's what we would do."

"You wouldn't mind if Dom visited? Probably only once a week. On Tuesday nights."

Tuesday. There it was, the missing word. My hands tightened on the steering wheel as the dot and the line finally joined to reveal what had been there all along. Now it all made sense. The Tuesday night tension that bounced off the walls upon her reentry; the short, hushed fights between her and my father that often woke me up; a glimpse of her sad face if I peeked over the half door to the kitchen, the scent of alcohol trailing instead of her perfume.

I took my eyes off the road to glance her way. "Mom, you were out every Tuesday night of my life. What. A. Coincidence." It could have been a line filled with bitter sarcasm, but it wasn't at all. It beckoned, lightly. It begged her to confide, reassuring her that I could handle whatever she chose to reveal.

She was silent.

"Really, just tell me. I'm all grown up. I'm on your side. I get it. Just tell me."

"Oh, Debbie, please. Enough." She slipped her hands from under mine and looked out the window.

"Mom, you've clearly known Dom for a while, or none of this could be happening. You've only been a widow for two weeks and in the hospital for one of them. Not even you could find someone that fast."

"What about my doctor?" She smiled.

I'd teased her in the hospital that the surgeon who had operated on both her and my father had fallen for her. "There's going to be a doctor in the family," I'd joke when he'd exit the room after spending so much time with her that it seemed she was his only patient. "And he certainly knows you're available," I'd repeat. "Wait for your first follow-up visit and then strike." I meant it too. For me, she existed outside of her relationship with my father. I loved him with all my heart but mourned him apart from her. And despite my grief, the need to make her smile was stronger at that moment.

"But it seems the doctor has competition I didn't know about," I added as we drove.

She smiled, still saying nothing.

"Mom, I understand what happened through the years. Maybe you don't realize how much I got you and Dad. Just tell me what's really going on." Like an out-of-body experience, I somehow felt like I was suspended above them both and could absorb it all without any resentment or blame.

"Well," she started slowly. "We had known each other before, and when your father died, he stepped in."

At last, a small admission but she wouldn't fully admit to their shared past. Even after I assured and reassured that I did not judge her in the slightest, and even after I knew him for seven years between our first meeting and our last.

Once freed from his under-the-table status, however, Dom became a presence in our lives, and anyone could see that they were a fit together. My mother bounced back quickly after that first mastectomy—within a month you would have never known what she had been through. One large new silicone falsie to replace what was lost and she was herself. She and Dom were a charismatic couple, and the chemistry between them was like a nearly visible lightning charge. But they were opposites too—she so polished and refined, appearing even more so in contrast to his rough, street-smart edges. But it worked. Even their mundane interactions often gave me pause. A simple, "Dom, what do you think?" could turn my head. For her to solicit advice was enough of an anomaly, but

the way she really did wait for an answer—curiously expectant—
told me just how much she admired him.

And every gesture of his did the same. So full of bravado and
self-confidence, he could admit his shortcomings and often appeared
astonished over his good fortune to have found someone who filled
his voids with sophistication and bridged his gaps with book-smarts.
These were attributes that went far beyond what anyone would
expect on his arm. "Dotty, you are just too much," he'd say beaming.

How my complete lack of judgment or anger was even possible, I'm still not sure. But it was genuine. I wasn't disenchanted
in the slightest and never, ever wavered from taking her side of
things. Anger toward any inconsiderateness never entered my consciousness. I never thought—let alone said—*Who would introduce a
new man to a daughter just days after her father died? Did my state of mind
at that gruesome time ever occur to you?* Willingly indoctrinated into the
cult of my mother, the lack of awareness of my own feelings versus
her needs was stunning. I was on her team forever and ever. Amen.

When I first met Dom, there was still so much I didn't
know—it would be twenty more years before I had the conversation with Annette about the abortion after the memory of that
Jamaica Estates house and my mother's despair returned to me.
Then, I just continued asking my mother questions, even though
her answers were usually short and incomplete.

"So, Mom, you really only see Dom on Tuesdays and maybe
one other night. Why is that?"

"He has a very busy life," she answered.

"Does he have any children?"

"Yes, one daughter."

"Ah. Just like me. Do you think you'll ever marry him?"

"I don't think so. I like it the way it is, and so does he."

"Is he married?" I knew I had to build up to that question.
"Is that why you don't see him more?"

A pause. "He is very unhappily married as a matter of fact.
But he's not the type of man to leave his wife."

Another time we were alone after he'd visited and I tried to
eke out more. "What is it about him, Mom?"

"Don't ask me to compare him to your father."

"I'm not! I just want to know more about Dom."

She opened her mouth, started and stopped. "Debbie, you're my daughter, no matter how old. And your father was your father. That's all."

"You know you want to tell me." I gave her a mirror image of her own side-eye smile.

She sighed. "We go together. He makes me feel something important. Now that's all, I said."

"That's a lot."

I had known Dom for two years when her remaining breast also succumbed to cancer. I was driving her to a doctor's appointment, and she suddenly asked me if I remembered the night I had read my poem to her at dinner in Maine.

"It all happened," she said. "I'm falling apart. I don't have my assets anymore." The same gesture of her graceful hand moving over her body.

"Mom, please!" I said lightly, for her sake—and mine, as I struggled with my own set of fears. "They were not your assets— you are the asset! You're the only fifty-eight-year-old woman in the world with no breasts whose married lover just gave her a new mink coat. And who still turns heads wherever she goes."

"Debbie, you couldn't possibly understand."

Afterward, it occurred to me that this was a phrase I was probably supposed to be saying to her. Wasn't that the natural order of things? Parents were supposed to do the reassuring when their children complained that they just didn't get it. But ours was a mother-daughter bond in reverse—the universal relationship turned upside down and jam-packed (or pack-jammed as she liked to say to be different) with so many strange reversals, missed beats, and lost opportunities to go deeper with one another before it was too late.

The Decline

The notion of seconds—from helpings to chances—is usually good. But the second time around for cancer never is. My mother's other mastectomy, two short years after the first, marked the start of a downward spiral that led to five years of horror for both of us.

Looking back, the first mastectomy was a breeze. Although it was a shock that struck at the heart of my mother's femininity, beauty, and power, the rest was good news. The lymph nodes were indeed confirmed entirely clear, and there was no further treatment because the cancer had been completely contained in the breast that was stripped away. A spear dodged, a battle won, my mother victorious. After her three months with me, she was back in her apartment right after the new year and valiantly adapted to life alone, taking care of all the dusty details on her own for the very first time.

Then, when we had moved far enough past the first incident that I no longer mentioned or worried excessively about it, my mother reached into her nightgown and cupped her remaining breast. We were alone in my kitchen on a weekend morning, and I hadn't seen the other half of the former duo for a while—since the operation's scar she was more restrained.

"Do you see how light this is? Do you see?" She was studying her nipple. "There's no lump or anything. But the color is changing." My stomach clenched as I watched her examining every inch of it, knowing she had probably already checked it hundreds of times, working herself into a private frenzy.

"I do see, Mom. I'm sure it's nothing. But it is almost white. Let's get it checked out." I was relatively calm, repeating to myself that no lump equals fine. And it was. After another mammography and a biopsy that was really just a biopsy, there was nothing bad to report at all. But because the doctor couldn't explain why the color was draining, the recommendation was a follow-up mammography in six months.

Even though the news was positive, it still felt as if a cloud, laden with rain, had appeared in a clear sky. I pretended not to see it, but its shadow hovered over days that had, until then, been unfolding so beautifully. I was in my motherhood groove and had never been happier—Richard was a four-year-old charmer, and we all were basking in baby girl glow with Elizabeth. My maternity leave had recently ended, but the three-day work schedule eased the transition back. I was in the rhythm of my own independent life—and then, that cloud. *It's nothing. It's nothing.* I repeated my silent mantra more to convince myself than to issue any command to the universe.

My mother stayed with me for a few days after the biopsy and the movie about a summer resort, *Dirty Dancing*, had just been released to Blockbuster Video. I decided that there could not be a more perfect story to distract us both—instead of a hotel in our "Italian Alps" region of upstate New York, the movie was set at a "Jewish Alps" resort in the same mountainous location—and I rushed to be first in line to rent it. After baths and bedtime, I hit play.

I fell right into the story despite how different the *Dirty Dancing* resort was from our own eccentric tiny hotel. What mattered to me was that it was the same landscape. But the cloud must have been lingering over my mother's head as well. Too tense to accept the movie for what it was, she seemed furious at the writer and director for getting it all wrong.

"Give it a chance," I urged. Her running critique was like a distracting subtitle under each scene, sapping my delight.

"I can tell already. It's terrible."

"Mom, it got such great reviews. Just watch."

"This wasn't what I was expecting at all," she added. "Who cares about any of them?"

She didn't see herself in the young characters, I realized, and therefore couldn't relate to any of their experiences or circumstances. She wanted her movie and got someone else's.

"I think it's great," I said firmly. As the minutes passed, the more she criticized, the more I defended. The more I defended, the more fault with it she found. I felt some dull ache being stoked. She was treading on my happiness with all of the worry, and now with opinions so different from my own. "Stop criticizing," I finally snapped, my eyes glued to the screen and surprising myself more than her.

"There's nothing left to say anyway," she responded.

I felt on the verge of tears and hit pause. "Remember when we went to Maine when I was little? And I got so sick, and then nothing felt right afterward? I hated everything?"

She nodded. "You were hard to handle that week."

The feeling of discontent from that trip was as present for me as if it had happened two weeks before instead of more than two decades. "It was rough for me too," I agreed. "I wasn't in the right frame of mind after being so unsettled. And now neither are you. I'm sorry, Mom, maybe this wasn't the best night to watch this."

My mother stared at me. "I *am* sure it's nothing. Everything will be fine. I'll be fine. Put the movie back on, Debbie." She smiled. "Let's see why such a mousey do-gooder would be interested in a dumb guy like him. Or why he would ever be interested in her."

I returned *Dirty Dancing* to Blockbuster the next day, and we watched no more movies during that stay. Life slowly returned to normal—she went back to her apartment, and we were able to push aside the state of her colorless nipple until the next doctor visit six months later. This time, the mammography did show something, but the consensus was that it was just scar tissue from the previous biopsy and nothing to worry about. As a precaution, though, they'd have to do another biopsy.

With no pull-to-the-side whisper from the doctor, I too believed that this would be just another annoying procedure. The morning it was scheduled we were in the same hospital with the same doctor, sure that everything would be fine just as it had been months before. We knew if something serious should be found they would again move forward with a spontaneous mastectomy, but we weren't listening to the litany of presurgical caveats, just nodding like glazed passengers ignoring a safety talk on an airplane.

So, we were both stunned when she woke up without a second breast. And the secret whispers to only me began again. The dire truth was what had been nothing six months prior was now a virulent cancer, different from her first, one that had already spread to more than half her lymph nodes. It was a situation that would have to be managed, not cured.

I stood by as she accepted another fabrication—that they had found cancer, and since there was just a trace in only one tiny lymph node, she'd have a little chemotherapy and be absolutely fine. "It's very minor," she reassured me. But of course, I knew differently. *My mother does not have long to live, my mother does not have long to live* . . . obsessive thoughts played like a chorus over and over and over in my mind, coloring everything. She was only fifty-eight years old, and I couldn't lose her. I needed her. I loved her.

But cancer did not care. New terrors to be managed cropped up every few months, starting right after the chemotherapy began. It was a powerful concoction due to the advanced stage, a recipe that was balanced with high doses of steroids to keep her as strong as possible. She stayed with me during the treatment, and about a month after it began, I found her slumped over the bathroom sink. "Something's wrong," she slurred. "Not the chemo."

A side effect of massive doses of steroids is high blood sugar, and her level was so astronomical that by the time I got her to the hospital, she was practically in a diabetic coma. "These things can happen," the doctor said. "We'll admit her and get this under control, and we'll have to reevaluate the treatment." But a call came early the next morning—she had been moved to intensive care after having a major heart attack during the night brought on by her diabetic state. Suddenly, the woman with no previous heart problems might not last the weekend. *My mother might die right now, my mother might die right now.* She was unresponsive, but I stayed by her side as much as they let me. By day two she was weak but conscious, and she made it through, getting a little stronger every day. But they couldn't restart the chemotherapy right away—*those cells are growing, those cells are growing*—and when they did, the formula had to be changed. The most effective ingredient had to be removed because it was toxic to the heart. *It's going to spread faster, it's going to spread faster.* Every few months from that point on, there would be another cancer flare-up in one part of her body or another. Those errant cells were waging a true revolution.

My mother's spirit was so formidable throughout that she inspired everyone around her. When asked how she was carrying on, she'd answer, "What choice do I have?" and smile. Maybe the belief that things weren't as bad as they actually were helped her to cope with each new incident—once it passed, she'd be finally free of problems. Or maybe she really knew the truth all along. I wouldn't know, because she and I never mentioned the possibility of her dying. I never said: *Mom, just in case, let's really talk. Tell me more. You have nothing to lose. And I have everything to gain.*

Although we never acknowledged out loud what was happening, as my mother's copilot, I was drowning in her cancerous world where everyone had it, everyone talked about it, everyone was suffering. The nights after my mother's chemotherapy usually brought the same dream since I was certain I would get it too—*how could I not?*

"Just give me some now, just a little dose," I begged the dream doctor hiding behind giant glasses. He would always oblige, mixing me up a little cocktail. First, the needle's pinch, then her poisonous liquid dripped into my veins in this fantasy that felt like reality, so finely calibrated with her experience was I. Just as I had immersed myself into every aspect of joyful pregnancy, I became consumed with preventing breast cancer. I had to forestall what

I felt was coming for me and bought into every health food craze that promised miracle benefits.

The harsh beat of her deterioration over the next few years marched her forward into oblivion. It was a fall from a great height, which made it all the more unfair, at least to me. She too often looked perplexed toward the end, as though she couldn't quite believe this was happening to her—*to her.* She'd be quiet, never voicing the fear. But I knew it was there, somewhere. That's why she never missed her sleeping pill—to wake alone in the middle of the night was just too terrifying.

My mother had never been religious, but one day, when she was about to be admitted to the hospital for another occurrence, I was looking for something else in her bedroom and pulled a delicate bronze cross from her nightstand.

When she saw it in my hand, she said, "Yes, Debbie, it's a cross. I pray every night now. It's very soothing."

"You actually pray?"

"Things have a way of changing."

That was the closest she ever came to admitting that her formidable self was actually facing down death. After that round of treatment, my mother came home with me once again—the many procedures designed to buy her more time had become so frequent that she was almost splitting that time evenly between our two residences. It became clear that she needed her own quarters with a bathroom, kitchenette, and sitting area. But our house was small as was our plot, so we had no choice but to refinish the lower level. Bob supervised the creation of a little apartment just for her, but no matter how it was cloaked, she was trapped once more in a dreaded basement—albeit one in the suburbs instead of the northern tip of New York City—a fate she'd been trying to escape her whole life. I wished I had been able to offer her a better option and chided myself for not having the wherewithal to provide more. I couldn't help thinking of her staring at those walls as she was contained once again by something that was beneath her from every angle. Just thinking about how devastating it must have felt made me cringe.

But she never once complained, even when I'd hear her on the phone with Dom and her coterie of friends, conversations that had been a part of her every day when she was alone in her apartment. And when she stayed at my house for longer periods, Dom and her closest friends would visit, and she would receive them upstairs. As her illness progressed, however, her world began to collapse in on itself like a black hole. In her last years, I'd watch her slowly raise her emerald-green mirror to glimpse if her wig was firmly in place, or to practice smiling with the new teeth that replaced the ones chemotherapy had brushed loose from her gums; or to just check and see if one more thing had gone wrong. Her mirror no longer reflected back an image of the most beautiful of all, but one of disintegration. A coming apart at the seams of life that no illusionist could obscure. Her absences from work became too long and frequent, so she eased her way out. She became less inclined to see people—even Dom toward the end—and preferred to just sit in a navy chair right off my kitchen in the den, a soft blanket in her lap, and her Nehru-collared bathrobe zipped high.

I had become, in a way, a mother and my aunts rolled into one. Sitting in that chair was a person I didn't know, dependent instead of independent, needing me not necessarily to love her but to care for her. She had shed her skin to reveal someone unrecognizable underneath, and I desperately wanted the old her back, the perfect one that I had chased and danced around. I often had to bite my lip, my hand to my chest, as illness slowly vanquished all I knew. Boiling vegetables to mush so she could eat them, I jumped one day when she suddenly belted out,

Amazing grace, how sweet the sound that saved a wretch like me
I once was lost but now am found, was blind but now I see.

Nothing could have been more unexpected; she never would have sung this into the microphone at the resort, or in a church along with others since she never went. In fact, she didn't even know all the words. Just that one verse over and over until she could sing it no more. I walked in and knelt before her, putting my head in her lap as she rested her hand on the back of my neck. We said nothing else that day, but I hoped she could feel how much I loved her. Frightened and overwhelmed daughters can seem like distraught or angry daughters—I hoped that she never sensed impatience, hoped that she never thought I was just going through the motions.

As her slip away quickened with so much unsaid between us, the car became my refuge. Not wanting my children to see me breaking down, I would cry whenever I was alone. All it took was one note of "Philadelphia," "Don't Let the Sun Go Down on Me," "Tears in Heaven," or so many other popular songs of the day to get me going. The car was my setting for a mobile, musical catharsis, but the moment I pulled into our driveway and arrived home to my family, it stopped.

At the point when cancer had spread throughout her body and taken up permanent residence in her brain, she had been transferred by the hospital to hospice. I came home after work and visiting her to a waiting envelope. I had needed her birth certificate for one of the mountainous details to be fielded. She spoke infrequently and haltingly now, and so had been of no help when I dug through all of her organized papers and found absolutely everything but that one critical document. So, I had no choice but to send away for a copy of the original. By the time it arrived, she had stopped speaking altogether, but when I opened it, I stared in disbelief and immediately needed her voice. It was the second time an official certificate contained a stunning surprise about a parent.

I brought it with me the next day. "Mom," I began, knowing full well that there was a slim chance of any response, "your birth certificate says you weren't born in July! You were born in August. Your birthday is August seventeenth, not July seventeenth?" A lifetime of celebrating together, of cakes for Dotty and Debbie, the conjoined twins separated only by years—and now this? All her comments about really being more of a Leo came flooding back. It all made sense now. She was a damn Leo! Even her love of green fell into place—peridot was her real birthstone, not my ruby. The color of her jade tree and the curio that housed it, the suit the gorilla responded to, her favorite velvet chair, and the watercolor of a woman with long red hair flowing over green robes on the wall beside it. My mother had surrounded herself with so many clues—that's who she really was, so that's what truly spoke to her.

August. Another illusion that had hidden who she really was. But who lies about their birth month? "Mom, if you really weren't born the day after me in July, why would you keep up the charade my whole life?" I demanded, showing her the paper. "Mom, try to talk to me." But it was too late.

This truth obliterated an essential part of our Dotty-Debbie narrative and dissolved some of the connective tissue between us. The reality beneath the fairy-tale surface of our relationship shook what I had always held on to so tightly.

And there was even more on that certificate—although it was nowhere near as distressing. My mother was actually two years older than she had claimed. She had initially lied to my father to make herself older, and then when she finally told the "truth," made her real age younger. My father thought she was twenty-four when they married, assuming he met her when she was twenty-one. But after they were married, instead of telling him that her real age was twenty, she lopped off two years and made herself eighteen. The story had stuck for the rest of her life.

When I would visit as she remained unresponsive, that August secret found its way into every conversation as I dished out slices of who my mother was to anyone who would listen.

"She sounds like a funny one," the hospice nurse said as she switched IV bags.

"She was. And this saga is proof that you really never knew what to expect next."

I lifted my eyes to meet hers on the opposite side of my mother's bed. She was one of my favorite nurses, sturdy, straight-forward, and no-nonsense Irish. In my almost daily visits, we had forged a loosely knit bond, knowing we'd soon never see each other again. Maybe having seen so many daughters in the process of letting go, she understood my longing to share just who this shell of a human really was before cancer had eaten her alive. We both knew that it was nearly done with her, bored and ready to move on now that there was nothing left for it to take.

I had placed framed photos of my mother around the room, more so others could see who she really was than to comfort her— she was beyond that now. We both stared at the version of the woman in the bed. I smoothed some wisps of hair off her high forehead. "She was exceptional. So incredibly beautiful."

"I'm sure. Like you." The nurse continued despite the shake of my head. "But it must have been hard to grow up under that kind of beauty."

I gave the same pat answer to that comment that I had when I was a child. "Actually, I always felt very proud that I came from her."

The nurse tilted her head as if she knew something I didn't; as if I might need a minute to reconsider my answer. Then she said, "Just lying here, even like this, she still looks different from everybody else."

"She was, always. And she always had a look that implied she knew something you didn't," I went on. "Thanks for letting me talk about her. When you live through something like this, you can't see past the illness anymore."

Someday, I hoped, I would recapture the woman she'd been before these nightmare years. Facing a future without her, I felt an urgent need to grab hold of the streaking spirit that was her life's through-line.

"You'll find a way to remember who she was." The nurse wiped my mother's arms and lifted her slack neck to slip a new pillow underneath. "It's in you. You're her legacy."

We had already talked for so long that I offered no comment on how ill-equipped I felt to carry her torch. Instead, I merely nodded.

"Let's try the feeding tube once more," the nurse suggested.

I winced. I had to leave the room the last time they had tried to force the plastic down my mother's uncooperative throat. The offer to try one more time caught me between holding on and letting go.

I looked at my mother's face as I was about to answer the nurse and saw a tear coming down from her left eye. Somehow, she found the strength to almost imperceptibly move her head from side to side. A clear no.

"We're not going to try the tube again," I said. "Look. She doesn't want this. Enough." As I stroked her arm, I felt it was just as well that my father hadn't seen her decline and fall into death. He wouldn't have been able to face the harsh reality. But having him there as she disintegrated certainly would have helped me. I had tried my best without him to navigate her care, but, as the years went on, even good decisions had bad outcomes. There was no one right road, ever. And if there was, I was never on it at the right time.

Near the end, I showed up to visit her hours late—with the rapid-fire demands of, by then, three children, a husband, a job, and her illness, I was never where I was supposed to be. I couldn't handle one more, no-win medical decision. So, I switched to spiritual measures. They were easier, no real right or wrong, no downside. If it didn't work, she'd be no worse off. Even though she was Protestant, I asked the Catholic priest who roamed the halls to come in and give her absolution for all her sins. Just wipe them away.

When he entered, the room was quiet with only the hum of machines for his choir. He spoke with the authority of the anointed, his voice resonant. Like the tenor at the hotel singing of fallen women and beatific virginal mothers, his words echoed in my throat and between my ribs. He made the sign of the cross on her forehead. "I absolve you from your sins in the name of the Father, and of the Son, and of the Holy Spirit. Amen."

"There," I whispered in her ear when the rite was over. "Now they're all gone. And we know you might have had a few big ones." That once would have made her smile. Did she even hear me or know what just happened? Did it matter?

I hadn't grown to be particularly religious despite my grandmother's best efforts, probably because my mother wasn't. But at that moment, I wished I was pious without question, without the sneaking suspicion that human nature drives us to create explanations and reassurances for what we cannot face—our own demise. Still, especially in those final days, I tried to believe. I watched the back of the priest disappear down the hallway, trusting that his absolution had given her something important, even if it was just comfort.

I had thought of inviting him in because of where I was in my own life. My half-Jewish/half-Catholic teenage niece, who was struggling to connect with something more than the limbo she was in, had suggested that we convert together the year before.

Still Protestant, I had married into the Catholic church, and my children had all been baptized Catholic. As Richard had his first Communion, I realized that my outlier status separated me from him. That didn't sit well with someone who was trying to be the best, most connected mother, so I had already made the decision to convert. Wanting to help my niece had pushed me to actually take the step, one that would have pleased my grandmother after all her Sunday effort, even though I was switching sides.

I sat in that first basement meeting with a priest and a mixed bag of people searching for something beyond what they had. I realized that while I had needed my niece to begin, she would definitely need me if she was going to stay. The process evolved into a welcome once-a-week relief that fueled the hope, as my mother slowly vanished, that there was more. Or at least the possibility of it. The conversion process took almost a year, and when I started, I hadn't fully realized these months would also be her last. It was a comfort beyond measure.

Just days after the priest's absolution, my mother was gone. I held her hand as she finally let go, sitting beside her and watching, as ever. She was there one second and gone the next. I waited for some cosmic reverberation that was bound to happen. But there was nothing. "Just give me a sign that you're still here," I whispered, "but don't scare me."

I reached for her perfume bottle alongside the hospice bed. Estee Lauder Youth Dew had found its way into every fiber that she touched, even penetrating the wood of her dresser drawers so that a pull on the filigreed handles let the spell loose. I didn't put it on myself—*never*—I just sprayed the tiniest drop and then stepped under the mist. One inhale, and I could almost deny what had just happened. It was very close but ultimately lacked the special alchemy that happened with her particular molecules.

She knew that I was still afraid of the dark and of all manner of things that go bump, so I hoped she would come gently. Just a little sign so I'd know that she was present in another way; that there was something beyond all this. I sat tight for two more hours, christened with her lifelong scent, but still, there was only the vacated, stiffening body on the bed. No curtain pull-back, no transformation, no dramatic reveal. Just silence.

Endings

The sickeningly sweet smell of too many lilies assaulted me as I entered the funeral parlor, so different from that perfume trailing behind my mother like a wake unsettling any boat upon her waters. I held on tightly to another framed picture that needed to be included with all the others. Her eyes looked back at me from within that frame, still full of dreams, innocent of the fact that cancer would end her life way before she was ready to hand over the keys. The dreams were of no consequence now. There were no illusions in a funeral parlor.

I peeked from a distance at the open coffin, needing to take my first view from afar. No rushing up, a slow build so I could adapt to the scene. Then a baby step closer. The side of her face. Smooth and waxed and serene, despite her ordeal. The teased hair dyed her exact shade of red and styled by her loyal hairdresser, who had insisted on time with her corpse to gift her the look she loved. The bronze sequined gown she had worn when I was married. All so surreal.

I'd decided that I would kneel before her after the visitors paying respects had left. Doing so first would crumble me; render me totally unable to stand watch and thank everyone on her behalf. I was already so tired, each blink of my eyes was a second too long. The night before, I'd had the first version of the night-mare that would haunt me for years—that she wasn't really dead, she was still sick, and I had abandoned her for months. Filled with panic, I had lain awake for the rest of the night despite the pill I took to sleep.

Forging on as she would have, I arranged all the pictures from her life on the tables alongside the coffin. The ones of her early years that I had transferred from the hospice. The magazine cover, the glamour shots, my favorites of the two of us together when I was little. Bubble baths, shared birthday parties, holidays. The Easter Parade photo of her, impossibly glamorous in a suit so like the one she wore to the Central Park Zoo that caused such hysteria. All younger pictures of her. The mother I needed to remember. The mother that wasn't always there yet was still the major force that shaped and inspired me. But now she was the invisible one, truly gone.

I had called Dom from the hospice after she had been pronounced dead. He made me promise to call him first when it happened, just as he had made me promise to call him with updates when she finally told him he could no longer visit. He understood that it was too painful for her to let him see her this way. But she knew it was too painful for him. Dom had loved all of her, even her self-centeredness and demands. Even in their last days together, he still shook his head and smiled as if he had never experienced any combination quite like hers. "Dotty, you are too much," remained his favorite line.

"She's gone, Dom."

"Did she suffer?" he managed to ask.

"I don't believe so," I answered, choosing to spare him the awful drowning sounds she had made toward the end.

When I walked back into the empty funeral home on the second day, I hoped the wake's last hours would be easier. But over-powered anew by lilies even more intense than the day before, I realized that the ripest bloom precedes the wither. I knew to brace myself. I heard only my own footsteps creaking on old wood, then turned toward the sound of a door opening in the rear.

"Thanks for doing this, kiddo." Dom took my hands in the fading light of the parlor's back window. "You get it," he continued. "Like I said on the phone, just need to say goodbye to her by myself." I did understand. He more than almost anyone else needed to be there, but even though seven years had passed since my father's death, he couldn't or wouldn't be seen by most of the other mourners. So, I had skirted the strict funeral house rules and coordinated an early half-hour private viewing. A little velvet hammer firm finesse from me, and Dom was in.

I looked down as he pulled some things from the pocket of his coat, which was topped with a sheared black fur collar. "Stuff I'm leaving with her," he said, choking up. "I loved her, kiddo. Love of my life."

I put my hand on his arm and offered a sad smile that he was unable to return. As always, Dom was well put together, looking extra sharp for his goodbye. His own cologne sparred a bit with all the flowers and won easily. He had only a few more lines and creases on his handsome face since I first met him; his hair was still wavy and thick, now just more gray than black. He hung his coat on the rack in the hallway to reveal a black pinstripe suit and crisp white shirt with a deep red tie. "For my doll," he said, straightening the knot.

Standing there alone with him—and his long shadow—a sudden firecracker thought hit me. Absolutely everything tracked back to that hotel. My mother's young girl exposure to the Canzoneri resort had cast a spell that made a relationship with a flash and cash man like Dom acceptable, even desirable. It had laid the foundation for choices that were unconventional in the real world, but conventional in its own.

"You know what I like about you, kid?" he asked me.

"What's that?"

"You always put your mother first."

"It wasn't hard to do."

"Good girl," he added, still distracted by whatever he was organizing. I caught a glimpse of a faded photo and a folded-over note on yellow lined paper. I wanted to reach out and grab them, knowing that I would never dare slip my hands into the coffin later. She wouldn't have approved of such an invasive move.

"And you never got mad at her about me. From day one. Put her above your father."

"It wasn't one above the other. I loved my father too." I had loved him, although, in truth, I had loved her more. But that was not for Dom to hear. My father was already too diminished in his eyes.

Dom's brow knit, then unscrambled. "Sure you loved him, 'cause you're a good kid."

"I just understood her more," I offered. *Had I?* I wasn't sure, but it sounded right.

"Dom, I wanted you to have this," I said, handing him a velvet pouch with a broach he had given her, an ebony warrior mask with a diamond crown, sapphire eyes, and a mouth of rubies. He said once that he'd had it made for her. "It was something only she would wear, Dom, so I thought it should be yours."

He held it in his hands, looking down at the pin and shaking his head from side to side. "A one-of-a-kind, just like her. I did good with this one, didn't I?"

"Yes, you did. She absolutely loved it. You keep it now. It will help you remember her."

"I don't need no help with that." He tucked the pin in his pocket. "Thanks for this, kiddo. I'll remember you too."

I smiled again at this leading man of her heart. He patted my hand and moved into the chilled room. It was time for his solitary vigil. When he knelt before her coffin and bowed his head, I closed the door on their last conversation, wishing that I could hear everything he mumbled.

I wondered if Dom's wife had any idea of her husband's intense love for another woman. But even more, how much my father—definitely the more enlightened man in this scenario—had really known or just suspected. I thought back to his collection of songs that I'd found when I was writing his eulogy. The ones written when he was older were full of sadness. As if he knew but decided to look the other way—the opening lines from five of those later songs clued me into the answer.

"Time Has Made Me See"
*Time has made me see what a fool I have been, I reached the end
to find where to begin
Time has made me see that this love so strong, looked too good
to ever go so wrong*

"Night After Night"
*Night after night here I am all alone
It seems wrong when my heart is yours to own*

"Remembering"
*You had your way and thought it was fun, I'm left to pay for
what you've done
Your memory will forever cling, so here I stay remembering*

"Moody and Blue"
*I guess you've got to be blue when you have loved and lost
There's no way out for you when you've been double-crossed*

"Lonely"
*Lonely, so lonely because my love has gone far away
Weary so weary, I'm so tired I have no heart to pray*

Maybe music was the only way he could express or come to terms with why he had lost her. Even if I had the chance to talk to him about why, I probably would never have shared my real thoughts with my father. They would be too painful for him to hear. The characteristics that made Dom a powerful man had reeled her in and anointed him "the best" in her eyes. On one level it was the allure of his success—respect that my father had not earned from her. But on another, Dom had mirrored her and took her higher. She was swimming in a reflective pool—when she bent her head to look at him, she saw herself.

His rougher edges even gave her extra footing; perhaps moments of superiority to balance the inequities embedded in a dependent relationship with a man like him. But if my mother had sacrificed some personal honor, it never showed. In fact, his love and financial support were badges that spoke to her desirability, for she was equally complicit in the cultural rules that governed pairings such as theirs. She bought into how it worked, all the more so because she loved him.

I always tried not to think about how Dom's success might have been at someone else's expense. I had to do that with my own Italian male ancestors. I'll never know what really happened on those rocky Sicilian hills in Palazzo Adriano, the town just beyond both Corlene and Prizzi where the Canzoneri clan was from. All I could do—if any of the uncommon personal power that made them rise flowed in my veins—was try to channel it for good. And seek the good in everyone and everything. My mother did the same, in her way, with Dom. She found the good in him and stayed with it. And she found the good in my father and never left him.

Dom emerged from his private goodbye twenty-five minutes later, red-eyed and wrecked, and left through the funeral home's side door with just a final nod to me. I never saw him again, but he did, however, call me two years later to borrow money. Business had taken a turn for the worse without her guidance and wise counsel, it seemed. Gently, I refused. I would not help him as my mother would have. His world was not where I lived.

The world I did occupy right after my mother's death felt foreign and dull, with little room for anything but sorrow. She died in January, and the final two months of my conversion program began to mean even more to me as I searched for some higher meaning and truth. The little stone church had the aura of the Methodist one of my youth: it was a refuge, its quiet meeting room a place of comfort, surrounded as I was by the conviction that she was everlasting. I willed myself to be less doubtful and tried to just go with the flow.

The conversion ceremony was a part of the Easter Vigil, held the night before Easter Sunday. The initiation rites are an important part of the renewal of the holiday, and all I really remember are candles and choking emotion that rose and fell with the searing music. Everything was still so raw, but I made it through the process and was done. Or so I thought. Afterward, the priest approached me to say that each year one person who converted was selected to speak to the entire congregation forty days after Easter about the transformation process.

"We've chosen you," he said.

"Me?" I certainly had the most secular point of view of the group, but maybe because the priest was a thoughtful Jesuit, or had heard it all before, he was patient with my questions.

"You have a gift to share. It will be real."

"But how can I talk to believers? What could I possibly say?"

He put his hand on mine. "You'll figure it out."

Very, very reluctantly I said yes. And then I wrote a speech that didn't profess to have answers, that didn't offer anyone advice—in fact, that didn't even have the word God in it.

On the appointed Sunday I took my cue and stepped up to the podium and began, "If you had told me a year ago that I would be on the altar of a church talking to the congregation during a mass, I would have said you were crazy. Yet here I am." And I just continued to speak from the heart about the parallels of losing my mother while gaining new perspective and comfort. When I looked into the pews, the congregation seemed to be going along for the ride.

"When I was nine months pregnant with my first child," I went on, "I was on a busy New York City street. An August sun was beating down, and the heat blazed up from the concrete in waves. Horns were blaring in the crawling weekend-escape traffic as hundreds of people walked in all directions around me. Then, suddenly, the baby moved—one of those big end-of-pregnancy lurches that you can see—and I instinctively touched my stomach, closing my hand around either an arm or a leg and holding tight.

"In a flash, I had an epiphany so unexpected and so profound that I had to lean against the side of a building. Here I was in all this bustling and noise, and here he was in his own very different world. In darkness. I knew that he would be born into all this light in a matter of days, but he did not. He was just floating, not realizing that at all. I was his mother with my hand on him, but he had no idea."

My lips and chin quivered in that way where you either have to stop or rush through with your voice cracking, as mine did. "It was a clue to life for me. The first time I truly understood that there could be other dimensions beyond what we know. That singular moment opened me up to a more expansive view, and that moment gives me hope now.

"Perhaps I stand here before you with my mother's hand on me, and I just have no idea that it's there."

Ascension

I stared at a picture of my youngest son Edward's first birthday, taken just two weeks after my mother died. There I am with him on my lap, opening presents. I have a vague memory of feeling that something had to be pulled together to celebrate him—and that I was sitting because I couldn't stand—but not much else. The time after the funeral remains a blurred apocalypse, like walking through rubble covered with ghostly white dust. Stunned and lost, I donned a mask to step my way through each day and cover pain that felt impossible to resolve.

Slowly, though, during that first year of coping, I began to realize that something was beginning to change for me professionally after my mother died. So marked was the shift that I see it now as a defining line, between BD and AD (Before with Dotty, and After without Dotty). My intense focus remained on the demands of my children, but now with my mother gone, I found that I needed more. Work became my secret extra distraction from the loss. I granted it new importance and meaning—my new idol to worship, to cater to and dance around. Even the stress it brought became my own amazing sidestroke away from the torment, for my mother haunted me in death. Not the kind of haunting where I was afraid I'd hear boo and see her standing there with her flesh peeled back to expose bone. It was more like a taunt—*it will be impossible for you to replace me, for you to exist without me.*

In this AD world, I kept moving to fight through it and began to take on bigger, more interesting challenges. My company had been purchased years before by France's largest global publisher, Hachette Filipacchi, and I was a little fish surrounded by very smart people in a really big pond. Nonetheless, I became known for having a way with people and ideas, with business and marketing. It seemed that what I brought to this pool party was a perceptiveness that got to the essence of opportunities. I had a particular insight and intuition that enabled me to connect the dots. This created value and I began to ascend the ladder beyond the magazine circulation division to the corporate level in marketing, international sales, brand oversight, and then the whole company's reinvented path for the future.

The start of my AD period was in the early 1990s, and although media had always been heavily female, it was not as much so back then, and definitely not in the higher ranks. Only a handful of women made it to the upper echelon, and even when we were "in," we were still mostly on the fringe of power with only a few of us actually holding it in our hands. It was old-school and conventional, and I thrived within it as one of the nontraditional outliers.

The opposite of today's open floor plans, our corporate headquarters was a vision of wood and brass, with doors everywhere to ensure that any palace-like plots were private and closed to all but the inner circle. The boardroom on the forty-fifth floor was a massive double-door enclave, with recessed lights that hit all the right spots on a lacquered table that sat thirty-five people comfortably. Sliding into one or another of those beige suede chairs was bliss. I was deemed worthy and allowed access, just like my mother. But this was a very different poker table. The stakes were much higher, and yet, I found that I knew how to play the game in a way that was completely authentic to me.

It was still the era of "walk like a man, dress like a man, talk like a man, and think like a man" if you wanted to succeed as a woman. It was also a crazy time when the fact that women were often paid less actually benefitted both sides—the company saved money, and a door opened for a woman that might have otherwise remained closed. *Oh, happy day.* It was a way in and up, a chance to prove yourself and to me, as a product of my time, nothing at all seemed wrong about it. The environment was tough—a pre–politically correct, highly charged world of negotiation with its fair share of shouting and cursing and cigars—but I held my own without checking my emotions at the door. I never hid my intuitive nature or pretended that I wasn't a mother. Every meeting benefited from the female leaders present, and I soon learned, as did the Boys Club, that estrogen is a necessary counterpoint to testosterone—its equal balance achieves the best outcome.

I loved being in the center of it all and, soon after my mother passed, I became the integrated marketing director under a new CEO. Right after I started, I had to get a budget approved for a costly project that the company didn't even know it desperately needed. My odds for getting a green light were slim—it was a big ask of nearly one million dollars that competed with too many other divisional needs. What the money would fund—a robust database of all our magazine readers—was a new concept that would not return the investment immediately. I was worried but stayed attuned to the forces and agendas behind-the-scenes, as well as to how difficult it was for the CEO to absorb everything and, Solomon-like, properly choose what did and didn't get funded.

On one of my weekdays at home right before the big presentation—a crisp fall day perfect for leaf-pile jumping and pumpkin picking—I took all three kids shopping for Halloween costumes. Richard (Batman) was ten and Elizabeth (Batgirl) was seven and Edward (Superman) was two. As I navigated the cart through the store's tiny aisles strewn with the considered but cast-aside choices of other children, the upcoming meeting kept flashing on a split screen in my head. To get to yes, I needed a creative approach so everyone would realize just how important this project was to the company's greater good.

I stared at rows of costume accessories along the back wall when a flash of inspiration hit, and I suddenly knew how to make the pitch relevant and memorable. "Mommy has a big workday tomorrow, and I have an idea," I told my dark-haired, dark-eyed adorable brood.

"Hate dumb stupid idiot job," a very verbal Edward blurted, his own unruly, curly halo bouncing as he gripped the cart's handrail.

My need to convey how they were number one also had a side effect—it de-prioritized the work part of my life. When they were young, their impression was that work was just the nuisance thing that took me away. I integrated them to impart lessons along the way, but back then, diminishing its importance felt best. I gave him a kiss and handed over his costume to distract him. "Come on now! I need all of you to help!" I told them my plan, and they giggled appreciatively. They loved picking out the props, and I got everything I needed.

When I walked into the boardroom the next day, there were about twenty men and one other woman seated around the gleaming conference table. I had often been commended for my ability to say pretty much anything to anyone—I believed it was all in *how* you said it—so I never held back. I found my seat and began to silently lay out my plastic Halloween stash: a knife, sword, hatchet, bow and arrow, handcuffs, and a gun (again, it was a different time). As they all bewilderedly looked at me, I said, "This is so important to where we need to go as a company, that none of you are leaving this room until it's approved."

A bold yet idle threat—but one that certainly got their attention. As I held up each weapon and described its properties, I revealed a particular aspect of why this project was so critical to our collective future. With the arrow, I talked about the value in targeting the right person at the right time; with the knife, how we could slice and dice content tied to a reader's preference, and so on. It was a stunt that seems cringeworthy silly to me now, but I got the money.

A few years later, I was promoted to lead ELLE International as the head of global sales, and my world really opened up. But I had to accept returning to a normal five-days-in-the-office schedule, with much more travel than ever before, most of it abroad.

At the time, Edward was seven, Elizabeth twelve, and Richard sixteen. I wasn't sure that I wanted to do it, or even that I could do it. Not only did I not have a passport, but I had only ever worked alongside sales and never seen myself as one of them—in my mind, other people did that schmoozy thing to bring in all the money and keep the company afloat. I was reluctant on all fronts.

"Shouldn't I get sales training?" I asked the CEO.

"No! Don't screw up a good thing. No one needs another traditional salesperson."

"But I've never even traveled abroad. And I don't speak French or any other language. What if I don't resonate?"

"Trust me. You'll resonate," the CEO assured me.

It turned out that he was right. A few years after that conversation, I was invited to speak at the company's global conference in Russia. On stage, images floated on a giant screen behind me as I brought the largest global advertising campaign in the magazine's history to life. Appearing in editions of *ELLE* all over the world, the initiative was envisioned, sold, and produced by my talented division with the help of *ELLE* US and the brilliant, remarkable woman who led it. Looking out at hundreds of applauding executives, it was a moment that I wished I could have shared with my mother. She would have looked fabulous in her enormous Russian mink hat at the Pushkin Museum dinner that followed.

Instead, I began to share my international experiences with my children, mostly with Elizabeth—adventures that took us to places like Paris, Milan, and Switzerland. Travel, foreign hotels and restaurants, and events with great goody bags were exciting and eye-opening experiences for her too and having her at my side brought me enormous joy. And I included her back in New York too; when we published John F. Kennedy Jr's political culture magazine, *George*, I brought Elizabeth to his floor on one especially memorable "Take Your Daughter to Work Day." Always incredibly thoughtful, John invited her and another girl into his office and chatted with them for a full ten minutes. I stood back, watching, my eyes filled with tears and feeling immensely grateful for this rare experience made possible for Elizabeth solely because of where I was in my life.

With success came a built-in dilemma and a layer of complexity for me, however. Chasing something because you have to is one thing. Chasing something because you want to is entirely different. My long-standing enemies, conflict and guilt, always knew that my income lifted our family, but now, they tightened their chokehold because they also knew that I loved to work. They were fighting mad when they saw how I woke in the middle of the night full of ideas, too passionate about what I was working on to sleep. They made me feel bad for being happy, and they made me hide from my children that work was incredibly fulfilling for me—I still feared that if they knew that, it would somehow affect their priority status.

For someone with such high ideals for the kind of mother I wanted to be, the downside of success was real—work took me away and brought pressure and more travel than I ever intended. It got easier over time, but conflict and guilt never really left me as my professional world continued to expand.

The opportunities kept coming, and life kept changing. When I became the publisher of *ELLEgirl*, it was my first brand to oversee and nurture with a truly amazing team. And I became an even cooler mom, granting Elizabeth—a member of the perfect target audience—the chance to participate in the work success requires. These opportunities ran the gamut, from the global *ELLEgirl* magazine conference where she represented the American *ELLEgirl*, to helping the marketing team with all of our events—checking in guests, or stuffing and handing out goody bags—to access that included LA TV show premieres, fashion shows, and music extravaganzas that our teen magazine would partner with. I was so proud as I watched Elizabeth's ease with each new experience. At such a young age, she already seemed formed and formidable, so sure of herself as she interacted with all, especially the women around me. It was a very different pool, but she was every bit as curious as I had been, wonderfully observant and always soaking up insights. I was certain that attitude would propel her forward just as it had propelled me.

My next assignment was the world of interiors as publisher of *Metropolitan Home*, which was so much more suited to me than the cattier fashion world. Interior design felt more substantive, and the people within it seemed genuinely welcoming and warm. Then, under a new CEO, I became the chief brand officer of both it and *ELLE Décor*, two brands with very different perspectives. *Met Home* was modern, and *ELLE Décor* was decorative—it was about fantasy, opulence, splendor, and ornament—but sometimes, it was all too much. *Met Home's* modernism, focused on form and function over flourishes, was interesting, but often too little. To me, a blending of influences—a little of each rather than the extreme of either—created the most appealing result. The middle lane. The in-between was indeed the best place to be. It offered more freedoms and fewer restrictive rules to follow, more possibilities hidden in the white space between ordinary and extraordinary. All you had to do was be open to it.

And I was. That openness ultimately brought me my most important corporate role, chief innovation officer for the entire company so that I, along with a whip-smart executive team, could reinvent its future. My need to seek distraction had paid off.

All along, I wondered if my success was born out of a need to prove something to my mother, and to myself. There was no doubt in my mind that she was in me as I worked my way up. Sometimes I even felt that I was channeling her now that she was gone. Walking the way she walked, full of confidence and guile. Talking the way she talked, full of statements and command. Perhaps I was replacing her by becoming her, in a way. But that wasn't quite right—it was more like now that she was gone, something finally had been unlocked to reveal . . . me. Now that I was no longer in her shadow, more compelling opportunities and experiences had unleashed a motivation that was absent before, a willingness to stand beneath my own spotlight.

To pull it all off, I realized later, what I had really become was an amalgam of the three different women who raised me. A blending of influences without question. Someone who could suit up glamorously and operate with a bit of confident bravado yet could come home and sink into cuddles and cooking and crafting. Whatever strange alchemy was working inside me, it made me a nurturing mentor who sometimes was also a corporate heroine, but often a corporate rebel—though always with the greater good of the company in mind, and my signature velvet hammer in hand. I bristled under authority and never did my best work with someone breathing down my neck. Those who knew me understood that I was best left to my own devices, with the freedom to go off and come back with more than what was expected. I listened and then didn't, and rarely asked for permission, preferring to apologize later. I spoke with an authority that resisted the rules in place and found a way around the outdated ones that prevented progress.

One of my bosses, a woman who I completely admired, once said, "If I had your confidence, I could do anything." Another said, "You're fearless." But I was neither. I had just had early training for doggedly pursuing dreams—a.k.a. the dream that was my mother. I do see now, that despite all her potential and assets, the stars just didn't align for my mother the way they did for me. Maybe it was the era in which she lived, or maybe it was the result of her own personal choices. Or—and this was the most shocking of all—maybe I simply had a flair, a gift for making the stars align that she had lacked.

Whenever these wisps of new awareness flitted through my brain, the little girl, still so alive inside me, would poke me and shout—*My Mommy lacked nothing! How can you even think that? She was perfect! And she had everything, everything!*

But now I can say to her, *Hush, sweet little one. I know, I know. But I know this as well. It's all right that some talents are ours and ours only. I love her now as much as you did then. I could never tell our story without hers—I could never even find our story without telling hers first.*

Awakenings

No one could see I was nervous as I walked down the hall. Head high, back straight, smiling, an eager stride. Even if they had glimpsed my hand opening the door to her assigned office, the tremble was so mild, it could only be known to me. A quick shiver that was there and then gone. But in truth, the fear of the dark, of the unknown, was never far. I quietly closed the door behind me. The prominent Manhattan psychic astrologer was already seated; her eyes fluttering, her mouth moving in prayer or ritual as she lit a new candle for her next appointment. Me.

I was an astrological skeptic but believed that psychic gifts were possible, so I went with the flow. From time to time, people had randomly popped up in my life who seemed to have something extra that let them know things well beyond what was knowable. An unknown guest at a party who took my hand and told me details about my life, another who stopped me in the street to share a thought about a real situation, someone who dreamt what then happened. Once you've been touched, once you've experienced it personally, denials come less quickly. So, I sat across from her, prepared to be accepting.

The session was a corporate holiday gift—Karen was commissioned for the day, and five of us were each given hour-long sessions with her scheduled one after the other. She had brought some esoterica—a clear sphere on a metal stand sat alongside her, and on the desk between us, several more candles burnt down to different heights next to white crystals arranged in a small glass dish. She was a vision in beige—ashy light blond hair with wispy bangs, pale makeup, and a flesh-colored lipstick that matched a creamy fringed shawl. Essential oils floated around her like a halo. She took both my hands and looked at me with warm mocha eyes that popped in contrast to her muted palette. "Welcome."

I had supplied the time, place, and date of my birth before the session, and Karen had a laptop in front of her, studying what, I assumed, was my chart. "Astrology is the gateway to who you are," she explained. "But in this session, it is only one source of information for me. I believe a reading should combine the metaphysical with the psychic. You may hear me refer to a spirit, my way of building your whole story."

At the word spirit, I was already unnerved, imagining frightening forces from the other side passing messages. "This is my first experience and before I can surrender to it," I told her, "I just need to mention a few caveats: no bad news, and not a moment's hesitation that would cause me to think for even one second that something could be wrong with one of my children."

"No worries," Karen reassured. "That's not the way it happens at all. This will be healing for you."

I tried to keep track of all she was saying about my planets and moons and houses, and what was rising or not—at one point, she turned her laptop around and what was happening on the screen looked as complex as the moon landing. Apart from the lingo that was new to me, it was clear she understood who I was to the core.

"You're not only a Cancer, but your chart shows Cancer planets as well, which makes the natural nurturer even stronger in you," she said, continuing to describe me as if we had been in each other's lives forever. And it wasn't just my personal history, it was what she said about work too. "In the next month, at the most two, you will make a critical decision for the project you're working on that has given you so much angst. And right after, a new opportunity—one that will appear only because of that project—will be the one to move on to." Every revelation was specific, right down to the people in my life. She often paused and looked away, then returned. "Spirit says that the woman you're working with will end up helping you more than it appears right now. Almost all of the difficulties will resolve themselves."

Karen went on to talk about more career shifts and how I would grow personally in the coming year. But what stunned me was one thing she said after listening to whoever was talking to her—that everything in my houses and planets, and whatever else was attached, was lined up with women and publishing. Apparently, I was on a mission that was my destiny, and I held that validation close.

"Before we end," Karen said, "tell me all of your children's particulars, and I'll tell you why each is in your life and what they need from you." I shared their own times, dates, and places of birth, and she continued. "Your oldest son is a truly content and independent person—you should encourage him to tap into an imaginative quality that he has. Your job with your youngest son is to tell him about his ancestors. He's a creative soul. Let him be around antiquity."

"And your daughter is precious—a jewel with many talents—and she's with you for a specific reason. What she needs from you is to help her develop her own strong identity."

Karen's words startled me. Elizabeth had only grown stronger and more independent as she became an adult with a career of her own. "I know her so well, and she knows herself even better, so hopefully, I've done my job there," I offered. "But I can't thank you enough. I was totally unprepared for how astounding all of this would be." Maybe it was the combination of the astrological *and* the psychic, but it was an hour of genuine revelation and insight, all spot on.

"Most are." She smiled. "You're very liquid for me, so I see more. You're intuitive yourself, so it makes you easier for me to read."

I loved that. No chance for misunderstandings; no need to explain my intent. I took her card and said, "This is not goodbye. You know me so well! You're too amazing not to see again."

"There's a lot ahead for you. The lotus has a thousand petals," Karen said as we parted.

The experience and all it revealed stayed with me, especially as things that she predicted actually happened over the next few months. And what she had told me that I needed to give my children became a framework for me, a window through which I looked at each of them.

One night, I fell asleep thinking about identity, and the closeness my daughter and I shared. I woke up startled a few hours later, and it hit me—*my mother. What had I needed from her? Who were the two of us together?* I made another appointment, this time with a specific agenda that I detailed in an email along with my mother's time, place—and real date—of birth.

"I'm glad you're back," Karen said when I entered. We were now at her private office in Manhattan, with a low coffee table between my sofa and her tasseled chair. She opened the computer on her lap after she lit candles and her eyes closed for a moment.

"I couldn't stay away," I told her. "I'm hoping you can read our charts together and tell me what you see and feel about us." I explained how discovering my mother's true birthday so many years before had suddenly taken on new importance. "It feels now as if her lie not only opened the door to an alternate view of our history but to another reality of who we were together, in a way," I added, unable to sit still, jittery from excitement or anxiousness or both.

Karen took a deep breath and began. "I explained last time that you had multiple Cancer planets in your chart. That's called a stellium, which means you have a cluster of your sign's planets. And your stellium is significant. You have five Cancer planets. That's rare."

"What does that mean?"

"You're an uber-Cancer." The nurturer. Intuitive, heartfelt, emotional, gentle. You're a Moon Child on steroids." She smiled and paused again, either for effect or because she was listening to whoever was talking to her.

"But the really rare part," she went on, "is that your mother has a stellium as well. Also one with five planets, but in her sign.

Her five make her an uber-Leo. The way her chart is configured mathematically, she is the narcissist—an uber-narcissist."

Karen peered at me from above her reading glasses. "Prideful, obstinate, the boss. Again, on steroids." She looked away and then back at me. "And you both have a cluster of like-moons as well. You have quite a few Gemini moons—this means you are lovely and light, free-spirited, clever. Her moon cluster is Virgo— as it relates to you, it makes her judgmental, critical, analytical."

She began weaving the story from what she saw or maybe heard. "You couldn't win," Karen told me. "You two are incredibly different, and it would have been a very difficult combination for you as the Cancer child of such a mother. You never felt as if you were the priority, important enough. Cancer is the giver, and Leo is the demander, the taker."

"I guess that's a pretty accurate portrait," I acquiesced.

"Narcissists are very alluring, so you had no choice but to be drawn in. And she has Neptune as well—there was always an element of glamour and deceit about her."

"Again, right on," I admitted. Uncomfortably so.

"Her influence on you suppressed your natural spirit when you were a child. The effect was not positive. In fact, it was dour, like a damper on you," Karen continued. "She put the kibosh on some of your truth. The aunts you told me about before softened all the blows and helped immensely. Otherwise, you might never have been able to be yourself." Karen shook her head at what she saw in our combination, or perhaps at what was being whispered.

I was starting to feel as if I had had enough. This was not my intention. I had come for the story, but I hadn't expected such a critical one. Karen was knocking my mother down. Her words were like an onslaught attacking sacred ground. My little girl was hopping—*how dare she!*

"It's not as simple as that," I defended. "Narcissism is a spectrum. She *may* have had some narcissistic tendencies, but my mother was never, ever cruel or outwardly critical in any way. She was so supportive of me. Never unkind."

"She didn't have to be unkind or outwardly critical, did she?"

Karen answered. "You anticipated everything. You knew. You could see through to the real her, and you knew how to avoid her unkindness. You needed to make sure that she was the center, always."

Karen stopped me cold. "Maybe she was never unkind because she recognized the difference between us," I finally challenged. "Maybe she chose not to damage my sensitive soul. That would be the opposite of narcissistic behavior."

"I believe that the reason that side of her did not come out was because you were always one step ahead," Karen answered. "She didn't have to crack the whip."

"You could have a point," I conceded, inwardly squirming. "I have to think about it."

"The good news," Karen went on, "is that you were born evolved. If you weren't, you would have been traumatized, you would have rebelled and repeated the cycle—you would have been the same type of self-centered mother. But you were not. You were able to process it all and actually use the strictures to your advantage."

"This is what's hard for me to accept, though," I persisted. "Because she was really a wonderful mother. The most wonderful. I loved her so much."

Karen then turned away and listened some more. "Spirit is here." She paused and said, "Women," then looked away again.

I was getting more agitated. What did saying "women" mean? What whispers were in her ear?

Finally, she looked me straight in the eye. "Sorry," she said. "But I'm not buying it."

"Not buying what exactly? That I loved my mother?" I stared at her, indignant.

"There was no way you could have with this dynamic," she said. "It's just not possible."

"What are you saying? Everything I've done my whole life was about her! About how much I loved her. She's at the heart of it all!"

"Listen to me carefully," Karen said slowly. "What you thought was intense love for her was actually your own desperate need to be loved *by her*."

I could feel myself turn inside out at the sound of the words. They were like ancient taboos and hearing them spoken released some primal fear. I felt like a bolt of lightning would strike my head at any second. They had unleashed a curse. A Pandora's box opened that should have remained closed.

"You were under the spell of loving her," Karen said forcefully. "But you did not. You could not. The intensity you felt was your own need crying out."

My crossed legs fully twisted around each other as she spoke, my left foot pressing against my right ankle, wrapped tightly with nowhere to go. "I don't know what to say," I finally choked out. "That thought has never, ever entered my mind for a second. Never. Not once."

"You couldn't let it. But reflect on this. It's the truth," she said.

The *truth*? More like a reversal of truth so complex that I could not grasp it. It was as if she were explaining black holes or some convoluted mathematical theorem. It was the opposite of every belief that had swaddled me my whole life, a fierce and dangerous reveal that made me want to jump up and put my hand over her mouth.

"What am I supposed to do with all this now?" I blurted.

"Deborah, the irony is that you thought you were the daughter of a goddess. But listen to me even more carefully. It is *you*. You are the goddess. You have the gifts."

They were words to me, just words. Words like spices in an unfamiliar dish that was impossible to digest; words so inside out and backward it would take years for me to fully unwind them. A lifetime of second fiddles played in my head. My way of being; my way of praising the higher power; my way of diverting any attention that came to me back to the source where it belonged. *You think I'm beautiful? You should see my mother. You think I'm smart? You should meet my mother. You think I'm something? Wait until you know her.* Now I was the goddess? Impossible. The house of cards that I had so carefully constructed over time had been toppled with a flick.

"One more thing," Karen said.

"I don't know if I can take any more!" I shouted.

"Was there a healing between the two of you close to when she died?"

I thought of the priest and the last rites, of washing away her sins. "I think so," I said.

Karen looked at me with kindness. "She was very grateful."

I clung to, and took comfort in, Karen's parting thought, but could barely allow myself to think about the rest. *I'm not ready. It can't be true.* But those new twisted words were in there, sticking me like pins.

I was thankful I had to leave later that afternoon for an overnight trip—now much more welcomed than it had been before. I needed to run away. It was a small New England hotel in a second building on the grounds that was dubbed "The Lodge." With full consciousness and more than a little amusement, I had chosen room 105 when I made the reservation weeks before. In all these years, it was the closest I'd ever come to reliving the old-age ripeness of our family's ramshackle resort. Door 105 opened to the same distinct scent—a funky and musty, damp and earthy smell of old wood and irremovable stains. A smell that flitted through my nostrils to the part of my brain that remembered my mother's fragrance, taking me back to a world that I wanted to reenter but could not.

Over the years I had fantasized about earning enough money to buy the resort and get that piece of our heritage back, but it had been razed a decade before. Now it was just like my mother and just like the little girl that once was me. Gone, but waiting to be rediscovered.

There's a certain distortion that happens when we lie in wait for something for a very long time. When what you are waiting for finally arrives, it has grown to such enormous proportions that it overshadows and excludes a hundred other moments around it. When I look back at my summers at the resort, memories of my mother's car turning the corner toward the hotel; of her bedroom door opening on Saturday mornings in my childhood apartment—and a thousand of her other arrivals and departures all flushed out in vivid detail—are more prominent than the memories of what happened in between. But as I stood in that hotel room, I realized that it was all there, just hidden from me in dusty corners sticky with webs. The truth of our summers, of all the seasons of our relationship. I set down my suitcase and turned on the light.

The Expert

The psychic astrologer's revelation was too enormous to swallow, let alone fully absorb at the outset. But I could not deny that she had awakened something. Slowly—and only when I was alone—I began to hold it in my mouth despite its bitter taste. I tried to say it aloud, softly, through clenched teeth—*I may not have loved my mother as much as I thought I did.* Propelled by the urgent need to know if it could possibly be true, I tore through closets and bookshelves, gathering every memory and fragment from the past that I could find.

I searched everywhere for an old folder I could see in my head. It was made of brown paper in an envelope shape, and hole-punched. My Aunt Lilly had handcrafted it with me one rainy afternoon to store childhood scraps. I remember pulling rust-colored yarn through the holes while my aunt's arias played in the background. Finally, I discovered the innocuous envelope deep within the night table's cabinet alongside my bed. When had I put it there? Ten years ago? Twenty? All this time, the past had been buried right next to where I slept each night.

I untied it and out spilled my carefully curated elementary school history, from report cards to spelling quizzes, from those birthday cards signed with my mother's beautiful script to my artwork labeled by grade. Suddenly, one kindergarten creation caught my eye. At five, I had painted myself alone and adrift in a boat on a deep blue sea. I was standing near the middle of the boat, an open black hole for a mouth, pleading arms outstretched, and my long black hair wild about my head. I was clearly frightened, with no hands and no oars. A perfect image of someone with zero control.

I could have been my usual lighthearted self and laughed that it was the type of cry-for-help painting that today might cause a school to call the authorities. But I didn't feel funny or want to downplay the emotion that the child I was must have felt. Unlike my seafaring great-grandfather, I was out of my element in the middle of nowhere, and every line of the image conveyed that. I wanted to scoop up that little girl and tell her it would be OK. That it was all part of becoming everything she would ultimately be. That feeling lost and lonely would produce a woman of depth and empathy and many facets who was able to create and succeed. That the dots really would connect to become something surprising and good. But that little girl could never have seen that then. She was too afraid. There was no denying how real the pain and confusion must have been; no way could I do my usual two-step around the truth. I had indeed been wounded.

Karen had spoken the essence of some unseen truth that, even though it was disturbing, offered me a completely new perspective. But it was an otherworldly one that I felt needed to be balanced with a traditional expert's view. As I looked at that painting, I decided to see a therapist.

A friend recommended me to Susan. We had a phone conversation before my first visit, and just clicked. She had a vivacity that wiggled its way into our question-and-answer back-and-forth and made me smile—quick lines and ready answers, just like the women around the pool. And I felt she could hold her own with me, that I would trust that she had the knowledge to potentially, and fully, open my eyes.

When I met Susan, she was very close to what I imagined—about my age and my height, but more bohemian, drawn to jewel-toned shawls and sandals. Even though we were in the suburbs, she had a Manhattan, Upper West Sider vibe. I followed her low ponytail peppered with just the right amount of serious gray into her inner sanctum.

"Tell me," Susan beckoned.

I sat back on the sofa and began to explain the essence of my mother and me (I probably should have put myself first, I realized, as she took notes). How I felt that as a child my mother never fully loved me, and how her perceived ambivalence might have affected me. How I never had anger or resentment toward her at all over anything. And although I wasn't sure how Susan felt about psychics or astrologers, how I'd been holding the essence of Karen's pronouncements up to the light ever since.

As one session gave way to the next, I mentioned the recurring dream that I had on and off for years since my mother's death—how I'd think she was really still alive and that I'd neglected her—but then couldn't remember her number.

"It's so clear," Susan said.

"What is?"

"You really didn't *want* to call her. You wanted to be doing other things. That dream represents *your own* ambivalence."

My mouth opened, but I said nothing. Just stayed that way for a minute, smacked into silence at the simplicity of the statement. Years of the same haunting dream and not once had I looked at it that way. *Not once.* In my mind, I was the bad daughter, too busy for her, a shirker of responsibility, and so many other slings that I threw at myself. I'd never thought my unconscious mind was sending me a little hint. That I really didn't want to be together. That my feelings for her were complicated and unsure.

"Your wish to connect and not connect—your guilt was assuaged by not remembering the number. You should call, but you really don't want to. As a child, you were always trying to catch her, and she was always floating away. In the dream, it's you pulling back."

My own version of tit for tat? Just thinking it felt blasphemous and I almost looked over my shoulder to see if my mother had heard. *Oh, God. How could it be true?* But that tingle was there; that prickle up my arms that told me there was at least the germ of truth; puzzle pieces of a Rubik's Cube snapping into the right places.

My eyes filled. "I need to absorb this," I said. "My whole life, I never thought I was ambivalent in any way. It's almost too much for me to take in. I've spent my life feeling that *she* was the ambivalent one."

"Do you remember any childhood dreams?" Susan prompted. "I always ask because dreams represent pieces of you and offer clues, just as this adult one did."

"I used to have a different recurring nightmare for years when I was very young," I told her. "It stopped maybe when I was around nine." I could feel myself start to sweat. "It was always the same. I was walking up and down my block in Queens, alone. I was about five or six maybe. Soon, the sound would start. A clang. It was a cup and saucer banging together every few seconds. An old woman behind me was clinking the two pieces of china over and over. She was stooped and withered, horrible looking. And she was coming for me." I was breathing heavily.

"Did she ever catch you?"

"No. She would get closer and closer. I would go faster down the street, and she'd gain on me. But she never caught me. I would always wake up before she did. But I had this dream night after night. She terrified me. I felt helpless and very alone. Out of control."

"So, what do you think the overall dream means?" Susan asked.

"Well, if you're into otherworldliness, you'd say the old woman was a spiritual guide trying to break through. That scares the shit out of me. That I'm intuitive enough to be on the membrane of something else, something that could take me over." My chest was heaving. "That's why I'm so afraid of the dark, I think."

"What else do you think it could mean?" Susan pressed.

"From a clinical perspective?" I asked. "I don't know."

"Close your eyes and hold the most frightening image of the dream in your mind," Susan said. "Let any thought or feeling come up."

I zoomed in on the old woman like a still frame. Suddenly

and unlike the original dream, other scary images started popping up alongside. It was as if my mind had wandered to anything that had ever unnerved me as I sat safely in Susan's office. The chandelier from my childhood hanging from the blood-red ceiling in my room. I remembered that when I was very young, I thought it spoke to me in a man's voice. My version of goblins had been over my bed instead of under. The sliver of light that caused shadows; voices from the kitchen that might have been my parents fighting. A glow next to my bed that felt like my mother.

I opened my eyes. "There was a fear party in there. And I had thoughts of my mother in the kitchen and in my room. Did I fear her?"

"Did you?"

"No. Not outwardly," I deflected. "I'd love to know what *you* think the dream and the fears mean. I'm here for an answer, remember?"

"The old woman in the dream could represent aggression or anger toward your mother that you repressed," Susan postured.

"Aggression towards her? That doesn't feel right to me at all. I was never even mad at her," I answered. *If it were true,* I wondered, *where did all this supposed anger go if I never allowed myself to feel it?* Playing hide-and-seek inside my body? Wrapping itself around my heart or maybe sprinkled throughout—an anger dot in my big toe, one in my lower back, one in my aching shoulder, a hundred dots, a thousand dots, holding their ground like warriors? Was my strong reaction to some sounds she'd make just my quiet anger at being so powerless with her? I raised my hand to the middle of my chest, my palm over my heart. It was a familiar gesture, a move to the center that I did whenever I felt stressed.

"Are you saying that this childhood anger is sort of the dark side of my moon?" I asked her. "There but unseen? Or is repressed anger just an easy clinical catchall?"

"Maybe it was your anger," she said. "Or maybe the old woman represents a part of yourself that was 'bad' coming to get you. The bad part that really was angry or resentful. You always tried to be so good."

Is that what I was really so afraid of? I wondered. *Myself?* All those numbered dots of hurt and anger connecting to form some bad creature living within. The real me. "I do think my true nature was to be good, though. Every memory, every picture I have or recollection from someone confirms that sweetness."

"Yes, but we all have dark thoughts," Susan said.

"If the old woman is either my bad self or anger at my mother, could what Karen said actually be true? That I may not have loved my mother as much, or in the way that I thought I did?"

"Well," Susan said, "this may surprise you, but I happen to agree with your psychic's general point. But I would say it slightly differently. It's clear to me that you loved your mother. But you also hated and resented her. And that buried hatred found its way into dreams."

"Hated! Impossible. I did not. I could not!"

"Given the details of your childhood, you had to have also had anger and resentment toward her. All children do as they grow. You just couldn't let yourself consciously feel it—you can't when it comes to your mother. And because it's too scary to blame parents, children can blame themselves and feel it's all their fault. It's especially hard for children of narcissists."

There was that word again. This time, I refrained from jumping to my mother's defense. But it stayed with me through the evening, and I downloaded a book about the children of narcissists. The examples were more extreme, like Rita and Denise, but I could find myself in their stories.

That night I dreamt of a time I was lying in bed crying because my parents were fighting. Their voices were coming through the half door's crack. I called for my mother. Aunt Lena tried to hush me, but I didn't stop. Finally, my mother came in, squeezing between Lena's cot and my bed, and leaned over me. I begged her to stop fighting. "Mommy, please!" There was no room for her to sit on my bed, so she simply placed her hand on my chest. Her touch made me hopeful that the fight was over and would never happen again. But she only said, "Debbie, that's just the way things are." My aunts encircled me then, wiping my tears and making everything right, just like fairy godmothers should. In the dream, we clung to one another, and I filled with pure, glowing love for them.

A thought popped in the morning I couldn't shake. *Was I angry at myself because I loved my aunts so much—maybe as much as I loved my mother when I was little, maybe more?* A bad betrayal. In some secret place, maybe I knew then that I might not really love my goddess as much as I should, as much as she expected or as much as the world thought she deserved. My dark side, the secret that made me want to punish myself. So I went overboard, obsessing about her to compensate, burying my feelings because I was so desperate to be loved by her. *Definitely part of the story,* I thought.

At our next visit, I showed Susan a handful of pictures of my aunts, my mother, and me, pulled from all the albums I could find. I wanted her to feel what was between all of us.

"That's a great insight about self-directed anger," Susan agreed. "But these pictures of your mother and you also tell another story," Susan said as she flipped through them. "They do show love and connection from her. It was all just so fleeting. And for you, it wasn't enough."

I stared at the infant and toddler pictures as she handed them back. I could see devotion in my mother's eyes. But it had come to me, I realized, in measured doses, like an antibiotic. Pills to be taken every other day or weekly, never curing me of the need for her, just making the absence tolerable. And I had been searching for the cure my entire life.

"She was who she was," Susan said simply. "The mind-bender here is that although you may not have loved her in the *way* that you thought—it could also be true that she loved you *more* than you thought."

I closed my eyes and inhaled her pronouncement.

"What we do know," Susan went on, "is that given your mother's childhood, it's quite possible that she didn't really know how to be a mother. She looked down on her own, who wasn't able to protect her from her father. So, it's very likely that your mother was not mothered well. When she became your mother, she didn't know how to let you feel what she really felt for you. The result was that you didn't get what you needed."

I stayed silent for another minute, thinking. "And yet, it all worked. It feels like I went through it to rise to another level."

"I don't want to borrow the psychic's words, but you did process it. You may not have understood it as you do now, but you moved through and came out the other side. I suspect that the fine china in your dream represents you. It's delicate, an object that could easily chip or break. Yet despite the woman hitting it together over and over, it never did. You didn't break. You're strong because you learned as a child to quietly manipulate your environment," Susan explained, "rather than be manipulated by it. You made everything work for you as best you could, which gave you incredible skills for later on."

"Even anger?" I asked.

"Even that. Matter has to go somewhere—the rules of physics can also be applied to emotions and the conscious and unconscious mind. You warehoused your anger toward your mother, stored it up, and repressed the impulses and emotions you felt that you couldn't risk expressing."

Stored like seed or grain in some internal silo. An image of the resort flashed through my mind, the silo alongside the barn and the stable. I had that prickly, true feeling. Velvet hammer seeds planted deep within me, slowly making it possible to come into my own light. "No outward rebellion, just an inward, quiet rebellion?"

"Yes, you toed the line on the outside," Susan said. "But inwardly you had another side that allowed you to find the way around your mother and push forward. It has made you resourceful, an effective persuader and negotiator, a mover and shaker in your professional life with the stubborn streak of a rebel that's still in there."

"I guess that agility is helping me now to grapple with the myth of my mother."

"I loved mythology too," Susan admitted. "This has been your quest. A heroine's journey. You are clearly a very different mother than she was."

Of that I was certain, and yet I had begun to wonder about the consequences of my own next-generation version of motherhood. For all of its glamour and glory, there was no denying that work had taken me away from the cocoon of my family—recently, I had realized that it also made me feel like my mother, and not in a good way. The combination of all my doing, doing, doing, reinforced—at least to me—that even though I started on the opposite end of the motherhood spectrum with vastly different intentions, I had inadvertently evolved into someone who was almost as absent as she was.

"I saw a cable show last night," I told Susan, "about how DNA is constantly mutating in good, bad, or neutral ways. At work, I deal with the concept of brand DNA all the time—the question of what's essential and what do we change. But it made me wonder about whether my own parenting 'mutations' have had a good, bad, or neutral effect on my children. What if I loved my children to a fault, in a way that healed my own wound, but risked creating a different one in them? What if, despite all my efforts to be the best mother in the world, I'm simply doomed to play out some genetic destiny?"

"We all make mistakes as parents, but you have not made the same ones she did," Susan reassured.

"Lately, I've been thinking more about which ones I did make." Karen's words about Elizabeth's strong identity had made me wonder. Now in her late twenties, Elizabeth had planted her feet firmly in editorial, my own original intent, and had evolved into my reflective truth teller and litmus test for almost everything. But all of the experiences and exposure to my work when she was younger had me at the core. Maybe that steered her path too much or made her feel like an extra on my stage. Maybe she felt she was always under my wing not only at work events but everywhere. I thought back to our own Saturday shopping excursions—I shifted the ritual's perspective to make it about her, but she still heard all the compliments coming my way when I tried things on too. The repetition of a cycle that had come before suddenly felt eerily similar. Did I unknowingly throw shade on her shine? "I wonder," I went on, "if Elizabeth ever felt that I had a shadow?"

"Why don't you ask her?" Susan challenged. "Open up together in a way your mother couldn't do with you? Get at what's real."

What is real? Such a simple question. The truth of all three of us swirled together in my mind alongside my own recent realization that what I had perceived for all these years might not have been true at all.

"I will ask," I promised. "Especially since I've learned that the world of children is as full of illusions as the world of adults."

"So now, as you let your own illusions go," Susan answered, "understand that back then you blamed yourself if you felt your mother didn't love you enough. Something had to be wrong with you because it couldn't possibly be her. Now you can share the blame, so to speak. What's true for you *both*—not just for your mother—is that you probably loved and didn't love."

"Some of it still feels elusive, but I do see my mother and myself so much more clearly."

"Goddesses aren't real," Susan said. "You've humanized her now, as well as your love for her. But first, you had to realize how angry you were at her. To see her for who she was and let yourself feel the hurt. And now you can forgive her."

"A part of my brain still says there's nothing to forgive. But I get it."

"If not forgive, just see through the illusions for what they are. Tempting and alluring, but also wounding and limiting."

New notions full of crackle and possibility snapped like twigs in the woods announcing an arrival. I could feel something shifting, that *Ah, yes, now I've got it* feeling. But nothing is ever so neat and tidy. I still needed to slowly reflect, turning the words and phrases over in my mind. Like shoes that need to be worn for a while to break them in. All sorts of internal tests needed to be passed before those thoughts would become second nature; before all the other deeply planted seeds and tightly held beliefs would fully vanish.

All these coexisting, contradictory feelings made my world grayer than ever. Two truths, three truths, four truths, five . . . there seemed to be no end to what could be revealed. I may never know what that little girl who painted herself alone and afraid on the ocean—in a boat, I now see, that was remarkably shaped like a teacup—was truly feeling. All I can do is allow myself to say, *Oh yes, that feels as if it could have been.*

The Women

I am now as she was then.

Those first words written in London the previous year had stopped me cold, like a car screeching to a halt to narrowly avoid a collision. That parallel-universe thought had forced me to the side of the road and continued to float above me, a hovering word bubble that no one else could read. It was a fresh intersection of my mother and myself, one that nudged me forward in my own midlife.

Our first visit to London had been as much of a whirlwind as the realization itself—short and unfinished—so I suggested a return trip the following year when Elizabeth and I both had time off from work. Just as if we had earmarked a page, the two of us reopened the book to where we had left off.

Back on foreign soil, I realized how many things had shifted in the year since those seven words had spilled from me. The recurring nightmares about my mother had disappeared entirely, and I was somehow less afraid of the dark. All of the therapeutic insights had helped me to temper pain from the past rather than tamping it down, as I began to see her—and us—in a more realistic light. And yet, there remained incomplete fragments in my mind, floating strands of feeling and memory waiting to be fully resolved.

"I love your curls," the woman behind the Mayfair hotel's reception desk said in her lilting British accent. During my AD period at work, my ongoing battle of wills with my hair had eased when I finally handed its care over to professionals. Not only did regular salon blowouts subdue its true nature, but they also saved me precious time while making my hair straighter and more polished. But lately, I had, on occasion, embraced my crown of tangled layers, fully loving the unruliness of my natural headdress for the first time.

Throughout the trip, I wore a gold bangle of my mother's in the modern way I always did—pushed up to my mid-forearm atop a long-sleeved shirt. I had inherited what little was left when she died, and I still carried pieces of her when I traveled—an evening bag, earrings, anything so she'd be experiencing it with me. But I was never able to just slip into something of hers and wear it as my own skin—first I needed to make it my own, to reinvent it and bring her into a new era. The vintage mink coat that I had sheared, adding cuffs and a shawl collar; the towering ring's stones reset into a smaller gold dome more suited to my taste; the classic pearls restrung with unexpected onyx in between. Each time, I cherished the reenvisioned piece, not only because it was infused with my own spirit, but also because it gave her renewed life. There was nothing I could reinvent about that simple, circular bangle, though—it was whole and complete just as it was, now as much mine as hers.

Midway through our week, Elizabeth and I were wandering through the regal rooms of Buckingham Palace, listening to our guide tell the backstories of royal paraphernalia—crested shields and coats-of-arms, gilt and sovereigns. As I heard the provenance of tradition, of customs and rituals, the year's discoveries played on silently in my head like my own new musical score.

Almost accidentally, peripherally in fact, I saw a white marble statue tucked in the corner alongside a staircase. Apparently, it was not one of the objects on the tour, so our guide was leading us by it without comment. The statue was of a beautiful woman with one child asleep at her breast and another one gazing up at her. She was on a pedestal, chiseled and eternal.

I lingered in front of it and thought of my attempts at soap carving as a child, trying to shape the woman I would become. The perfect woman of polished stone before me was looking down at the baby in her arms. I bent to get a better view of her face. Although it was arrestingly beautiful, it wasn't just the sculpture that caught my eye—it was the naming placard at the base. It said simply, "Mrs. Jordan." An ordinary woman among monarchs.

"Excuse me," I called to the guide who was already ushering us into the next room. "I was just looking at this statue. How did a nonroyal person end up here? Who was she?"

"Ah. Yes," said the guide. "Quite interesting, quite. Mrs. Jordan was a leading eighteenth-century actress in a long-standing, unconventional relationship with the Duke of Clarence."

"A.k.a. his mistress?" I clarified with a smile, to get a rise out of the other tourists with whom we had bonded.

"Yes, so to speak. They were together for twenty years, and Mrs. Jordan had ten children with him. When he became king unexpectedly, he left her and married another. She died alone and penniless two years later. Full of remorse, the duke had the statue commissioned as a tribute to his greatest love."

There were nods as everyone glanced at the statue and moved on to the next stop. But I was intrigued even if no one else seemed to be, lured by what was in between the lines of Mrs. Jordan's story. How had it been possible for her to live such a life outside of so many social layers and conventions—especially when status and gender were everything? What was it about her that had earned his love, and him hers? Excited little snippets of thought hopped around in my head like exuberant toddlers given too much sugar.

I caught up to Elizabeth, who was focused on the guide, completely absorbed. She was wholly herself but a miniature of me, literally—graceful arms and long legs formed a frame that, despite my height, stood at only five feet tall. But it was never the size of Elizabeth or a single exquisite feature of hers that impressed me— it had always been the depth of her. Almost as if she were meant to surprise the world with just how much could be contained within such a delicately petite package. In recent years more than ever, she had become a woman of scope.

We left the palace, and I took her arm as we interlocked our tucked hands—a trademark move—on our way to lunch at the National Portrait Gallery. The gallery's modern restaurant, Portrait, had sleek window walls that framed the spectacular rooftops and sights of historic London. We slipped into our slate gray leather chairs as artful nouvelle cuisine breezed by on stylish plates carefully balanced by waiters. We broke our gaze only to order, and then returned to the postcard views.

"The Mrs. Jordan statue made me think of Nano," I finally said. "Something pulled me in and made me ask for her story. I guess they were both women who lived by their own rules in different eras."

"Even though I was only seven when Nano died, I have such distinct memories of her," Elizabeth reflected. "I can't remember her voice, and yet I remember everything she said. I totally fell under Nano's spell. Her style, her way—she still inspires me today," Elizabeth went on, "Although I'm sure for you, it wasn't always easy."

"I know I was such a different mother. And yet . . ." I drifted. "Did you ever feel that I had a shadow that you had to come out from under?"

Elizabeth looked at me just as my mother had the day I realized that her hair wasn't really red. "Of course you did!" She laughed. "You *are* the best mother! But I'm the product of someone who had it all *and* who did it all. Your shadow might have even loomed larger than hers!"

I was stunned but laughed with her. "No way! That's impossible."

"It absolutely was possible. Whether we were out shopping on Saturdays, or with family, or at every single work event, over and over I heard how wonderful you were and that I looked just like you. It felt clear to me from every angle that I should be just like you too! We know history does repeat itself." She smiled.

Suddenly I felt like I was seeing my own story through a different lens. A little girl looking up and hearing her mother complimented, except this time, that mother was me. All the air-kiss flattery and required corporate homage spoken to her and in front of her—I ignored it, but my daughter probably could not.

"Well," I said, "for every other generation in history, it was easy to surpass your mother in the natural order of things. But, you're one of the daughters of the first generation of mothers who had full-fledged careers, so it's probably challenging for all of you. So, you're right," I agreed. "I guess a shadow is a shadow."

"Yes, but some things are specific to the three of us. Your love is a constant and the best sort of security," Elizabeth said quickly. "But because you grew up always chasing similarities with your mother, you loved that I was your mini-me. I needed to work at finding the ways I was different from you and to build my own legacy."

It was true. Sameness equaled love for me. I saw for the first time that—however unwittingly—I might not have fully granted Elizabeth the freedom to be different from me. I was certain about who she was as a young girl and conveyed that before she had figured it out herself. It seemed that all mothers both succeed and fail and cast shadows of their own where their daughters are concerned. But when we see them, we can evolve.

"Your generation's legacy will finally be about doing what feels authentic in a balanced way and not just following along," I commented as we both stood up from the table. "But for anyone to reach their potential or find their true self, all the myths and misperceptions they hold must come undone."

We locked hands again as we made our way out of the restaurant. "Maybe I was right to never blame my mother for anything. And here I tried to be so perfect," I teased.

"You're perfect for me, and I really am so grateful for everything," Elizabeth reassured.

We headed into the main galleries, this time without a guide, meandering as individuals as we contemplated room after room of Renaissance and Enlightenment era paintings. Elizabeth and I continued at our own pace, separating and then coming back together in the different spaces whenever our interests converged.

At one point, I ventured into a side exhibit, and suddenly there I stood—alone and facing a giant portrait of Mrs. Jordan. This placard carried her full name: Dorothea Jordan. Dorothea, the eighteenth-century version of Dorothy. I stared straitjacket still. Mummy still, as if invisible hands had wrapped sheets around my body, making it impossible for me to move.

The notion of synchronicity has existed for centuries. When I was younger, it didn't happen as often for me as it does now, or if it did, I wasn't as aware. Back then, I wasn't sure how I really felt about such coincidences, because if you accept them as meaningful, you have to accept a whole lot of other things too. Like destiny or something guiding all of us. But now, standing in front of that painting, I believed.

I couldn't take my eyes off the portrait, so I don't know how many minutes actually passed before the whole of the exhibit registered. Slowly, as I looked around the room, I realized that I was surrounded by paintings of forgotten, groundbreaking women in history. I circled among them, reading the biographical information below each piece, enthralled by the faces and accomplishments of these women, all of whom had lived in Europe in the late 1700s. They had all made remarkable strides at a time when little was expected from them; when they had few rights; when they had to navigate enormous cultural obstacles to achieve anything. They were novelists, playwrights, actresses, painters, musicians, and bluestockings—women like Mary Wollstonecraft, Angelica Kauffmann, Fanny Burney, Olympe de Gouges, and Germaine de Staël—all of them outliers, mavericks, and trailblazers who had accomplished so much despite the restrictive rules of the day. At a time when the appearance of convention was everything, these nonconformists somehow knew that forward motion required unconventionality.

I was enjoying just being in their midst when the truly unexpected happened. I first imagined my mother in the eighteenth century, her red hair piled high. Putting her faux Adams surname aside, she was fully English on both her Thayer and Stockton sides, just as many of these women were—could she be a descendant? Then it dawned on me that this circle of women must have all known one another. And it felt possible that what they had in common—a certain backbone, a shared root system that connected one to the other—could give me a new frame through which to view my mother and myself.

Their portraits seemed to whisper, "Debbie, come sit by me." And so I did, sinking into a virtual lounge chair to huddle around their pool, instantly eager for all I would hear.

Inspired, I found books on the most prominent of the women in the gift shop and was never without their presence for the rest of the London trip. In fact, I read about three women simultaneously, one book tucked in my bag for train rides, a book on a different woman early in the morning before we left the hotel, and another waiting on the night table for me when we returned. As if cramming for a test, I absorbed the lives of each one while still in London and a fourth on the plane ride home.

I soon realized that skirting the rules in place to survive and thrive—rules they didn't make but had to live by—was the constant between all of them. Back in New York, I went deeper, ordering all I could find online and, as I chronicled the flawed perfection of twelve of them, I slowly began to see my mother fully in a way that I never had before. Abstractly, spending time with them began to feel like spending time with her. The reasoning behind their choices helped me to see beyond the personal effect of my mother's decisions to how she had managed to sculpt herself in another era so different from my own.

Through their life stories, I gained an appreciation for the struggles these kindred spirits faced as they strove to become who they wanted to be. The age they lived in was as distinct as their more basic desires—to be fully heard and seen, to have rights, to live an independent life outside of the domestic sphere—but somehow, their long-ago tales made me see my own mother even more clearly. How she was born into a world where she had no control, so she created a new one—a world of her truths, her secrets, her rules, within which she was its queen. The anointed celebrity. As was the case with Mrs. Jordan and all of these other women from history, the limiting rules of the day and the life she had been handed simply didn't suit my mother, and she had to rebel and carve out her own path.

These early feminist heroines earned my gratitude for paving the way for generations to come, which made me even more grateful for all of my mother's unconventionality—I saw that in her own way, she had provided not only a road map for me but the resilience and aptitude to navigate life and emerge as a strong woman as well. I began to wholly reconcile her far-from-traditional life choices with my experiences as a child and to see that their true impact had not been as somber as I had once thought.

There are stages to healing, the early ones so much more raw and intense. But once you get through all of the initial pain and inflammation, there is a quiet, gradual renewal. As I began to realize her genuine love for me and understand my own for her, an idea I could not ignore filled me: *Write about her. Write about us.* The histories of these women made me want to try to articulate my mother's legacy and, in so doing, close the book on the hurtful "truths" that I had held as gospel for so long, now toppled by new insights.

They made me want to write so my love for her could finally be untangled and exist apart from my childhood longings and idealized versions of our lives together. I had to turn inward even more as I wrote, to sit quietly and make peace with all of the revelations so they could implant themselves firmly. As words floated from my head to the page, so did the full awareness that the story I had told myself all my life hadn't really been true at all. The writing of it was the final healing step that connected the dots and made me come full circle, just like our shared bangle. And full circle with my own daughter as well—my pilgrimage helped me see our relationship in a new light that has been freeing for us both.

As it turned out, my mother's gifts helped me reinvent my life at just the right moment. My corporate world did indeed dissolve, but its unspooling gave me another chance to see who I wanted to be, how I wanted to go forward, and what I wanted to serve. My winding journey of discovery along the road paved by our dynamics had, surprisingly, turned out to be mostly about me after all. I transformed an old story into a new one and discovered that I was the heroine of my own life. It seems that by reexamining her story, I reclaimed my own.

My life now looks nothing like the one I was living when I went on that first trip to London. It is a creative life, a writer's life—ironically, one my father would have loved to live. My whole world changed as I did, as I realized just how many gifts she had given me, even the ones that remained unopened until now—the ones that I didn't even know were presents. It was as if her hand was on my shoulder as the myth of her became undone. As if she were singing "All of Me" on the resort's little stage: "It's time, Debbie, to know all of me."

My excavation into the past—and the writing it spawned—liberated me and restored the undeniable, unquestionable love for her that I had as a child, and that I still have. It's just no longer an obsession. I honor her, but no longer through the eyes of that adoring little girl on the sidelines, breathlessly watching and waiting for that dressing room curtain to pull back.

Dorothy. My mother. I loved her. She was my muse.

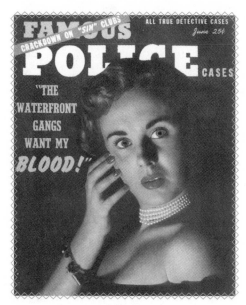

Dotty's Detective Magazine Cover

Photo from Dotty's modeling portfolio

Dotty in the Canzoneri Country Club cocktail lounge

Dotty when she got her nightclub job

The Canzoneri Country Club hotel

Dotty and Jay behind the hotel reception desk the summer after they met

*Jay (left) and his champion brother Tony
at the entrance to the hotel*

*Jay singing one of his songs at
the Canzoneri Country Club*

Dotty and Jay cavorting by the resort pool

Dotty preparing to marry Jay

*Wedding family portrait—Dotty, Jay, her middle brother (left),
mother, father, and aunt (right)*

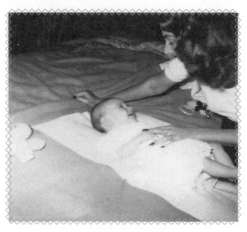

The author with her mother

The author with her Aunt Lilly

The author with her Aunt Lena

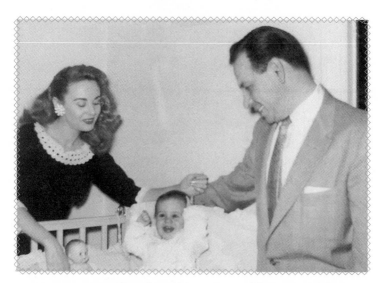

The author with her mother and father

Mother and daughter

Mother and daughter and bubbles

The author goes to the Easter parade with her parents

The author with her mother and aunts

The author between her mother and beloved family friend Annette (front)

Saturday's Child

Reading Group Guide

Throughout *Saturday's Child*, author Deborah Burns asks herself questions about the relationships and events that shape this story. Below are some questions for your book club to kick off discussion and help you delve into the many issues about love, family, and career that play a role in this memoir.

1. The author writes that her mother crafted a world where all of her domestic and childcare needs were taken care of so that she could be out in the world. This seems like a very modern solution. How do you think it impacted the author's feelings about herself, her mother, and her caretaker aunts? What is the upside (and downside) of an unconventional household or of a mother whose parenting style is outside the lines?

2. A parent's inner thoughts are usually hidden from children, making this author's life a sometimes colorful, sometimes shocking backdrop full of illusions and people who were not

always what they seemed. Every family has secrets. How did any in your family's history shape who you are today? Have you ever experienced a complete change in opinion of someone after learning their secrets?

3. The marriage of Dotty's parents was one filled with strife, and perhaps was the first place that Dotty learned how to forge the emotional armor that would be a key part of her identity. How might Dotty sharing her own mother's secrets have changed the way the author felt about her grandmother's experience? Are there still similar threads today about women and their choices? What's changed and what's remained the same?

4. When her future sister-in-law, Rita, infers that Dotty is lying about her age, she states that she, Dotty, and Jay are "three of a kind." How does the truth (or lack of it) impact Dotty's relationships throughout her life?

5. Deborah realizes that in her work at the factory, her mother is "an extraordinary woman living an ordinary life." How do you think this lesson impacted the author's own career goals and aspirations? And how did the author's need to give unconditional love to her children compromise or enhance her own career?

6. When the author reminisces about the mother-daughter relationships she has been privy to, she realizes that her conflict-free relationship with her own mother is unusual and perhaps troubling. How do you think Dotty might have dealt with a more rebellious or vocal daughter, like Denise with her mother, Rita?

7. The author is stunned by the psychic astrologer's assessment of her relationship with her mother. What did you think of the astrologer's analysis? If you're a skeptic, why do you think the astrologer's reading had such an impact? If you're a believer, have you ever had a revelation so powerful that you changed course, questioned your path, or sought new answers?

8. The author's therapist guides her to understand her mother's behavior and her own reaction to it. She references narcissism and helps reframe the story of the author's childhood. Have you dealt with narcissistic family members, or people in your life who are seductive and charismatic but self-centered?

9. Deborah's father is a quiet, loving presence in her life. In another relationship, as a creative songwriter from an outsized culture and well-known family, he might have been the star. How do you think his relationship with Dotty changed his trajectory? Can there be two stars in a marriage?

10. The author grew up under the shadow of her mother's beauty. What are other attributes or accomplishments parents have that could make their children feel inadequate? How can modern boomer mothers who have achieved career success make sure that their millennial daughters don't feel the same success is out of reach?

11. Would you read this book with your mother? Would you read it with your daughter? Why or why not? Much was left unsaid between the author and her mother, but the author and her daughter were able to discuss their feelings—what conversations do you think this book would start for you?

12. Unlike harrowing memoirs of abuse, this is a subtle story that resonates precisely because most people live in the gray of life where things are often uncertain or have shades of meaning. The author looked back on her life to move forward and, in so doing, came to terms with perceptions that may or may not have been true. What one relationship in your life—and the beliefs you hold from it—still affects you today?

Acknowledgments

This book was the creative journey of my life, a wild ride full of the unpredictable and the unexpected. But it all led me here with a heart full of gratitude.

To the most perfect parents for me and to whom I owe everything—my mother, Dorothy Adams Canzoneri, and my father, Jasper (Jay) Canzoneri. To my aunts, for your love and presence in my life—Lena Canzoneri and Lilly Canzoneri. To my grandmothers for creating such unique parents for me, and for the wisdom you imparted—Margaret Thayer Adams, and the grandmother I never had the chance to meet, Josephine Schiro Canzoneri.

To my family for their unwavering love and support—my husband, Robert Burns; my children, Richard Burns, Elizabeth Burns, and Edward Burns, and their loves: Theresa Burns and Corrado Pulice; and to my granddaughter, soon to be part of the mother-daughter continuum. You all are my heart, hearth, and home.

To my sisters-in-law who became my sisters—Kathleen Kass, Marie Simoneschi, and Virginia Badstuebner. And to my extended female family always at my side—Antonia Burns, Barbara Roan, Cheryl Patsos, Cynthia Burger, Denise Freeman, Kristine Dugan, Leah Brower, Liz Barcia, Lorraine Pulice and all the Pulice girls:

Deborah Burns

Lauren, Jaci, Katie, Cali, and Anna, Madison Burger, Marci Burger, Marie Costelli, Nicole Dugan, Rachel Kass, and Shirley Katz.

To my childhood pack of daughters and mothers who knew us then and never let us go—Anita and Mary Martire, Annette and Kitty Musacchia, Barbara and Barbara Canzoneri, Carina and Mary Canzoneri, Cathy and Josie Trinca, Diana and Marina Chaboty, Gina and Arline Randazzo, Judy Amdur, MaryEllen and Candy Gilbert, and Melanie and Sylvia Schneider.

To the publishing experts who lent their wisdom and brilliance to take me higher—Ann Campbell, Brooke Warner, Crystal Patriarche, Holly Corbett, Julia Coblentz, Meghann Foye, and Michelle Matrisciani.

To my pool of women, those early believers and supporters who shared their lives, time, and talents—Anne Janas, Amy Griggs-Kliger, Anna Marlis Burgard, Ashley O'Brien Reilley, Carol Smith, Catherine Flickinger, Cindy Livingston, Dawn Erickson, Eileen McMaster, Ellen Breslau, Ellen Oppenheim, Laurie Costantino, Lena Greenberg, Lisa Arena, Jane Kosstrin, Jill Montaigne, Karen Thorne, Laurie Meadoff, Mary Conway, Maria Maldonado, Michelle Berman, Pam Henning, Patti Burns, Randy Susan Pollard, Romina DeNicola, Rose O'Brien, and Zvia Herrmann. And a special thank-you to the extraordinary Francis Cholle for surrendering to an idea and encouraging me to live from my writing heart.

To the Fine Arts Work Center and its memoir writing workshop led by the transcendent Dani Shapiro, along with all the amazing writers in the group, especially Katie Devine, Karen Gentry, and Sally Donaldson.

To the Long Island writing workshops led by the talented Barbara Novack, Beverly Kotch, and Florence Gatto, along with all the aspiring and published authors, especially Florence Tannen and Sheri McKee.

You all will remain forever in my heart.

About the Author

Deborah Burns is a former women's media chief innovation officer and brand leader for *ELLEgirl, Metropolitan Home, ELLE Décor,* and *ELLE* Global Marketing. As an industry consultant, she helps brands and executives reinvent themselves, and she then did the same with her own life through the process of writing this debut memoir.

Beneath her business career beat a writer's heart. As the digital age changed the face of the magazine industry, Deborah found herself in midlife yearning for some changes of her own. She began a creative journey of discovery to tell her unconventional mother's story and a year of serendipity and revelation followed, full of twists and pivots as Deborah looked back to move forward. The experience was so personally transformative, she earned her professional coaching credentials and founded *Skirting the Rules®* to help other women reinvent authentic futures full of meaning and purpose.

The author lives on Long Island, New York, with her husband, Robert, and close to their three treasures, Richard, Elizabeth, and Edward. Ever fascinated by the forces behind change and connecting the dots between people and ideas, Deborah is continuing to write about women's relationships through the generations.

deborahburnsauthor.com

SELECTED TITLES FROM SHE WRITES PRESS

She Writes Press is an independent publishing company founded to serve women writers everywhere. Visit us at www.shewritespress.com.

The Butterfly Groove: A Mother's Mystery, A Daughter's Journey by Jessica Barraco. $16.95, 978-1-63152-800-2. In an attempt to solve the mystery of her deceased mother's life, Jessica Barraco retraces the older woman's steps nearly forty years earlier—and finds herself along the way.

Scattering Ashes: A Memoir of Letting Go by Joan Rough. $16.95, 978-1-63152-095-2. A daughter's chronicle of what happens when she invites her alcoholic and emotionally abusive mother to move in with her in hopes of helping her through the final stages of life—and her dream of mending their tattered relationship fails miserably.

The Space Between: A Memoir of Mother-Daughter Love at the End of Life by Virginia A. Simpson. $16.95, 978-1-63152-049-5. When a life-threatening illness makes it necessary for Virginia Simpson's mother, Ruth, to come live with her, Simpson struggles to heal their relationship before Ruth dies.

Veronica's Grave: A Daughter's Memoir by Barbara Bracht Donsky. $16.95, 978-1-63152-074-7. A loss and coming-of-age story that follows young Barbara Bracht as she struggles to comprehend the sudden disappearance and death of her mother and cope with a blue-collar father intent upon erasing her mother's memory.

Don't Call Me Mother: A Daughter's Journey from Abandonment to Forgiveness by Linda Joy Myers. $16.95, 978-1-938314-02 -5. Linda Joy Myers's story of how she transcended the prisons of her childhood by seeking—and offering—forgiveness for her family's sins.

The S Word by Paolina Milana. $16.95, 978-1-63152-927-6. An insider's account of growing up with a schizophrenic mother, and the disastrous toll the illness—and her Sicilian Catholic family's code of secrecy—takes upon her young life.